GRAPHIC COMMUNICATIONS IN CONSTRUCTION

DENNIS FUKAI

University of Florida

Prentice Hall

Upper Saddle River, New Jersey
Columbus, Ohio

Library of Congress Cataloging-in-Publication Data
Fukai Dennis.
 Graphic communications in construction / Dennis Fukai
  p. cm
 Includes index.
 ISBN 0-13-060552-2
 1. Construction—Drawing and design. 2. Field Drafting—Drawings.
 3. Preconstruction modeling. I. Title

Editor in Chief: Stephen Helba
Editor: Ed Francis
Production Editor: Christine M. Buckendahl
Design Coordinator: Diane Ernsberger
Cover Designer: Mark Shumaker
Cover photo: FPG
Production Manager: Matt Ottenweller
Marketing Manager: Mark Marsden

This book was set in Palatino by Carlisle Communications Ltd., and was printed and bound by Banta Book Group. The cover was printed by Phoenix Color Corp.

Pearson Education Ltd., *London*
Pearson Education Australia Pty. Limited, *Sydney*
Pearson Education Singapore Pte. Ltd.
Pearson Education North Asia Ltd., *Hong Kong*
Pearson Education Canada, Ltd., *Toronto*
Pearson Educación de Mexico, S.A. de C.V.
Pearson Education—Japan, *Tokyo*
Pearson Education Malaysia Pte. Ltd.
Pearson Education, *Upper Saddle River, New Jersey*

10 9 8 7 6 5 4 3 2 1
ISBN: 0-13-060552-2

Preface

This book was written for a new generation of construction professionals who face a new world of complex expert relationships. I refer to these professionals as "constructors" because they include the technically literate members of the increasingly broad and diverse construction industry. These men and women are, or will be, part of a highly educated work force aided by the computer and somehow distanced by the complexity of the information that will result. They can be young or old, novices or seasoned professionals, but they should all share the desire to manage their construction projects more effectively.

The goal of *Graphic Communications in Construction* is to introduce these constructors to a visual approach to problem solving using drawings to focus the efforts of various specialists on the resolution of a single problem. Drawings have the power to build consensus and teamwork for one simple reason: they minimize redundancies and misunderstandings because they allow everyone to see the same information.

I believe a drawing, as visual information, will be even more valuable to constructors in the near future. First, construction drawings have always been the primary interface for construction information. Second, the rapid advances occurring in networked and Web-based graphical information systems mean there is more data being generated than can be put into practice efficiently. In a fast-paced age of iconic integration, drawings give constructors the ability to communicate quickly complex ideas to various team members.

At the same time, one of the fundamental premises of this book is that basic two- and three-dimensional hand-drawings will continue to be important in this newly competitive digital age. The ability to draw by hand involves understanding details such as line weight, lettering, dimensioning, and scales. These are the basic ingredients in a graphical construction information system that must be understood to use drawings effectively as communications tools.

Two-dimensional plans, elevations, and sections are a fundamental part of construction drawings and are indispensable for communicating layout dimensions and information to workers in the field. Three-dimensional drawings also bridge a visualization gap for unskilled workers, lay clients, and other nonprofessionals.

Being able to draw these drawings is important because I believe that even the roughest arrangement of lines scratched in the dirt of a construction site can convey lots of information that cannot be expressed in any other way. It also means that you can grab a pencil or a soapstone and mark descriptive lines on a piece of drywall or some odd scrap of wood or metal. With such materials, your message is not only immediately portable but it continues to be available for ongoing reference and can be added to or modified as the work progresses—sometimes in very interesting and imaginative ways. Most important, when those same spontaneous lines are applied to a piece of paper in even the roughest form, they can be dated, faxed, copied, mailed, and filed to confirm an understanding, document a conversation, or act as a written record. Rough field drawings have saved hundreds of thousands of dollars in miscommunications and can be very useful in helping to initiate formal change orders or to justify back charges during final negotiations.

A second premise of this book is that the process of producing a design for a building, or any other object for that matter, follows a specific sequence of disclosures and discoveries. This process begins with a programmatic description of the problem, rough schematic sketches of possible solutions, scaled preliminary drawings that can be used to estimate cost and assess general feasibility, and engineered drawings with details and specifications that are as important to preconstruction and project planning as they are to the actual work.

Adapted from the work of architects and engineers, this sequential process is the core of a visual approach to problem solving. This visual approach uses drawings to analyze problems, visualize solutions, graphically exchange ideas, establish common understandings, and transform rough concepts into usable field instructions. With this approach, a team of professionals can see the same problem, collaborate to define solutions, and graphically record the resulting agreements.

When this interaction and exchange of ideas flow fluidly and are properly managed, the result is almost always a well-coordinated and clearly composed set of instructions. What follows is a straightforward construction project with minimal requests for clarification and a clear understanding of scope and values. Most important, the final outcome is almost always a sound building for our customers, something I honestly believe everyone wants to see in every aspect of a construction project—no matter how tense things sometimes get on a jobsite.

This book is therefore more about using drawings to communicate and solve problems than it is about either the drawings or the problems themselves. The learning strategy is to present something that is real enough to represent the complexities of an actual construction project, while at the same time keeping things simple enough to be useful to a wide range of interests and drawing skills.

The challenge is to set up this interaction with a problem that might be found on a real jobsite. This is not easy, because in actual practice a real building usually means a large one. As you can imagine, it takes a lot of time to solve the problems associated with a large building, and not all of these problems can be figured out in one or two drafting classes.

Most constructors will never need to draw a full set of construction drawings, and many have absolutely no interest in understanding how to do so. Setting aside the growing trend toward design-build and single-source project delivery, this perception misses the role of the drawings as a problem-solving and management tool. Drawings are forms of communication that can be indispensable to defining a problem and reaching a workable solution. Larger buildings also have their own particular construction methods. They use special techniques for assembly and detailing that take years of field experience to learn and thousands of dollars in consulting fees to put into practice. This is not a simple exercise for even a college-level drafting class.

As a result, the traditional way to teach drafting is usually to assign a basic wood-frame building and walk through the production of the drawings intended to explain its construction. For some, this includes designing the building and drafting base sheets such as the floor plans, elevations, and sections. And though some determined students will push beyond these basic drawings into details, schedules, and specifications, the learning experience is often reduced to a series of isolated exercises. Sometimes the students will lay out the stairs or a few wall sections, but these drawings will not reach the level of detailed complexity that constructors regularly face in the field.

Another problem is that this traditional approach gives the student a feel only for woodframe construction. Some argue that woodframing is out of date for modern construction professionals and try to mix lightweight steel framing and masonry techniques into drafting assignments. After all, most of the woodframing techniques found in a large custom residential home are so standardized that they do not need to be explained to an experienced contractor.

Drafting these simple buildings in isolation is problematic also because it suggests that individuals put together construction drawings without input from clients, engineers, contractors, and other consultants. As a classroom exercise, they imply that design professionals sit down by themselves to draft the drawings as fast as they can without consulting, communicating, or coordinating the information on those drawings with all the people who must contribute their insight and skills to a design process. This approach misses the potential of a drawing to integrate visually the input of the design and construction teams, and the resulting drawings are often fraught with frustrations for everyone concerned.

This book therefore specifically attempts to set up the interaction necessary to define and solve a problem that has no obvious solution or predetermined construction. It begins with what at first seems like a simple building but quickly grows into a three-dimensional puzzle with unlimited alternatives. The goal is to provide a detailed example to illustrate one possible solution to a set of verbal requirements presented in this book. The problems embodied in this example reflect many of the same conditions found in a large multistory building, including almost all the structural forces one might find in complex construction such as cantilevers, moment and shear connections, suspension rods and tension, and various foundation loads.

The result is a building with several unusual conditions, including curtain wall panels, atypical roofing details, weatherproofing problems, and a collection of difficult structural relationships. It also requires shop drawings for its steel and precast concrete members, as well as an assortment of submittals to verify finishes and field conditions.

It's also possible to go beyond the work in this book. For example, the building could be value engineered to improve its constructibility. Although few have found a more practical solution, you could use such an effort to explore alternate assemblies, structural systems, or modifications that still meet the basic program requirements.

It's also possible to study electrical and mechanical designs that incorporate solar power, geothermal transfers, and robotics. One group of students even went so far as to build their version of the trainer to see if it could really be constructed according to their drawings.

Any approach to problem solving will inevitably lead to some deadends or major revisions. That's the point of an investigative process. If the channels of communication are kept open to different points of view, however, revisions to the construction drawings or changes to the entire design become an integral part of the visual process. Thus, the drawings represent the changes and allow everyone to share a common vision because of the ongoing interaction. Each exchange is an opportunity for fresh input from a new perspective, which means the potential always exists to improve the quality of the information on the current drawings.

The outcome is a visual consensus represented in a set of drawings as a collaborative effort, ready for use as a dynamic communications tool that continues to be fully discovered throughout construction. With new visualization software and hardware just now becoming available, I am certain that construction drawings are destined to evolve into something far more interactive and useful than a fat roll of large print paper and an unreadable stack of specifications. My underlying goal in this book is to introduce some of the skills that may be necessary for future generations of our industry to make this transition.

Acknowledgments

I would like to thank the following reviewers for their helpful comments and suggestions: Dana Hobson, Oklahoma State University; James Jenkins, Purdue University; Laura Lucas, Indiana University; Madan Mehta, University of Texas at Arlington; James L. Otter; Pittsburgh State University; and Chris Ray, Purdue University.

Contents

Introduction

A Brave New World

With the appearance of educated men and women like you on jobsites, old ways and sometime casual attitudes have begun to change. Today, most of these constructors have their own ideas about what they will do on a project. Some even design and engineer their own buildings. They are active negotiators and interact aggressively with design and construction teams. They have their own opinions about how things should be done and are quick to suggest what the best ways are to implement their own responsibilities.

Although true to their contracts, constructors no longer blindly follow drawings and specifications and perform their duties according to command. They are now responsible for much more than what is shown on the drawings and must be careful to protect their own liabilities and the safety of those who work according to their directives. More and more often, they question illogical approaches, provide alternative solutions, control the pace of their work, and use the latest programs to make sure their work takes the direction they want.

A modern construction practice involves more than just constructing buildings. This industry thrives on advanced equipment and techniques driven by a tradition of competitive practices. Although sometimes slow to absorb new, computerized ways of doing business, it is continually moving toward greater complexity and relies on the collaboration of hundreds of different trades and specialties for all but the simplest buildings.

As a constructor, you will work with a loosely organized group of people with different skills who are assembled as a team to build a single project according to a specified scheduled. Your actions are subject to all the political, environmental, economic, social, and technical unknowns that can occur in a world of diverse viewpoints and motivations. Worse yet, the work pace is becoming faster and becoming even more complex. No one has the time to sit down and talk anymore. E-mails must be answered, Web sites visited, and video or single-shot digital images delivered.

To work in this industry, you have to be fast and you have to back your words with documentation. These documents carry your decisions and directives into the field because you cannot be everywhere and do everything for everyone. You must be able to leverage your management skills with every tool at your disposal, but you must also be able to use those tools to account for your actions and demonstrate your professional responsibilities. These documents include printouts from computerized management programs, submittal and transaction logs, and field drawings.

In addition, as the industry continues to expand, the role of architects and engineers is becoming even more narrowly defined. As a result, the new generation of constructors has begun to broaden their influence on the shape and form of the buildings that they build. Constructors are beginning to assume responsibilities that go well beyond the boundaries of the traditional general contractor. In many cases, construction managers control every aspect of the design and construction process, including everything from site selection and facility operation to operations and maintenance once the project has been occupied.

In fact, some constructors now manage designers, engineers, and architects like they would any other subcontractor. They must also interpret the needs of owners, government inspectors, realtors, and financial investors, as well as direct the labor of both skilled and unskilled workers in the field. Constructors must also be able to discuss cash flow and schedule conflicts with corporate owners and be sensitive to community concerns about the aesthetic quality and environmental impact of the total project.

To this diverse range of responsibilities, add daily duties like keeping up with hundreds of pages of project submittals, issuing requests for information or clarifications, calculating requests for change orders, publishing project information on project Web sites, and reading reports and bulletins pumped out by computers, faxes, or e-mail attachments. The output from these technologies can include schedules and estimates, material spreadsheets, memorandums and letters, and computerized presentations. These new devices allow constructors to express themselves with charts, graphs, and illustrations that meet or exceed the requirements and expectations of increasingly sophisticated owners and regulating agencies.

Use of this technology leads to file drawers full of specifications, contracts, spreadsheets, and reports that must be produced regularly to keep projects coordinated and running smoothly. Add also new technologies like project Web portals, e-business portals, materials tracking, palm pilots, 4D CAD, preconstruction modeling, computer visualization, and animations, the growing complexity of keeping up in this industry becomes increasingly clear.

Why Do Constructors Need to Draw?

The quick answer to this question is that the ability to draw makes it easier to communicate with all members of the project team and to document project activities during the flow of the work. In addition, drawings are extremely important to answer questions from workers in the field. Most of these questions will be requests for clarifications of information already on the drawings. These questions are easy to handle because all you need to do is read the drawings to find the answer. Something that is quite surprising is that most people on a jobsite do not bother to read the drawings—after all, they assume, that's your job.

Other questions will come from subcontractors or suppliers asking for verification of their interpretation or suggesting alternatives to the specifications in the contract documents. Questions like these will mean reviewing the drawings and specifications carefully to verify that the necessary information is in fact not already on the construction documents. Depending on the situation, most of these questions can be answered by the design team.

A few questions come directly from the workers assigned to a particular task. Every project is different but, in general, any question that cannot be answered by an obvious reference to the project documents must be coordinated carefully with the other field managers. First, it is important that responsibilities for the work being completed remain tightly controlled. Second, it is easy for too many people to become involved in giving directions, increasing the possibility of conflicting information and wasted effort.

The more important questions will come from the supervisors who do read the drawings and may therefore have identified an error or omission that needs careful examination. Good supervisors make it their business to read the drawings thoroughly and are usually the first to find the real problems. These questions will mean reviewing the documents carefully to find the information necessary to do their work.

Once a review is completed, any immediate answers must be relayed to the appropriate person in the field. You can do this orally or in writing, depending on the importance of the question. Deciding what is important takes experience, but on many projects even the simplest question and answer must be logged for future reference. In construction, seemingly simple problems have a way of coming back to haunt you when you least expect it.

If a review of the project documents does not turn up an immediate answer, members of the project team who might know the answer should be contacted as soon as possible to prevent any delay in the work. Most important, you must be certain that the work implied by the question is included in the original contract. If the information is incorrect or missing from the original drawings, then even a simple answer might require detailed coordination of related or even unrelated portions of the work. Any error in interpretation could mean lost time in the schedule and additional costs to remove and replace incorrectly installed pieces of the building.

Any time a question suggests an answer that goes beyond the scope specified in the contract documents, it raises a red flag. An answer that suggests work that was not included in the scope of the original contract must be regarded as an extra and should be considered for a possible change order. Keeping track of even the smallest changes to the contract is one of the primary responsibilities of a building engineer.

Almost every answer has to be coordinated with many other members of the management team. This team, of course, includes those directly responsible for that portion of the work, but it also means informing the estimators, schedulers, and purchasing agents who may be indirectly involved in the project. The objective is to keep everyone informed and give them an opportunity to comment on how any particular question or answer affects the overall flow of the work. In other words, it's just as important to keep the rest of the project team informed as it is to answer the question and get the work done.

As you might imagine the ability to read the construction drawings and thus be able to respond to these questions includes the ability to visualize a block of construction activities on the schedule and see how it relates to the overall sequence of the work. Your response could range from giving directions to workers who may or may not have the ability to read the construction drawings, to executing a major request for a change to the contract or, even worse, a stop order that interrupts the work until a definitive solution is found. Reading the drawings therefore means much more than visualizing the drafted lines.

First, no matter where the question originates, all members of the project team should be informed of any interpretation that is not clearly shown on the drawings or the specifications. And even with minor comments, a note in a log referring to the location of the answer may be standard procedure for a particular project.

Second, a straightforward answer to a simple question will sometimes require clear instructions and follow-through to make certain that your interpretation was understood correctly. Some answers are more important to get right than others, and special attention should be given to make sure no error occurs.

Third, answering a question usually involves much more than a verbal response. In many cases, the ability to diagram the answer for a group of workers will increase their understanding and their efficiency in executing the solution to the problem. A simple diagram can reduce the need for continuous supervision and help workers see the scope of their tasks without a lot of additional questions.

Add to this the fact that quick hand-drawings with simple and straightforward diagrams are often produced spontaneously in the field. They are usually drawn on something found laying around the jobsite. Drawings are also important in preconstruction meetings with subcontractors or other field personnel. They might be rough sketches on a white board in a conference room or scribbles on scraps of paper so that they can be copied and distributed to everyone affected by the project.

Field drawings are important because oral or written instructions may be misinterpreted, impractical, or tedious to use in the field. Few want to read a memorandum if a simple illustration can explain something more clearly. The drawings are therefore clarifications or diagrams that support, reinforce, or facilitate the construction process. These are not architectural or engineering drawings, but diagrams that explain the construction itself.

Drawings can therefore be at the heart of a well-managed construction project. They are part of a graphical language spoken on the frontline of the work force to back up all other forms of communications. Whether chiseled in stone, scribbled on a napkin, or plotted from a computer, drawings have always been the universal language of construction. They are the most fundamental way of communicating the work clearly on a jobsite. If you can draw, no matter how crudely, you can communicate your ideas and solutions in construction management. If you cannot, you allow others to speak for you, which is not a very good position to be in if you plan to control the flow and quality of your constructions.

Drawings Are Your Voice in the Field

Of course, as a constructor, you do not get paid to draft buildings. You draw because it is important to your role as a construction manager. You draft in trailers, in the middle of an excavation, standing on scaffolding, eating lunch, or late at night in a hotel room preparing for the next day's work. You will not carry a drafting board around with you, and T-squares, parallel rulers, and CAD workstations are not always found on a jobsite.

Unlike the work of an architect or engineer, field drafting is directly related to a construction activity, and it must be quick and to the point. It might be drawn to scale and lettered neatly and legibly. However, no one in the field will expect the drawing to do more than get your point across.

Not all drawings are the same. Some can be colorful, beautiful, impressive, stylish, and—to a constructor—a complete waste of time. On the other hand, drawings can save time and increase the efficiency of your work without becoming an obsession as the total focus of your attention. The goal of field drafting is to communicate construction, and you should use drawings as any working professional would use them.

Whenever possible, your drawings need to be clear and precise. They should look professional, with neat and legible lettering, good line weight, and the correct use of symbols and callouts. These drawings reflect your management style and will represent you in your absence. If they're sloppy and difficult to understand, they may suggest that your directives are not as clear as expected. Most important, your drawings must "speak" so that workers can follow them in the field. The drawings must adhere to the traditional format of all construction drawings. They should be arranged so that the information they contain is clearly visible and includes all the information necessary to do the job at hand.

Why Field Drawings?

More often than not, constructors in a hurry to get work done will not communicate their instructions clearly. They will try to explain something verbally in the field, ignoring the potential of a drawing to help manage their work. Even though they may have received the wrong answer from someone else or discussed alternate solutions with outside consultants, they have no documentation for their actions and no drawing to support their management directives.

Field drawings can be fundamental to good construction management. First, they communicate ideas quickly and do not need a lot of words, if any, to get their point across. If someone tried to describe the construction of even the simplest project with text or spoken words, they would spend a lot of time saying the same things again and again. At the same time, a drawing that contains a lot of extra information or long descriptive sentences clouds the information that someone needs to know to do the job. Field drawings should be concise and to the point.

Second, field drawings are a form of documentation. If you can draw it and someone can understand it, you have a record of that understanding. That same drawing can then be attached to a memo or inserted in a letter to cover you in case of a future disagreement. Of course, these drawings cover the other party as well. As most soon discover, good documentation is a two-edged sword. But the need for documentation is the reason why most experienced workers will insist that you put your ideas on paper.

Third, in some jurisdictions, a building engineer may be required to produce drawings to get permits for formwork, scaffolding, public walkways, equipment, falsework, or other temporary structures to build the building. These field drawings describe work that is not explicitly shown on the contract set of construction drawings. In many cases, they will have to be drawn at a required scale and on specific size paper so they can be microfilmed and added to the permanent records for the building. As such, they are included with the rest of the project documentation but have little or nothing to do with the finished building.

Fourth, field drawings can support your effort to visualize and communicate three-dimensional assemblies. As discussed above, these drawings can explain abstract details to workers in the field, diagram a unique process or particular assembly to owners or consultants, and justify payments for materials or subassemblies. They can reinforce your position in negotiations for extra time or money to complete the project. And with a little imagination, many drawings can be colored and animated easily to reassure lenders or a board of directors that a schedule can be met.

Fifth, and most important, field drawings are at the core of a visual approach to problem solving. Drawings can represent the outcome of a conversation about the definition of the scope and details of the work to be performed. Drawings are the focus of a dialog that slowly evolves into an agreement. They document the information you need to do the work. Each step in this visual process leads to the next step, with modifications that continue to clarify the final drawing. The drawings emerge from an ongoing communication process where each revision is evidence of a series of conversations that document the resolution of a problem.

Field Drafting as a Visual Approach to Problem Solving

The idea that a three-dimensional object can be resolved on a two-dimensional drawing in a visual problem solving process is probably the most important advantage of field drawing. Using drawings to resolve problems and to come to an agreement are common practices in construction. For example, shop drawings are submitted for review to convey the intent of a subcontractor or material supplier before they manufacture a product. Specialty contractors or suppliers submit shop drawings to show what they intend to build, manufacture, or supply to a project.

Constructors review these drawings or have the project consultants mark them up with comments before thy send them back for fabrication. The drawings are often revised and resubmitted for final approval a second (or third) time to make sure everything is right. Once approved, the shop drawings form an agreement for the work that they describe. The drawings are the basis of a binding agreement with the subcontractor or supplier who will do the work.

In this visual problem solving process, the drawings are exchanged as the focus of a technical conversation about the work that they describe. In other words, they are the focus of a series of interactions where, each time the drawings are exchanged for verification, all parties take a step toward an agreement on the extent of the work they describe. Both the communication and the resulting agreement are thereby facilitated by the visual information on the drawing. The final drawings, with their notes and details, emerge from the interaction as comments and modifications are added. The drawings therefore act as the media for communications between the constructor and the subcontractor. They communicate and then record the final resolution of each conversation.

This visual process is similar to that used by the design team to create the construction drawings for the entire project. The drawings are the result of a long series of interactions that cannot be captured on a single sheet of paper by a single individual. What we see on a floor plan, an elevation, or a section is the result of a sequence of exchanges and conferences, confirmations and modifications, verifications and final or at least semifinal approvals, all leading to the graphical information shown on a completed set of working drawings.

When the drawings are confused and the information is not clearly coordinated—which is sometimes the case—the opposite has most likely occurred. In other words, the cause for the loss of quality in the construction drawings is probably because the communication process was either rushed or nonexistent, the designers miscalculated or mismanaged their fee, or project coordination broke down during the design's production.

When this occurs, someone may have actually sat down and tried to draft the drawings as fast as possible, without any outside input and without consulting, communicating, or coordinating the information on those drawings with all the people who could have contributed their insight and skills to a design process. This technique might succeed with a simple building, but it is fraught with frustration for the kinds of building you are likely to build in your career.

Construction drawings use a standard format, a unique collection of graphic symbols and codes that, at least in theory, transfer technical information so completely that they form a binding contract and become the basis for the services of hundreds of people working in different trades. We depend on construction drawings to be clear and concise, with minimal errors or omissions, so everyone understands what to do, and the work can be performed quickly and efficiently in the field.

A Visual Approach to Problem Solving

Demonstrating how drawings come together is one of the primary goals of *Graphic Communications in Construction*. This objective is important because it means having a hands-on feel for the production of the drawings and not necessarily the volume of information or details referenced on their pages. This book is therefore more about understanding how to use drawings to communicate and solve problems than it is about either the drawings or the problems themselves.

You will take a vague conceptual idea and move programmatic diagrams toward schematic sketches in an attempt to define a problem well enough to begin scaled drawings. These scaled preliminary drawings will be important for pricing and evaluating feasibility before eventually detailing the entire building for construction. The challenge of this book is to produce a set of drawings for a fairly complex building that fully describes the scope and quality of its construction. Once your drawings are complete, you will be able to test them by preconstructing the building on a computer. Considered by most to be the tool of designers, the advent of the computer means drawings are fast becoming an essential communications tool. Constructors must be ready and able to work with this tool to express their ideas or they will be left out of the conversation.

Chapter 1, "Seeing from Dimension to Dimension," begins with a discussion on how construction requires you to shift your perspective constantly from two to three and back to two dimensions in an ongoing process of visual interpretations. As you move from dimension to dimension and back again, each shift brings new insights and a new perspective of the construction process, but it also introduces an ongoing potential for error. As documents that describe a process, construction drawings represent a sequence of events that come together over time. Understanding how to read drawings therefore means understanding how to visualize time, a different concept than simply understanding how to enclose space. To a constructor, time is a process that requires interpretation, communication, and management.

Chapter 2, "The Basics of Field Drafting," introduces the idea that drawings emerge from a collaborative effort and are founded in the basic formats of 2D field drafting. It covers simple topics like basic drafting tools, line weight, and lettering, but also the kind of information that needs to be included on a sheet of construction information and how to plan the organization of visual information. Drawing takes a lot of practice to get exactly right, but almost anyone can use a drawing to communicate more effectively in the field.

In Chapter 3, "Field Drafting," you will work through a series of exercises to understand how field drafting defines a visual approach to problem solving. This chapter covers the first three steps of a seven-step process. Step 1 sets up the visual investigation with a written description of the problem called a program. This written description is often supported by conceptual diagrams. Step 2 involves schematic sketches of at least one idea that meets the requirements of the program. The objective of this step is to get a general direction for further detailed analysis. It is often better to push for several schematic ideas rather than one that is well developed but possibly incorrect. Step 3 takes the rough sketches and design direction defined in step 2 and lays everything out to scale, as preliminaries, including the plans, elevations, and sections that will become the base sheets for the final construction drawings that will go to the field.

Chapter 4, "The Field Drawings," covers steps 4 and 5 of the seven-step visual problem solving process. Step 4 is the design development phase. It involves revising the scaled preliminaries according to input that was received from their review at the end of step 3 and making some basic assumptions for early outline specifications so that a conceptual estimate can be made to confirm the budget prior to beginning detailed engineered drawings. Once the costs are confirmed, the actual engineered drawings are produced in step 5. This step is the longest and most detailed in the visual problem solving process because it prepares the drawing for the input of engineers, consultants, and other specialists. The objective of this step is to gather the construction information systematically and add it to the engineered drawings as a lightly laid out set of alternatives, which can then be verified prior to punching them out and finalizing the drawings for details.

In Chapter 5, "Construction Details in 3D," the construction details necessary to build the building shown in the engineered drawings are resolved in three dimensions.

In step 6, you build three-dimensional details rather than draw them. The chapter introduces three 3D hand-drawing techniques and uses two of them, the isometric and axonometric, to help visualize and illustrate the way the building fits together. Isometrics and axonometrics are drawn to scale in a Cartesian coordinate system.

The value of three-dimensional drawings cannot be overstated. They give you the ability to communicate almost instantly in the field because they are quick to visualize and can effectively convey management directives, including reports to owners, memorandums to architects and engineers, and quick diagrams to workers on the jobsite. Though many constructors may consider 3D drawing an art, it is much more a tool that gives you a unique advantage in facilitating your work.

Finally, in Chapter 6, "Preconstruction Modeling," you will use the 2D field drawings and the 3D details to build a 3D preconstruction computer model. Unlike architectural models, preconstruction models include all the pieces of an object's construction, assembled according to the same work breakdown structure used in the field. This chapter therefore introduces an approach to computer modeling that simulates the construction process. It includes benchmarks, workpoints, and stringlines and proceeds through chalkline layouts and installation of the foundation, framing, roof, and walls. In traditional buildings, this step can include the installation of drywall and cabinets and painting. In preconstruction modeling, the 2D and 3D hand-drawings are tested for errors and omissions that often cause delays, cost overruns, and unsafe conditions in the field. The value of knowing how to draw in 2D and 3D is that it makes it easier to understand the potential of computer modeling for preconstruction analysis and project management.

When you finish reading *Graphic Communications in Construction,* you will have had a hands-on experience with the visual approach to problem solving for a uniquely complex project. You will be able to move an idea from a vague verbal description through conceptual sketches, budget estimates, engineered drawings and details, and, finally, preconstruction modeling in preparation for actual construction. You will learn this material in a series of progressive steps, tying related bits of information into a cohesive set of construction documents.

The most important outcome is that you will understand how construction documents emerge from a series of interactions and exchanges. A poor set of construction drawings is the inevitable result of a poorly managed visual problem solving process and sets the stage for conflict and contradiction on the jobsite. An efficient set of construction drawings, on the other hand, can be your voice in the field, with all the information necessary to communicate the construction process clearly.

Chapter 1

SEEING FROM DIMENSION TO DIMENSION

Living in Flatland

In the 1880s, Edwin Abbott wrote a book about seeing different dimensions. He used an allegory to tell a story about a society of shapes that lived in a place called Flatland. There were no solids in Flatland, just two-dimensional rectangles, squares, polygons, and circles. These two-dimensional geometric shapes lived flat on a two-dimensional plane, like those shown in Figure 1-1. They couldn't look up or down from their flattened point of view, and they could see only the edges of other shapes as they moved along the plane. To the citizens of Flatland, who could look only at the edge of the other objects in their world, it meant that everything looked like a line, like the coin shown in Figure 1-2, shown first standing on its edge with its face visible in three dimensions and then laid flat on a table. Flatlanders see only the last image.

As you look at the coin standing on its edge, it has a three-dimensional shape and form. But as it drops down onto the table, it joins a two-dimensional plane and loses one of its dimensions. When viewed from the perspective of a Flatlander, only the edge of the coin is visible and it looks like a line. But the overall shape and size of the coin remain, even when it is visible only by its edge, and the same is true in Flatland.

In Flatland, "space" was therefore measured according to one dimension, the length of the edge of a flat object. The shapes had more than one dimension and existed along the two axes of a flat plane, but only a single dimension was visible. Most Flatlanders just saw a line and everyone looked the same.

A line in Flatland could be almost any shape, even when it looked like a line. For example, in the upper part of Figure 1-3, the edge view of a circle, square, a triangle, or even a line always remains a line when viewed from a Flatlander's perspective. Without being able to see the corresponding top view, a lot is not visible to the average Flatlander. In fact, there is an entire dimension missing from this restricted point of view. There were a lot of things that many Flatlanders just did not understand.

Abbott's parable shows us how difficult it is for anyone to see another dimension from a fixed world-view. But as you can see in Figure 1-3, this dimension is quickly

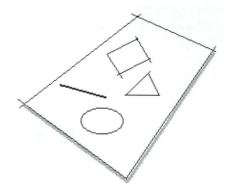

Figure 1-1. Two-dimensional shapes in Flatland.

Figure 1-2. Three-dimensional objects drop into Flatland.

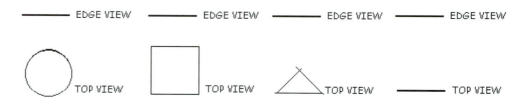

Figure 1-3. All geometric shapes in Flatland look like a line.

revealed by the addition of another view. When we label the lines as edge views and give each of them a corresponding top view, we use two 2D images to define the shape of the same object. The top view is a projection of each edge view. The addition of this simple projection means we can suddenly see a lot of things that could not be understood with our originally restricted one-dimensional view.

If the Flatlanders understood how to draw top views of the lines they saw around them, life would have been a lot different in their one-dimensional worlds. But a top view would mean they would have had to understand an entirely new dimension. Any notion of another dimension was not possible without understanding a third dimension. After all, how could there be a top view if there was no up or down and if one's point of view was confined to a flat plane?

A Sphere in Flatland Redefines Space

A sphere is a three-dimensional shape. The idea of a sphere in Flatland changed everything Flatlanders knew about their world. Unlike a circle, a sphere has volume. It also has a width and a height and cannot be represented within the world-view of a Flatlander. With a sphere, there is much more than meets the eye, and its total volume was beyond a Flatlander's perception.

A sphere could move up and down through the two-dimensional edge view of the surface of Flatland. To Flatlanders the visible line that described the sphere as it passed through their world changed its length according to the part of its three-

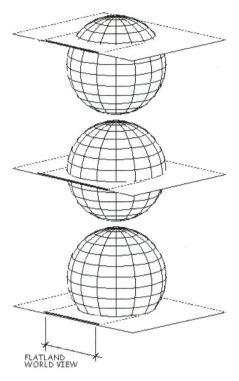

FLATLAND
WORLD VIEW

Figure 1-4. The 2D line visible to Flatlanders grows and shrinks as the sphere moves through the plane.

dimensional shape that was passing through their two-dimensional plane. See Figure 1-4. As the sphere rose, it got shorter and shorter until it disappeared. Worse yet, as it descended from this elevated position, it got longer and longer, only to get shorter and shorter as it passed through its equator.

Of course, the same would be true of any other three-dimensional shape passing through Flatland. A box, pyramid, or even a house would all look like varying lengths of lines that would suddenly disappear as they passed through a Flatlander's two-dimensional world-view. To a Flatlander, the very possibility of this vertically upward direction could only mean there were views of the world that were impossible to imagine. To understand a sphere passing through their world meant that they had to shift their minds from their one-dimensional thinking and visualize an up and a down from within their flat plane. The very idea would have been impossible for them to consider.

None of this is difficult for us to imagine because we live in three-dimensional space. The fact that there is an up and a down only means that we can see a top and a bottom to everything around us. We can add another dimension to two-dimensional space by giving the objects around us a corresponding height. See the rectangle in Figure 1-5, for example. If we imagine that we can "extrude" the flat two-dimensional rectangle vertically, the height of the extrusion becomes the height of the box. This new vertical direction moves the two-dimensional rectangle into the third dimension. Now, the edge view is really a side view and a top view shows the new object in two related 2D drawings. One drawing represents the length and width of the box from above, and the other drawing represents the height and the width of the box from the side. Knowing the length, width, and height of a box means that all three dimensions are represented in a set of two 2D drawings.

People in Flatland would not have understood what these two drawings meant. It's hard enough trying to see two dimensions from their limited edge view of the world, but three dimensions was absolutely impossible to imagine. To understand the significance of a set of 2D drawings means having the ability to see in three dimensions.

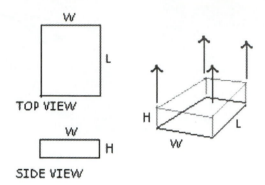

Figure 1-5. In three dimensions, height is an extrusion of the two-dimensional object.

Three Dimensions in Two-Dimensional Drawings

Almost every living creature with eyes has the ability to see in three dimensions, but only human beings have the ability to visualize three-dimensional shapes when they are viewed as projections on a two-dimensional plane. This act of perception means that we can imagine the shape by aggregating the total form in our minds from abstract information.

With this ability, we can understand the shape of the simple box from the two 2D drawings shown in Figure 1-5. As you can see in Figure 1-6, however, slightly more complex objects require more information before we can understand them. In other words, we also have the ability to recognize the lack of complete information and know when we cannot visualize the objects that the 2D drawings represent.

The additional information necessary to understand these shapes could be provided with additional notes or even detailed descriptions of the shape of the lines in the drawings. This information could take a lot of text, however, and even then words may not be adequate to understand fully the total form. Reading a written description means that you have to shift from yet another level of perception, this time, to and from the written word. Text would be used to supplement the graphical image, and you would combine those words and lines on the 2D drawings to form a picture of the three-dimensional shape. Sound complicated? This is exactly the challenge presented by a set of construction drawings.

It would be a lot simpler to add at least one more view and avoid the need for a lengthy description. For example, when a side view is added to some of the objects in Figure 1-7, the shapes of all objects are easier to understand. In this case, the third view of these objects is derived from the other two views. These are called orthographic projections.

To build an orthographic projection, parallel lines are drawn from the top view and turned down to intersect with lines projected from the side view. The length (L) lines in the top view pass through a 45-degree bounding line to make a 90-degree turn down to intersect the height (H) lines from the side view. The horizontal H lines are projected across to the side view to mark the heights in the new view. The third view is called a projection because it is taken directly from the two other views.

Note that the additional view clarifies the shape of the three-dimensional objects because it gives you more information about the original shapes. You can visualize the three-dimensional shape only when you have enough information to imagine its complete form. In fact, without the third view, you wouldn't really know enough about the object to understand it. You would have had to ask a lot of questions to get it right.

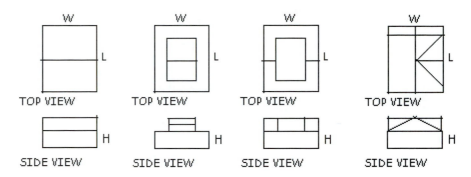

Figure 1-6. Two 2D views are often not adequate to describe a three-dimensional object.

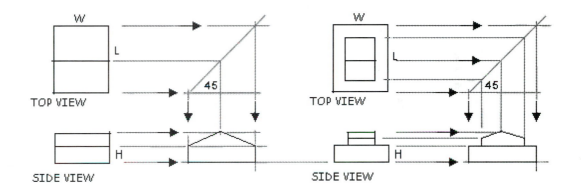

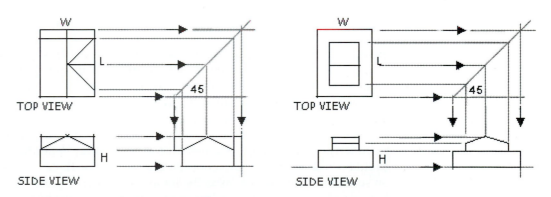

Figure 1-7. Three 2D drawings give you more information about the object's shape.

Two Dimensions in Three-Dimensional Buildings

For a building, these same 2D drawings are the basic ingredients for almost any set of construction drawings. The top view is called a plan, and the side views are called elevations. There are many other kinds of plans, including roof plans, floor plans, enlarged plans, foundation plans, framing plans, site plans, and grading plans. There are also two basic kinds of elevations: interior elevations and exterior elevations.

Plans and elevations have one thing in common: they are oriented to the Earth by a north arrow as a symbol of the plan on the title of the elevation. Without a north

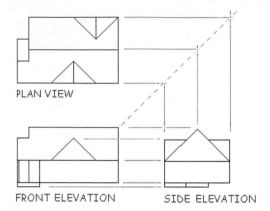

Figure 1-8. The plan view and elevations can be confusing when they are not oriented by a north arrow.

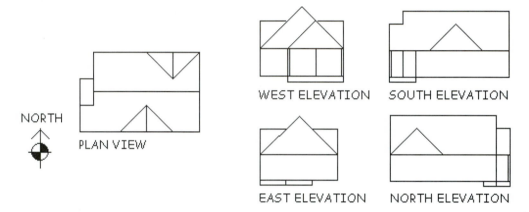

Figure 1-9. A north arrow means that the sides can be referenced from a common direction.

arrow, a building, road, or bridge could not be built. This orientation and the surveyed benchmarks associated with it locate the structure on its site and become a fundamental reference for almost everything found on the construction drawings.

Without some indication of the orientation of the building in the three 2D drawings in Figure 1-8 there is no way to understand its construction. You need to know which way the building faces to be able to reference the top, front, and side views as elevations. Without these references, the orientation is arbitrary and the building could be built facing any direction. And if these same three 2D drawings were found on separate sheets, as they usually are in a set of construction drawings, you would have no idea which drawing represents which side of the building.

As you can see in Figure 1-9, once the plan view is referenced to north, all the side views or elevations have a corresponding orientation. Five 2D drawings can describe the shape of the three-dimensional building. Instead of the three 2D drawings in the original projection, you now have a plan view and four side views to represent the building. The plan view shows the roof with its ridges and valleys, and each of the elevations shows how these ridges and valleys fit together on their corresponding sides. The challenge now is to visualize the building from this plan and these elevations and to understand how they fit together as a three-dimensional object. As you can see in Figure 1-10, visualization is not too difficult for a simple house when all the views surround the object in a 3D drawing, but it can get confusing when the plans and elevations are scattered throughout a set of construction drawings, especially when the building is complex and has a lot of special features.

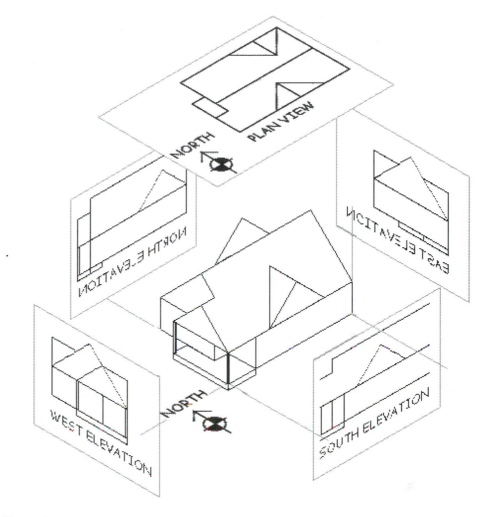

Figure 1-10. Five 2D drawings are necessary to visualize this three-dimensional building.

The Three Challenges to Visualizing Construction Drawings

There are three underlying challenges to visualizing a set of 2D construction drawings. The first is in your ability to change your point of view. Like Abbott's Flatlanders, changing your point of view from one dimension to another can be disorienting because visualizing an object from a 2D drawing is not so much about understanding any one drawing, but more about understanding how several drawings fit together to describe a single object.

For example, note how difficult it is to understand the shape of the building in Figure 1-11 from the five 2D drawings when the views of the building are fragmented. You have to match each of the elevations to one of the elevations of the plan. In fact, to visualize the north elevation, you even have to think upside down.

But in Figure 1-12, the elevations for the same building are oriented according to a plan. This simplifies the relationship of the elevations and even if you covered the image in the center, visualizing the three-dimensional object is easier because the drawings are directly referenced to each other. In other words, they work together in your mind because they are juxtaposed as you view them.

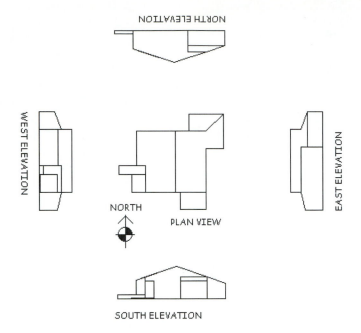

Figure 1-11. Visualization is easier when the plans are oriented around the same plan.

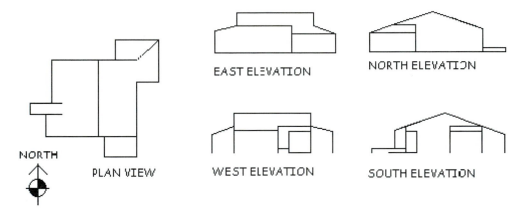

Figure 1-12. Visualizing the shape of this building is difficult when the elevations are not directly associated with the plan view.

The second challenge is to keep in mind that it is just as difficult to draw the 2D drawings as it is to visualize them after they are drawn. For example, it's obvious in Figure 1-13 that good drafting takes special training and a lot of practice, but at the same time, you have to keep in mind that the drawing is of an object that does not exist outside the imagination of the designer who drew it. For someone to draw lines and abstract shapes on a flat piece of paper to describe an object that has to be constructed by another person, he or she must shift their three-dimensional imagination into a narrowly defined, two-dimensional way of seeing.

Drafting is an art because it involves the ability to project a three-dimensional object onto a sheet of paper. When it is done correctly and the views are closely related, the interpretation is facilitated. But when done incorrectly, with missing information and images and details that are fragmented and seemingly unrelated, it is

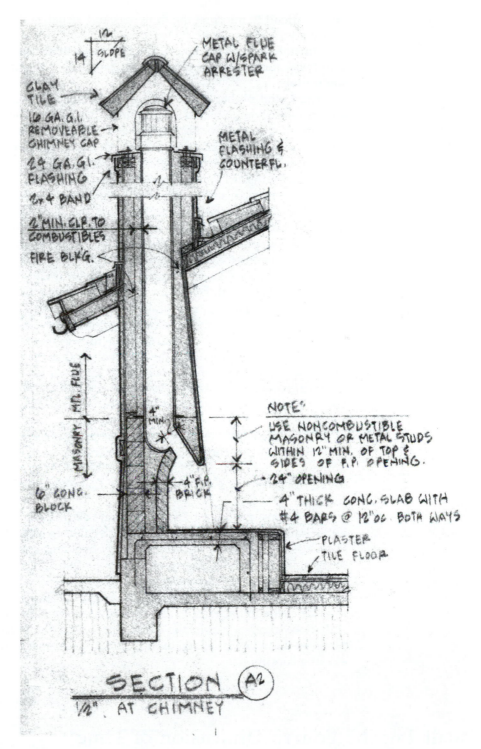

Figure 1-13. Drafting is an art that takes a great deal of training and practice to visualize two-dimensional drawings from a three-dimensional concept. (Drawing by Jarvis Architects, Oakland, California.)

more difficult to interpret the drawings and visualize the scope of the work. Faulty drafting will lead to requests for more information and further clarifications to prevent misinterpretations. Poor drawings mean that construction will be a challenge simply because there is not enough information on the drawings to complete the visualization.

Third, and probably most important, is that 2D drawings do not reflect the sequence of time embodied in the drawings themselves. They are static forms of graphical information that contain a great deal of superfluous details that are not always relevant to the immediate task at hand. All this extra information produces a lot of visual noise that makes visualization difficult. The challenge is to place the drawing within the context of the construction process.

For example, in a floor plan like the one shown in Figure 1-14, you can see references to the frame of the building, room finishes, electrical wiring, and furnishings on the same drawing. This is an overload of information, but it is the most practical way to draw a floor plan. It would be much more efficient if this plan showed just the framing, or just the finishes, or just the electrical wiring. In other words, the visual noise in the drawing would be eliminated if the irrelevant information for any one phase of the project could be hidden from view. While this is now possible using animation on a computer, it is not very practical for printed drawings.

This is resolved in the field by the constructor's skill at interpretation and visualization. In other words, to read the drawings, a constructor must be able to read the sequence of work implied by the information that the drawings contain. It is therefore much more than simply visualizing space, which would be relatively easy. For these drawings to be useful to workers in the field, the information relevant to the task at hand must be extracted and repackaged so that each individual can understand it.

Invariably, when the information is taken out of the base drawing according to the sequence of construction, missing information or gaps in the details of the construction will begin to appear. This is where field drawings become important to the flow of the work. Clarifications must be made that place the details of the construction in real time.

For example, Figure 1-15 shows a field clarification drawing that is as complex as the information it is attempting to clarify. In fact, almost all the information it contains already exists on the contract drawings and specifications. But because the original information is fragmented onto the floor plan, interior elevations, and the specifications, it has been redrawn as a single clarification drawing to facilitate the work. And because the drawing is produced in real time, in the flow of the work, it is much easier to understand and immediately useful to the workers making the installation. In other words, the detail comes after the framing for the building is in place, so it can be visualized in the context of its construction and supported by the existing conditions.

Visualizing the Fourth Dimension of Time

The construction process described on any set of 2D drawings implies time. No matter what the drawings show, the foundation always comes before the roof, the roof comes before the walls, and the finishes cannot be applied until the walls have been sealed. There are exceptions, but anything that changes the logical sequence of the construction must be communicated explicitly with a note or a detail on the drawings.

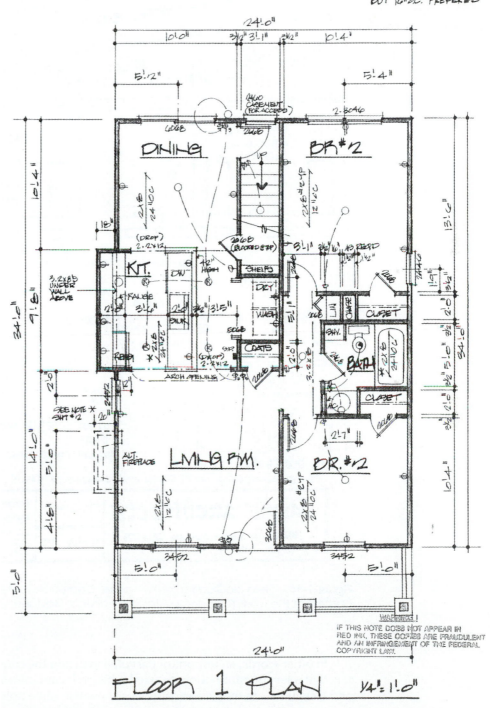

Figure 1-14. Two-dimensional drawings take careful interpretation because they deliver a lot of information all at once. (Drawing by Rick Thompson, architect, www.thompsonplans.com)

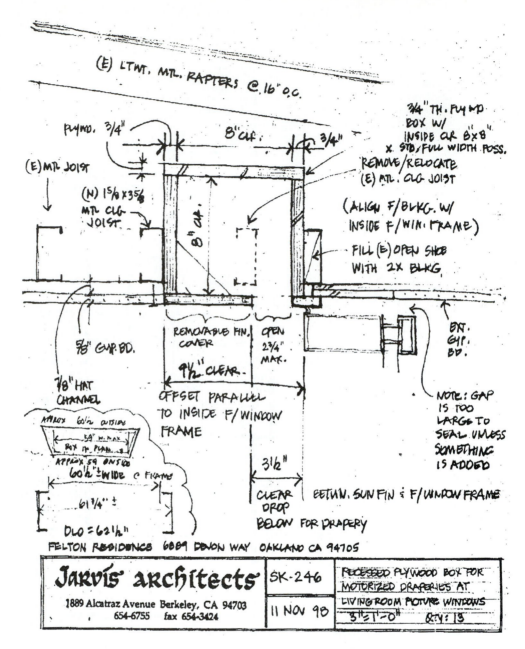

Figure 1-15. Field clarification drawings are clearer because they are drawn in the context of the work. (Drawing by Jarvis Architects, Oakland, California.)

In other words, an important part of visualizing the construction drawings is the fact that relevant information is mixed with irrelevant information on the same plans and elevations. As the project continues to evolve, some notes and dimensions are no longer necessary, and new notes and dimensions become more important. The constructor must be able to read and extract this information from the construction drawings to understand the evolution of the three-dimensional shape of the object under construction. This is where experience counts because the sequence of construction is not always immediately apparent. In fact, sequential information is often buried in the notes and details on a single 2D drawing. For example, a foundation plan like the

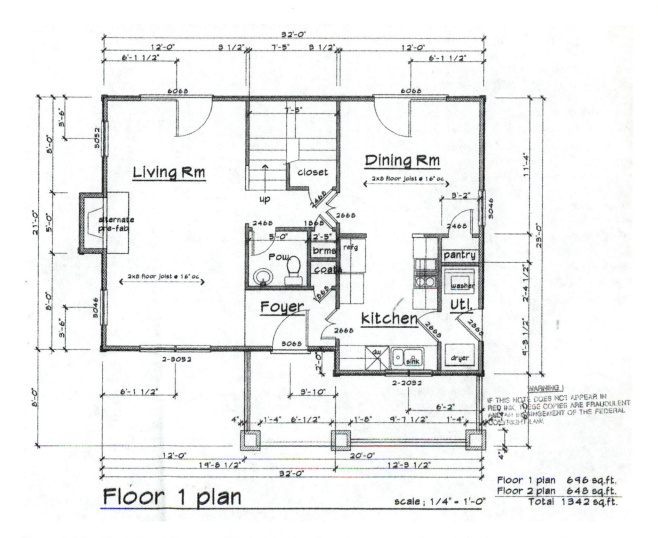

Figure 1-16. The information on a 2D drawing implies a sequence of events that occur over time. (Drawing by Rick Thompson, architect, www.thompsonplans.com)

one in Figure 1-16 has many layers of information, but each layer must be interpreted as part of the visualization process.

In fact, as shown in Figure 1-17, the time implied in the foundation plan in Figure 1-16 is extensive. For example, site preparation must be completed before anything can be started. Site preparation includes basic clearing and grubbing, laying out the field, setting batterboards, identifying staging and laydown areas, locating and installing temporary power, and even placing field toilets for privacy and servicing. All of this must be completed before excavations can begin, and none of it is explicitly shown on the drawings. The overall size and location of the building are the most important pieces of information to be extracted from the foundation plan before construction even begins.

Once the preparations are complete, the excavation can begin. During excavation, the depth of the cut must be checked continually against the drawings because an error of a few inches will mean more formwork and concrete, possible time delays, and cost overruns. For example, the elevations for the bottom of the footing and the top of the wall must be found in the drawings so they can be checked in the

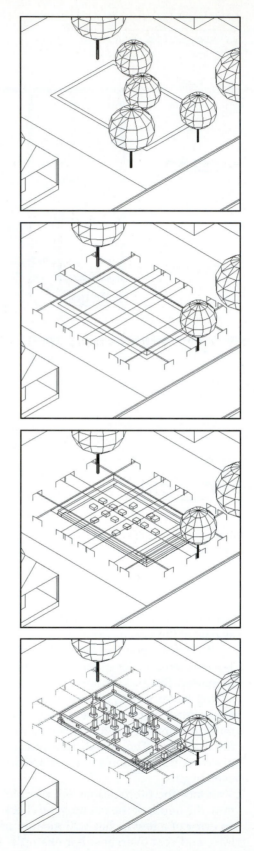

Figure 1-17. Time and the sequence of construction is not clearly represented in the foundation plan.

field. Since this information is not on the plan, it must be clearly referenced to a detail section.

When the excavation is complete, the footing must be laid out, formed, reinforced, inspected, and poured before the stem walls of the foundation can even begin. The details for each of these steps is embedded on different sheets of the 2D drawing. Again, the constructor must extract the relevant information by reading a combination of notes and details. It is up to the constructor to interpret this data and break it down into a sequence of work activities.

Of course, any variation from the logical sequence of construction must be noted on the drawing so that it can be considered, ordered, and then constructed in the field in a timely manner. An omission in this information could be critical to the success of the construction and usually causes requests for information and possible change orders. For example, the location of the sewer line coming out of this building is not shown. If the foundation walls were constructed before this omission was discovered, it would mean extra work to cut a hole in the footing or the wall to drain the building.

Time can be drafted into a set of 2D construction drawings to reduce potential conflicts. The inclusion of time means simply arranging the drawings and their details according to the sequence of their installation. This chronological sequence puts the graphical information in a logical pattern for easier interpretation and means that the drawings may be easier to follow during construction.

A Visual Approach to Communications

Construction drawings emerge from the collaboration and cooperative efforts of a team of design professionals because the construction drawings, with all their notes and details, are the tangible result of interaction and communications among designers, engineers, architects, suppliers, building inspectors, owners, and constructors over the time they are drawn. When the communications between these professionals are well coordinated, the resulting drawings will reflect their collective thoughts clearly and completely. When communications falter or break down, the drawings will reflect disorder and muddled thinking.

The drawings evolve over time. This is different from the time implied in the drawings for the construction. It is a design development process where vague ideas are solidified by almost continuous interaction with owners and consultants according to a specific sequence of services. This interaction is standardized by industry practices and contractual relationships. In each step, drawings are exchanged and discussed to confirm tentative ideas and to establish direction and approvals before continuing to the next step.

This process is valuable to a constructor because it is a visual approach to problem solving that can be applied to many field problems. In fact, it can be used whenever a constructor is faced with a vague idea and no clear definition of a specific solution to a construction problem. As you can see in Figure 1-18, the process starts in step 1 with a program. A program is a verbal or written description of the project and often includes rough diagrams showing general relationships and orientations. This is important because it sets up the basic requirements for the solution and establishes the scope of the work for all the steps that follow. It should be as complete as possible. Major changes could mean starting all over again with a new program.

Step 2 includes rough sketches called schematics. The schematics generally describe any number of possible design concepts. The intent is to suggest a physical form that meets the program requirements. The goal is to establish a general direction for design development. This often takes more than one set of schematics, and you

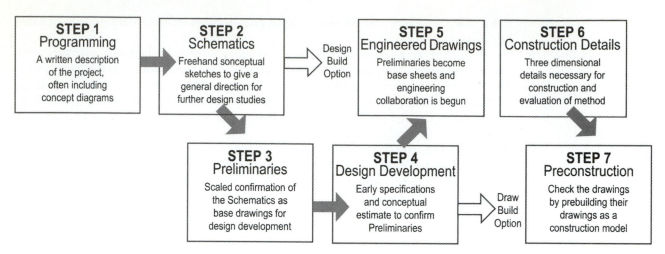

Figure 1-18. A visual approach to problem solving involves seven steps: programming, schematics, preliminaries, design development, construction drawings, construction details, and preconstruction.

may find it most productive to have at least three totally different ideas to choose from with the initial schematic submittal. The schematics should be about ideas and not pretty pictures.

Once approved, the schematics are carefully drafted to scale as preliminary drawings in step 3. These scaled drawings are the base sheets for the construction drawings and give you an opportunity to make sure that the features shown in the schematics actually fit together. This is a design feasibility phase, to confirm that everything works together and that the schematics were interpreted correctly. Some of this should have been considered in the schematics, but the preliminaries give you the opportunity to be certain that nothing is forgotten. The objective of the preliminaries is to get final approval prior to proceeding to step 4.

Step 4 is the design development phase. In this step, the preliminaries are expanded with early specifications so that the drawings can be estimated and checked for financial feasibility. The design development phase is important because it is the last step before the drawings are actually engineered and detailed for the construction. Up to this time, the majority of the interaction has been with the owner or principles that are making the decisions about the project. This is the first time the drawings should be studied carefully for cost by an outside consultant to verify the budget numbers and make sure that everyone agrees with the conceptual estimates. This is also a key point for a construction management company to provide a guaranteed maximum price for a draw-build contract.

The engineering drawings begin with step 5. This is the step that takes the most skill to produce because it means thinking through the information necessary to actually build the structure being designed. The project is engineered in this step. The main structural, mechanical, and electrical components must be reviewed with outside consultants, and their input is coordinated and drafted into the base plans and elevations. Some of their suggestions will change the preliminary design. If the changes are major, it may mean resubmitting preliminaries for an additional approval. If there are no major changes, the plans and some of the details for these components might be drafted for inclusion in the final drawings.

In step 6, the engineered drawings are detailed with the notes and dimensions that will be required for assembly. For obvious reasons, this step is where the most skill is required to complete the drawings. Detailing is no easy task. It means understanding the nuances of the entire project as well as being able to show the best ways to put the results together in the field. These details look at every piece of the construction in an attempt to anticipate every possible contingency in the field and head off any questions that might slow the project down. This step also includes the specifications. These follow the early specifications and are usually compiled from notes and memorandums gathered from the owners, consultants, and design team. Final specifications require a great deal of expertise to put together, even with a computer, and will not be covered in this textbook.

Step 7 is the preconstruction phase. In this book, preconstruction means prebuilding the project on a computer from the 2D drawings. This step will allow you to test the drawings to see what information they contain and to see if any additional details may be necessary. Preconstruction can also include permits, bidding, negotiations, value engineering, and final contract definition. In fact, it can mean anything and everything, up to and even including groundbreaking, and is often an overlooked stage in the preparation of construction drawings.

Note that step 2 is the turning point for many design builders. For example, many residential design builders working in small, tightly knit construction communities do not need much more than a set of rough schematics to begin the permit drawings necessary to build the project. And even these drawings will be minimal, just enough to show general code compliance. In other words, instead of drafting numerous drawings, they will use their experience and perhaps a few field drawings to guide them through the construction process.

The break after step 4 occurs in more complex buildings and is often referred to as the starting point for a "draw-build" contract that sometimes includes a fast-track component. To get the contract, a construction manager gives a guaranteed maximum price based on the design development drawings and early specifications. Although the concept seems risky, it actually allows the builder to control the final engineering and detailing for the project and, at least in theory, more easily control the final cost of the project. It takes a great deal of experience and an excellent team of constructors to execute a draw-build fast-track project. With the computer, however, we are entering an age of management complexity unheard of just a few decades ago.

In summary, the same seven steps can be used as a visual approach to solve almost any construction problem:

1. Start with a clear description of the problem.
2. Generate some rough sketches of at least three possible solutions.
3. Draft the best solution to scale to make sure it works.
4. Price the scaled drawings to make sure the cost is acceptable.
5. Engineer the drawings to make sure all systems are included.
6. Carefully detail and specify the construction represented in the drawings.
7. Check the drawings and the details prior to construction.

The Value of a Visual Approach

The seven steps listed above are valuable for three reasons. First, the resulting illustrations can be used to manage the construction and will be more effective than any amount of written or oral communication. In fact, the less clear an idea, the more important drawings become in construction management, but even the simplest parts of a project can benefit from an illustration. For example, compare the field drawing in Figure 1-19 with the verbal description of the same detail in the textbox below.

Like the proverb that says a picture is worth a thousand words, it's obvious that construction communication can be expressed and understood much more quickly with a drawing than with words alone. As a construction manager, this is an important skill for effective management.

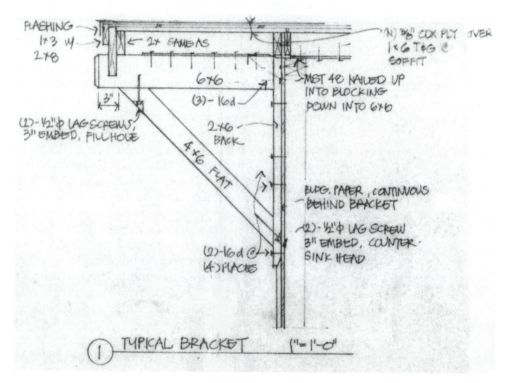

Figure 1-19. A drawing of a bracket can explain the construction much more clearly than a written description of the same bracket. (Drawing by Jarvis Architects, Oakland, California.)

A Simple Shelf

The bracket supports the new $3/8$" CDX plywood deck that goes over the existing 1×6 tongue and groove soffit. You need to support the existing deck with a continuous 2× that sits over the top of the 6×6 horizontal member of the bracket detail. This 6×6 has a 4×6 knee brace under it at 45 degrees. Install the knee brace flat so that the 6× width matches the 6×6 itself. Nail the 6×6 with three 16d nails to a 2×6 backing that attaches to the exterior wall. Use two $1/2$" diameter lags screws, countersunk and embedded 3" deep at the base of the bracket, and two $1/2$" round lags screws, countersunk and embedded into the attachment at the top of the bracket. Fill the countersunk holes for painting. Attach the bracket over the top of continuous building paper on the exterior wall with pairs of 16d nails in four places along the vertical face. Nail a 48" metal strap up into the 2× blocking in the wall and down onto the new 6×6 horizontal member for the bracket. Notch and fit a 2×8 fascia over the 6×6 and nail to the 2× resting on the 6×6. Apply a 1×3 over the fascia and use a strip of continuous sheet metal flashing to seal the edge.

The second reason that a visual approach is valuable is because the interaction means you must continually shift your point of view to understand the problem from the perspective of several related specialists. In other words, every drawing literally makes you look at the problem from a different set of eyes. To establish consensus, you have to incorporate the concerns of everyone involved in resolving the problem. You must communicate with them to get their opinion of the direction that the construction documents are taking.

The drawings therefore become the focus of the communication that finalizes the resolution of the problem. The information in a detail evolves as it is passed from player to player and from phase to phase. For example, the detail in Figure 1-20 was initially drafted to show the general profile of the continuous footing for one portion of a building. When the detail was checked by an engineer and reviewed by a construction manager, it changed as specific dimensions and notes were added.

Figure 1-20 shows the suggested sizes for the footing as well as the type of reinforcement recommended by the engineer. At the same time, the construction manager suggested that the depth of the footing be raised by 2" to reduce the cost of the foundation and the excavation. It seems like a minor change, but a 2" difference in the depth of the footing changes the height of the wall to a masonry dimension, and thus no concrete block needs to be cut by the mason.

Obviously any change that makes construction easier or less costly is a valuable consideration. But when a change occurs, the final suggestions should be distributed to everyone on the project so that it can be reviewed and confirmed. For example, for the changes made by the engineer and construction manager in Figure 1-21, a review by the mechanical engineer could point out that the 2" change in the bottom of the footing would make an already tight crawl space impractical for his installations. This error would be critical if discovered in the field because it was not properly coordinated as the drawings were being developed. But when caught early in the interactive process, it is a simple adjustment that can be handled easily with a phone call and a correction to the dimensions shown on the drawings. Once all parties agree, the final solution becomes a derivative of the communication process.

The final reason this visual approach is so important is that the drawings that are sent back and forth for comment and confirmation actually record dated submittals and reviews that could become valuable if it became necessary to verify the scope of the work when the project is under construction. In other words, the markups used

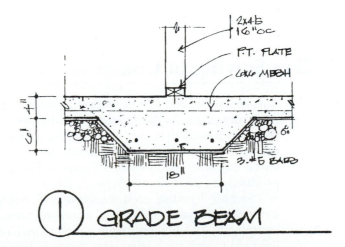

Figure 1-20. This detail is a suggestion for a solution that must be confirmed by an engineer and reviewed by a constructor prior to installation. (Drawing by Rick Thompson, architect, www.thompsonplans.com)

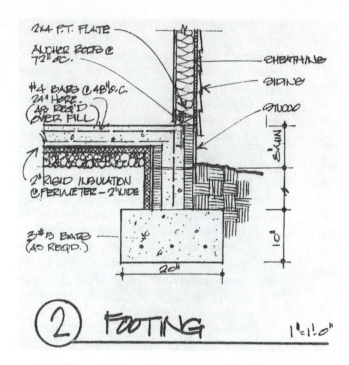

Figure 1-21. The final detail documents the evolution of the communications about the detail. (Drawing by Rick Thompson, architect, www.thompsonplans.com)

to finalize the drawings record the comments of the players involved. Most important, these comments keep track of what was said or not said in the process. For example, if the mechanical engineer did not adequately review the drawings as requested and missed the fact that the crawl space was too small to complete the installation, it would pinpoint where the breakdown in communications occurred. Depending on the cost of the change or the potential for delay in the schedule, it may well be a costly error on the part of the engineer. Without documentation, however, arguments and fingerpointing could lead to even bigger problems and more costly delays to the actual construction.

Visual Problem Solving in Construction

This visual problem solving process is important because it gives constructors the opportunity to join in the interaction that shapes their work, first, because recognizing the steps means that they can contribute their ideas to the design team in a timely manner. Construction management and design-build projects have clearly shown that a constructor can make a valuable contribution in all seven steps of a design's production.

Second, because even the crudest drawings will get your point across much more clearly than words alone, a constructor who can contribute to the design's development with illustrations is much more likely to be heard. For example, look at the field sketch for a television alcove in Figure 1-22. Even without a lot of words, you can see almost exactly how the profile of the alcove changes with different types of television sets. Without a drawing, you might have been able to explain the requirements of this detail, but it would have taken longer. In the meantime, your

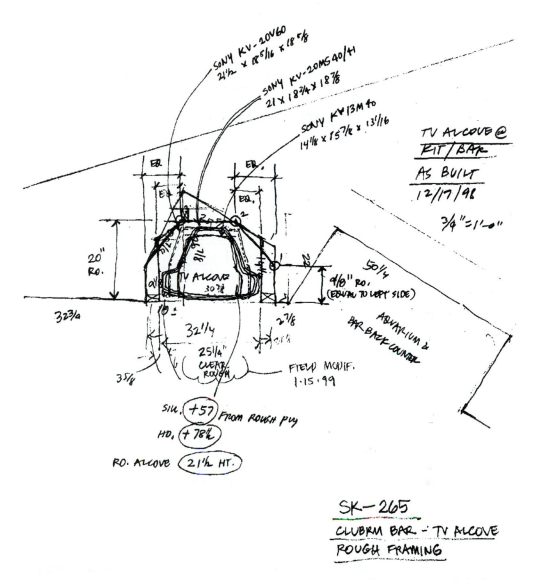

Figure 1-22. A field drawing for a television alcove makes sense without a lot of descriptive text. (Drawing by Jarvis Architects, Oakland, California.)

words could easily be misinterpreted and the potential for additional comment and for exchange of ideas would not have been possible with the carpenters who will have to build the alcove.

Third, as the design develops, the dimensional shift from two to three dimensions can provide new insight. This is a form of visual abstraction that often reveals some hidden detail or problem that may not have been spotted in a single drawing. Participating in the evolution of the design means seeing it change from step to step. Any drawing means some degree of abstraction, and interpreting that drawing always means making some visual adjustment to see the information it contains.

For example, note how the 2D site layout in Figure 1-23 forces you to "read" the lines and notes to understand what is going on. In fact, you have to review several sheets of the drawings to see the building associated with this plan and how the site layout might influence its construction. This 2D drawing forces you to shift your perspective to a two-dimensional world, changing your point of view so that you can interpret what the drawing has to say about the layout dimensions or the general

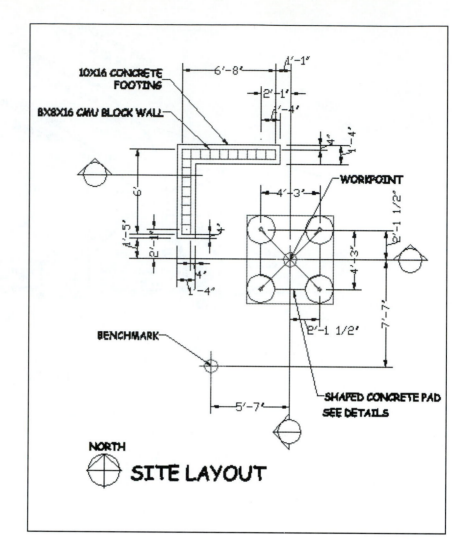

Figure 1-23. You have to shift your perspective and "read" a 2D plan to understand the information it contains.

location of the work according to the benchmark. This is important information, but like the coin in Flatland at the beginning of this chapter, this dimensional point of view has its limitations.

Figure 1-24 shows how the same information on the 2D drawing comes alive with a different sense of the scope of the work for the project when it is viewed in 3D. The extra dimension means vertical information is easier to understand, improving the speed and efficiency of communications and broadening the audience of those who can understand the resulting image. The need to visualize the work still remains, but it now includes new information that may be critical to how the site relates to the final construction.

When you are able to use this shift to illustrate your ideas and express yourself clearly as a construction manager, you can become an active member of both the design and construction process. Each drawing contains different kinds of information. As you will see in the chapters that follow, they are all equally important to communicate your ideas about construction.

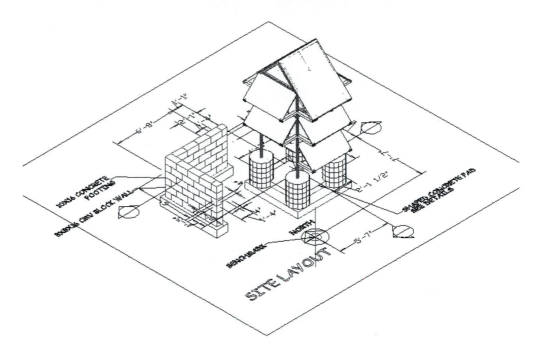

Figure 1-24. Adding the third dimension means a faster and more efficient understanding of the information because there is no need to interpret the plans.

Chapter 2

THE BASICS OF FIELD DRAFTING

Field Drawings and the Same Seven-Step Process

It's important to note the difference between a set of construction drawings and the construction contract documents. The contract documents include the construction drawings, construction contract and general and supplemental conditions, specifications, addenda, and any specified attachments to these documents like a cost breakdown, performance schedule, budgets or allowances, or listing of milestones as deadlines for completion and payment for specific portions of the work. These documents are obviously important because they describe contractual relationships and designate responsibilities for the project.

Construction drawings are therefore an integral part of contract documents. They incorporate early specifications, but usually only enough to clarify the kinds of materials shown on the drawings. The construction drawings give the dimensional relationship and details of the construction, but you cannot build the project with just these drawings. Construction drawings are not design drawings, but they are the derivatives of the seven-step visual problem solving process described in Chapter 1. For building construction they will contain all the information necessary to lay out the work and assemble the building, but they must be used in conjunction with the specifications. The specifications give exact descriptions for the materials and specific procedures that must be followed for their installations.

On the other hand, field drawings are drafted to support or clarify the construction drawings. They contain just enough information to complete the work that they are describing and are specifically related to the completion of a designated task in the field. These drawings usually come in the flow of the work. In other words, they are produced either spontaneously in a field conversation or they are drafted to clarify a particular installation. The level of detail in these drawings and the way they are drawn will vary with the task and the crew.

For example, if the drawings are for a skilled crew whose members know exactly what to do, you do not need a lot of detail or explanation. In fact, the overall dimensions and a general reference or a copy of a specific detail in the construction drawings or a page number in the specifications is often enough for most experienced crews to complete their work.

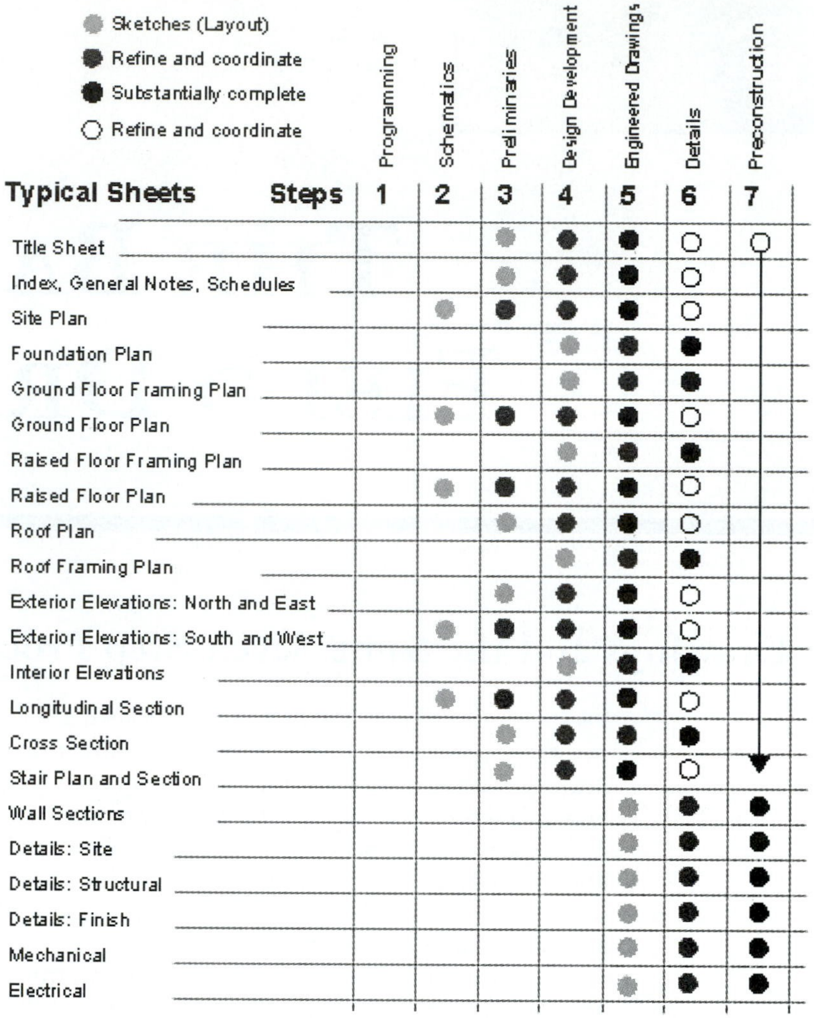

Figure 2-1 — Chart of Typical Sheets vs. Steps

Legend:
- ◐ Sketches (Layout)
- ◕ Refine and coordinate
- ● Substantially complete
- ○ Refine and coordinate

Typical Sheets	Programming 1	Schematics 2	Preliminaries 3	Design Development 4	Engineered Drawings 5	Details 6	Preconstruction 7
Title Sheet			◐	◕	●	○	○
Index, General Notes, Schedules			◐	◕	●	○	
Site Plan		◐	◕	◕	●	○	
Foundation Plan				◐	◕	●	
Ground Floor Framing Plan				◐	◕	●	
Ground Floor Plan		◐	◕	◕	●	○	
Raised Floor Framing Plan				◐	◕	●	
Raised Floor Plan		◐	◕	◕	●	○	
Roof Plan				◐	◕	●	○
Roof Framing Plan				◐	◕	●	
Exterior Elevations: North and East			◐	◕	●	○	
Exterior Elevations: South and West		◐	◕	◕	●	○	
Interior Elevations				◐	◕	●	
Longitudinal Section		◐	◕	◕	●	○	
Cross Section			◐	◕	●	●	
Stair Plan and Section			◐	◕	●	○	▼
Wall Sections					◐	●	●
Details: Site					◐	●	●
Details: Structural					◐	●	●
Details: Finish					◐	●	●
Mechanical					◐	●	●
Electrical					◐	●	●

Figure 2-1. Construction drawings come together gradually as design team members resolve unknowns and contradictions.

But if you are preparing drawings for an unknown or inexperienced crew or for an open bid from an outside manufacturer or fabricator, you may need to detail carefully every piece of a particular project. Some field drawings become miniature sets of construction drawings in themselves, sometimes complete with specifications. For complex fieldwork or especially large temporary installations, you may need to hire an outside engineer or architect to produce field drawings for special building permits.

Figure 2-1 shows a list of the drawings that would probably make up a set of field drawings like the one you will be working on in this book. It may seem extensive, but an experienced building engineer could put together all the drawings for these seven steps in a couple of days. In fact, some members of a construction team might point out that such a task is what a building engineer is supposed to do.

Note that the drawings in this list evolve from the same seven-step visual problem solving process shown in Figure 1-18. The program is most important because it defines the requirements of the solution. It is obviously important to have a clear understanding of exactly what the problem is you are trying to resolve.

The drawings will be discussed in detail as they are prepared, but in general, the schematics should include a site plan, floor plans, and at least one elevation and section of as many different ideas as seems practical for the project. The more ideas that you can include in these sketches, the more successful you will be at reaching a solution. Again, schematics are loosely drawn sketches. The purpose of the site plan is to lay out the work and orient it to anything else around it. The floor plans show the horizontal relationships of the interior of a building, and the elevation and sections give the height of both external and internal construction.

The preliminaries are the base drawings for the main set of drawings. As such, they should include a cover sheet with the name of the project and relevant information like dates or control numbers for billing purposes. The second sheet contains general notes like an index, abbreviations, and addresses for the project. The rest of the set is a scaled version of the schematics, probably with additional elevations, sections, and other plans that may be necessary to prove that everything fits into place.

Once the preliminaries have been finalized, the drawings for the design development phase should include whatever refinements and sketches are necessary to establish early specifications and a conceptual cost. What this entails will of course depend on the project and the needs of the estimator.

The engineered drawings that follow the approval of the costs associated with the design development phase take the preliminaries as base sheets and begin foundation and framing plans. The preliminaries are continually refined to reflect any changes that occur as the project is engineered. If there are major changes or revisions, preliminaries may have to be resubmitted for approval.

The objective of the detail drawings is to study the actual assembly of the pieces of the project: what is known about the structure and the mechanical and electrical systems. Again, detailing takes a great deal of skill and experience, but once it is complete, the field drawings should be a set of well-coordinated sheets of information that can be tested in the final preconstruction phase.

Limit the Drawings, Not the Content

You may not need all of these sheets for every project. In fact, all the notes and dimensions for a field drawing could ideally be found on a couple of sheets of paper. This would reduce the number of sheets in the set and make it easier to coordinate the information. As you can see in Figure 2-2, a single sheet of drawings can provide a lot of information, and the details that a single sheet contains are easily referenced because they are juxtaposed on the same sheet of paper.

Of course, it's important not to reduce the content of information on the drawings or cram so much information onto one sheet that it becomes overloaded and difficult to read. The key is to keep the level of detail for each sheet reasonable for the task you are trying to explain without duplicating information or providing superfluous information on more sheets than is absolutely necessary.

A good way to do this is to separate the information into logical segments so that it is easier to understand chunks of information without overwhelming workers with details they do not need to know. As a rule of thumb, follow the order and sequence of the construction itself. For example, in Figure 2-3 the details for the construction of the overhangs and rake edges of the roof are placed right next to the elevations. This way, the carpenters working on the sides of the house can refer to the work necessary to complete their installation.

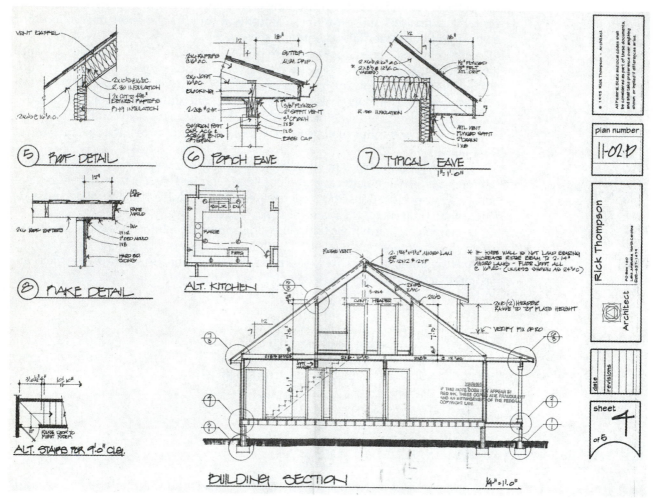

Figure 2-2. Sometimes a single sheet in a set of drawings can provide a lot of information. (Drawing by Rick Thompson, architect, www.thompsonplans.com)

When you have more that a few sheets of drawings, the biggest challenge is to get all the drawings to work together as a single set of instructions. Figure 2-4 illustrates how all the elevations can be shown on one sheet. More often than not, however, these elevations will have to be referenced across several sheets in a set, making it more difficult to visualize the building because you have to flip from sheet to sheet. Each time you change the page, your mind has to remember the previous image while it incorporates new information into that image. You can cross-reference the sheets to guide workers to other places in the set to find related infor-

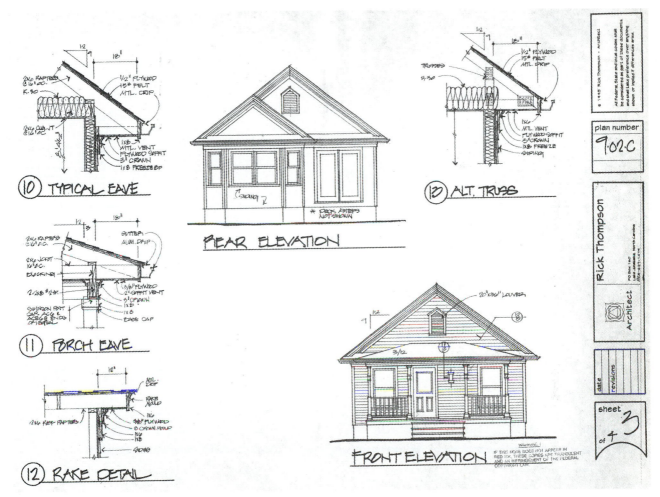

Figure 2-3. Placing details where they can be referenced quickly and easily will help workers in the field find the information they need. (Drawing by Rick Thompson, architect, www.thompsonplans.com)

mation. By limiting the level of detail found on each drawing and making these cross-references as clear as possible, you can efficiently guide them to the information that they need.

The visual flow of information in a set of drawings is a function of the way they are organized and referenced. When a set is drawn efficiently, workers should be able to move from sheet to sheet as they interpret the drawings without feeling like they have to hunt for the information they need. When field drawings follow the same standard format of all construction drawings, workers will be able to anticipate the location of the information within the set.

Figure 2-4. Multiple elevations can be referenced easily when they are shown on the same sheet of the construction drawings. (Drawing by Rick Thompson, architect, www.thompsonplans.com)

Field Drawing Is Not Drafting

A field drawing is a much more immediate form of communications than is a set of construction drawings, even though they come from the same kind of interaction. It's probably already clear that even the simplest sketch increases your ability to communicate more clearly and improves the efficiency of your work in the field. Without it, you may have to explain the same set of instructions over and over again or, worse yet, ask a worker to remove and replace something that he or she did because you did not explain yourself clearly.

In a field drawing, you therefore draw to convey ideas and information that facilitates the flow of the work. A field drawing is something you produce on the spot or in a job trailer for clarification or to manage an immediate situation that workers face during construction. The construction drawings are quite different. They are the base reference to the project's designated scope and the specific details necessary to complete the work according to the contract.

For example, in Figure 2-5, a field drawing for a planter can be drawn quickly to relay immediate construction details in the field. This same information might be found in the contract documents but may be spread across the site plan, landscape plan, building elevations, and specifications. The advantage of having all that information in one place is fairly obvious. Without it you would have to spend a lot more time coordinating a very straightforward installation or you would have to turn over the complete set of plans and specifications for the workers to follow as they built the planter. Both methods would be time consuming and inefficient.

A field drawing allows you to compile the information in one place on a very quick sketch, perhaps fax it to the architect for final verification, and then give it to the workers as a single sheet of instructions as they tackle the task of actually building it. In fact, with a copy machine, very little drawing may be necessary. You can simply add a few notes to the right detail on a copy of the construction drawings. Either way, the steps are still the same:

1. Define the problem as a program so you know what you are trying to do.
2. Use the base contract documents to sketch the information you found as a quick schematic, perhaps suggesting alternatives that would be more efficient.
3. Confirm that this information is generally what they want and quickly draft the result as a scaled preliminary.
4. Verify costs and specifications.
5. Check the construction drawings for engineering information and include that information in your field drawing.
6. Include details. If there is any doubt, refer the field drawing to the project architect or engineer for further input.
7. Check your work to make sure it is correct.

In working through the seven-step process, you should find out during the schematics if there is enough information in the contract documents to complete the field drawing. If there is not and you have the time to make a formal request for information, you may want to have the designers draft the clarification. Depending on the contract, the complexity of the problem, and the scope of the project, you may have no choice. No matter who actually drafts it, the end result is still a field drawing.

Field drafting is therefore something much more deliberate. It is purposeful and preplanned, and it focuses the problem solving process on producing graphical information that describes a tasked-based solution, as the workers need it in the field. The drawing still emerges through a series of progressive interactions, and the results are not unlike the construction documents of architects and engineers; it is simply quicker and more to the point. In fact, field drafting is guided by the conventions of these professions simply because the drawings that result communicate similar information, but do not involve computer or hand-drafting equipment. It is directed more at getting the job done as efficiently as possible using a drawing as a management tool.

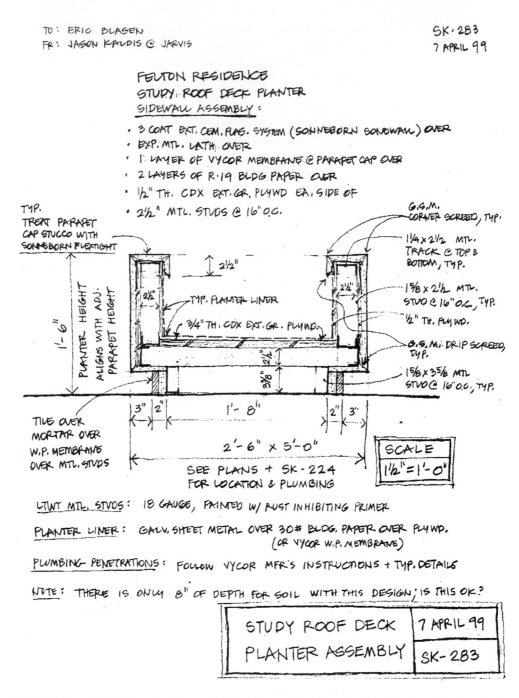

TO: ERIC BLASEN
FR: JASON KALDIS @ JARVIS

SK·283
7 APRIL 99

FELTON RESIDENCE
STUDY ROOF DECK PLANTER
SIDEWALL ASSEMBLY:

- 3 COAT EXT. CEM. PLAS. SYSTEM (SONNEBORN SONOWALL) OVER
- EXP. MTL. LATH OVER
- 1" LAYER OF VYCOR MEMBRANE @ PARAPET CAP OVER
- 2 LAYERS OF R·19 BLDG PAPER OVER
- 1/2" TH. CDX EXT. GR. PLYWD. EA. SIDE OF
- 2 1/2" MTL. STUDS @ 16" O.C.

TYP.
TREAT PARAPET
CAP STUCCO WITH
SONNEBORN FLEXTIGHT

G.S.M.
CORNER SCREED, TYP.

1 1/4 x 2 1/2 MTL.
TRACK @ TOP &
BOTTOM, TYP.

1 5/8 x 2 1/2 MTL.
STUD @ 16" O.C., TYP.

1/2" TH. PLYWD.

G.S.M. DRIP SCREED,
TYP.

1 5/8 x 3 5/8 MTL.
STUD @ 16" O.C., TYP.

2 1/2"

TYP. PLANTER LINER

3/4" TH. CDX EXT. GR. PLYWD.

PLANTER HEIGHT
ALIGNS WITH ADJ.
PARAPET HEIGHT

1'-6"

2 1/2"

2 1/2"

2 1/2"

3 5/8"

TILE OVER
MORTAR OVER
W.P. MEMBRANE
OVER MTL. STUDS

3" 2"   1'-8"   2" 3"

2'-6" x 5'-0"

SEE PLANS + SK-224
FOR LOCATION & PLUMBING

SCALE
1 1/2"=1'-0"

LTWT MTL. STUDS: 18 GAUGE, PAINTED W/ RUST INHIBITING PRIMER

PLANTER LINER: GALV. SHEET METAL OVER 30# BLDG. PAPER OVER PLYWD.
(OR VYCOR W.P. MEMBRANE)

PLUMBING PENETRATIONS: FOLLOW VYCOR MFR'S INSTRUCTIONS + TYP. DETAILS

NOTE: THERE IS ONLY 8" OF DEPTH FOR SOIL WITH THIS DESIGN; IS THIS OK?

| STUDY ROOF DECK | 7 APRIL 99 |
| PLANTER ASSEMBLY | SK-283 |

Figure 2-5. A field drawing for a planter shows how the planter is to be constructed when the workers are ready to make the installation. (Drawing by Jarvis Architects, Oakland, California.)

The Tools of Field Drafting

The only real tool necessary to do a field drawing is a stick. With it you can scratch a diagram onto the ground to explain just about anything on the spur of the moment. It isn't a very permanent or professional document, but there may be occasions when it will serve the purpose. Of course, as a constructor, you may want to improve on this

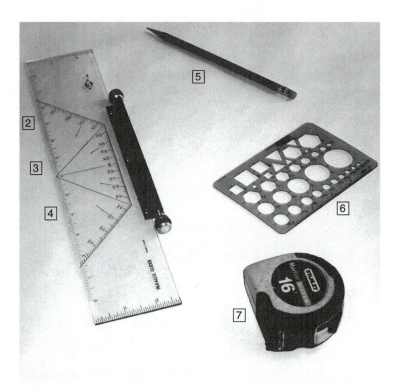

Figure 2-6. Simple tools for the constructor.

rather ancient method with the addition of the simple tools shown in Figure 2-6, which are explained below:

1. The first is an ordinary sheet of paper. Since the trick to field drafting is to keep your resources as simple as possible, a sheet of plain, 11×17 copy paper is the best option because it is readily available and will fit in almost any office copy machine. You will find that you can do a lot with this size sheet. Whatever you draft can be easily changed and recopied—even in color—and used immediately in the field.

2. A parallel glider is a tool that combines the utility of a T-square, triangle, straightedge, and protractor in a single drafting instrument. It rolls easily to make lines and stays parallel when rolled with even pressure. In addition, the straightedge on the parallel reads in inches (or millimeters) because it has a built-in ruler. This makes drawing to scale even easier.

3. The protractor works by tilting the parallel glider so that its straightedge aligns with the angles engraved in its transparent face. Once the angle is aligned with an existing line, roll the straightedge to the position where you want to draft the angle.

4. The ruler along the side of the straightedge allows you to draft parallel lines quickly. Draft a line and then move up a specific distance using this ruler to measure the distance. This tool is especially useful when you want to draft a series of guidelines for lettering.

5. Any ordinary pencil and eraser will do. The pencil doesn't even need to be sharp. For field drafting, it is not necessary to worry about different line weights or fancy pencils. In fact, the most useful pencil in the field is a carpenter's pencil. It can be sharpened with a penknife, can be shaped to draw thin or thick lines, will not break easily, and stays put when it is placed on a sloping surface.

6. A small shape template is all you need to draft the circles, arcs, triangles, and boxes necessary for field drafting. Obviously, these shapes include round

objects like light fixtures, but you can also use them to draft detail bubbles and section symbols common in construction drawings. The circles in the template have centerline marks at the quadrants that help you to position the circle over a particular location.

7. Using a measuring tape instead of a drafting scale might be too cumbersome if you do a lot of drafting or plan reading, so you may want to substitute a real engineering or architectural scale. But for a constructor, a measuring tape is almost mandatory on a job site and should be as readily available as a hard hat. You can use it to measure existing construction and to check clearances of an installation, as well as to scale drawings when a dimension has been omitted and you need to evaluate the intent of the drawings.

Pencils Are Pencils

There are pencils of all different types with many different kinds of leads. These leads vary in hardness (or softness). Pencils can be wooden or mechanically retractable. For field drawings, you can draft everything with one pencil. As you can see in Figure 2-7, this takes a certain skill, but it's certainly not as difficult as building a building.

The trick is to find a pencil with an average hardness—not by any coincidence, the most popular is a plain #2 (or H) pencil. If you stick to this one type of lead, you will soon learn that you can vary both hand pressure and tip sharpness to create the kind of line you want. A sharp pencil will produce a thinner line and a dull one will give you a thicker line with just about the same pencil pressure. Pressing firmly will make the line darker and pressing lightly will make it lighter. You can also use sandpaper to make a chisel point by flattening one side of the pencil tip. In the age before the computer, many professional draftspeople used a chisel point to give their lettering a crisper and more readable look, but most constructors find this unnecessary.

So here is a basic rule: you need only one pencil to produce all the lines you need to draft for a field drawing. You might think, "Well if that is true, I can do it with a pen." But on a job site, with all the dust, dirt, and sweat, a pen will quickly clog.

Lines Are Not Just Lines

When you draft a line, it is important to hold your pencil at a slight angle from vertical as the point makes contact with the drawing surface. This is the natural position of your hand and a pencil. To prevent the lead from flattening with every stroke, roll it continuously in your fingers. Rolling sharpens the tip as you draft. Drafting with a flat point will cause your lines to become fuzzy and irregular. Rotating the pencil keeps the shape of the tip even, so that the line weight remains constant for the length of the stroke. When you master the art of drafting with a pencil, your consistent line weights can be used to represent various objects in a single drawing. The result is a clear set of field drawings, as you can see in Figure 2-8.

There are two factors in good line quality. First, there is the sharpness and clarity of the line, reflected by the width of a line. The line must be drafted distinctly using a pencil lead sharpened to the appropriate thickness. If a pencil tip is too soft, it will

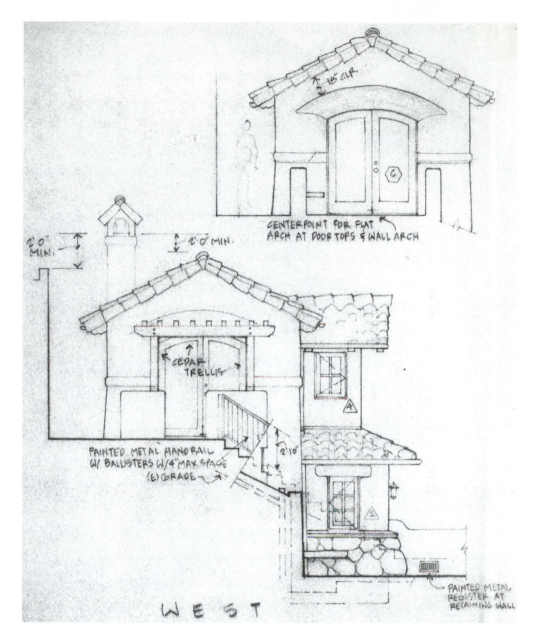

Figure 2-7. Varying the pressure on a single pencil can produce a variety of line weights. (Drawing by Jarvis Architects, Oakland, California.)

break down quickly and lose its clarity. At the same time, a lead that is too hard and too sharp may tear the paper.

Second, there is the darkness of the line. This is the tonal value or density of the line when compared to other lines on a sheet of paper. The darkness of the line is controlled by pressure on the pencil plus the hardness of the lead. If you keep the hardness of the lead constant (one pencil), you will find that changing pressure is all you have to do to vary the density of the line.

Good line quality takes practice and is a skill that comes naturally to very few constructors. What is important in field drafting is that the lines are clear and distinct from one to another. Darker lines will also appear to be more dominant than lighter

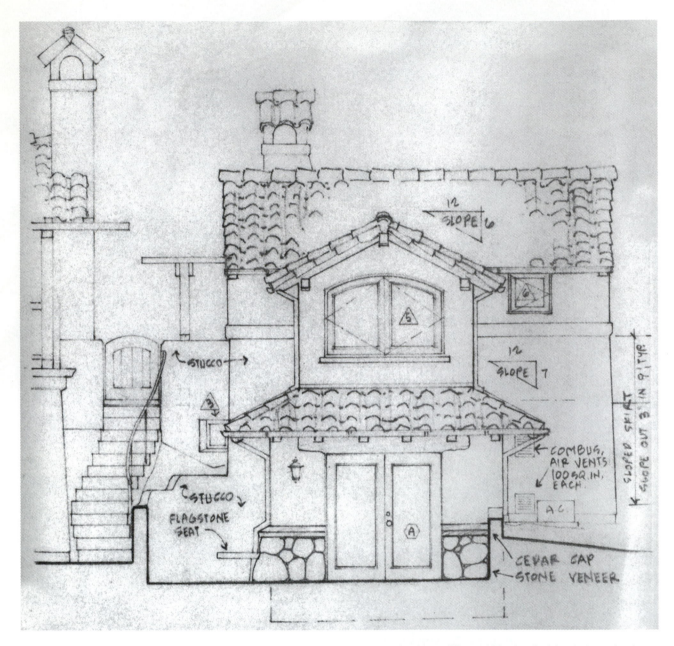

Labels within drawing: STUCCO, STUCCO, FLAGSTONE SEAT, SLOPE, SLOPE, COMBUS. AIR VENTS 100 SQ. IN. EACH., A.C., SLOPED SKIRT, SLOPE OUT 3 IN 9 TYP., CEDAR CAP, STONE VENEER

Figure 2-8. Varying the line weight means that you can represent many different kinds of objects in a single construction drawing. (Drawing by Jarvis Architects, Oakland, California.)

lines, so varying the density of the lines will make the drawing more readable. Readability is important because the drawing will communicate information more accurately. For example, the construction details in Figure 2-9 show how heavy lines can outline the profile of objects that have been cut by a section, while lighter lines show objects in the distance or in elevation.

It has long been understood that line quality moves the eye of the observer, creating a flow to the visual information being delivered. In other words, dark objects stand out, drawing the eye because they dominate the lighter ones. Thus, you have the ability to visually order the way your drafted objects are seen. You can create a hierarchy of graphically relevant information.

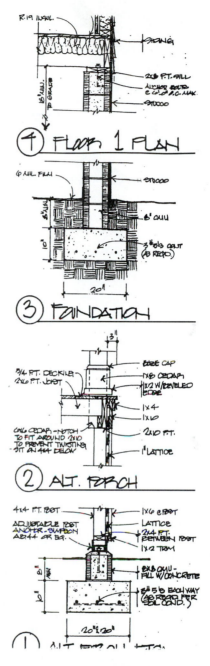

Figure 2-9. Line weight can emphasize certain parts of a drawing, clarifying the image for the workers in the field. (Drawing by Rick Thompson, architect, www.thompsonplans.com)

Types of Lines

The lines on a construction drawing are an integral part of the coded diagrams that represent a project's construction. They are as important as the symbols and other drafting conventions on any set of construction drawings. To avoid as much confusion as possible, the lines on the drawings must follow certain standards. The type of lines you use have meaning to experienced workers. As such, they must be drafted so that they make sense to those who have worked with other sets of construction

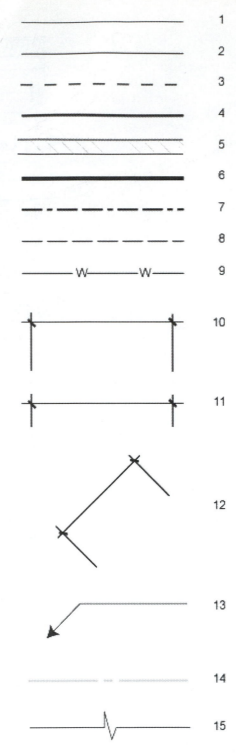

Figure 2-10. Types of lines.

drawings. If everyone drafted differently, every set would appear to be speaking a different language, which would add to the communication problem already faced in the field. The numbered lines in Figure 2-10 correspond to the numbered items in the following list:

   1. Layout lines are drafted lightly. They act like chalklines and serve to lay out the project on paper just as they would on the ground. Layout lines position the building or parts of the building on the sheet before they are actually "punched in," or darkened. They should be drafted lightly so that they fade away as you draft over them with other lines. You do not need to erase a layout line.

2. Object lines are drafted darker than layout lines. These lines define the primary information for the plan, elevation, or section and outline the object that is the subject of the drawing. These lines are punched out after a layout is completed.

3. Hidden lines are sharply drafted short dashed lines similar to object lines. They show the parts of the building that are hidden or omitted from a particular view. For example, hidden lines are used for cabinets or other furnishings omitted from a particular view or blocked by a wall or some other feature of the building.

4. Cutting plane lines are like object lines, only darker. They show the outline of objects that have been cut by a section through part of the building. Cutting plane lines are usually the heaviest lines on the section.

5. Hatched lines mark the surface within these cutting plane lines. They indicate the inside of the object. Hatched lines are drafted differently, depending on the material cut by the section. For example, use diagonally parallel lines, spaced close together, to indicate a section through masonry.

6. Borderlines are dark lines. On a site plan they show the footprint or outline of the building or objects—without the interior walls. Borderlines include the outline of porches or decks and any major part of a building. Footprints do not usually include overhangs, patios, driveways, or landscape features. Borderlines are also used to draft the title block of the sheet.

7. Property or boundary lines are also very dark lines. These lines define the legal limits of the property on which the building or project sits. On the site plan, they are usually lettered with the surveyor's metes and bounds description of that particular property line.

8. Setback lines or guidelines for the construction are sharply drafted dashed lines similar to hidden lines. They show the distance away from a property line where the local codes restrict certain kinds of construction.

9. Utility lines are like setback lines but with a letter designating the type of utility being shown, for example, "W" for water line, "E" for electrical, "S" for sewer, or "T" for telephone.

10. The extension lines for dimensions are thinly drafted lines that extend perpendicular to, but do not touch, the object they are dimensioning. It is important that extension lines do not touch the object so that they are not confused with the object they are dimensioning. These lines are lighter than object lines but sharp enough to be permanent.

11. Dimension lines are exactly like extension lines except that they run parallel to the face of the object being dimensioned. They are usually slightly longer than the object so that end markers can be added to denote the extent of the dimension.

12. End markers can be open or closed arrowheads, but it's quicker and easier to draw them as heavy diagonal slashes. They mark the extent of the dimensions and should stand out on the drawings to indicate clearly the length of the dimensioned object.

13. Leader lines are special-purpose extension lines that connect a note or detail symbol with some part of the building. These lines should be drafted like dimension lines, but they should point toward the object with a line and end marker. The end marker can be an arrowhead or bullet that touches the object to which the note refers.

14. Centerlines are sharply drafted lines similar to extension lines. They mark the center of an opening or object, such as a window, door, or electrical fixture hanging on a wall. When locating the center of a hole or cylindrical solid, you use two centerlines, one vertical and the other horizontal. These lines extend from the centerpoint to the dimension line.

15. Break lines are sharply drafted, light lines similar to dimension lines. They indicate that part of the object has been omitted. This omission is usually made because the object is too long to be drafted completely at an enlarged scale, but it could also mean that the portion omitted by the break line was not important to the detail itself. A Z- or U-shaped symbol interrupts this line at least once in its length. There are usually two break lines to define both sides of the break.

Planning the Drawings

Nothing will signal disorganized thinking more clearly than a poorly planned drawing. For example, if a plan runs too close to the edge of a sheet or if a set of details or elevations are haphazardly placed on the sheet, it's a sign that someone was in a rush and may have just thrown the information together on the page. Planning the drawing is important because it means thinking about what you need to communicate.

The schematics will give you some idea of the kind of information necessary to lay out the scaled preliminaries, but getting this information right usually takes a lot of practice. To make planning a little easier, this book uses a five-step OLPAP checklist of issues to think about for any drawing or detail in any of these phases. OLPAP is an acronym for:

1. **Orient** the worker. There should be some benchmark or reference point from which workers can begin the work. This orientation includes pointing out which way is north.
2. **Lay out** the construction. Provide the dimensions required for the work, including both overall dimensions as well as dimensioning the location of the pieces that need to be installed.
3. **Pieces** and processes are identified. Call out the names or descriptions of every piece and activity that will be specifically installed or fabricated using this drawing.
4. **Assembled** pieces are correctly positioned. Check to make sure the relationship of the pieces shown in the drawing fit together the way you want them installed.
5. **Presentation** is clear and professional. The resulting drawing does not have to be perfect, but it should be clear and concise so that it reflects the quality of your management directives.

For example, in Figure 2-11, the OLPAP checklist is used to verify the content of a simple site layout:

1. The site layout is **oriented** to the Earth and to the rest of the drawings in the set. This includes detail and sheet numbers for this sheet and related sheets. A reference point is shown to orient the work to existing conditions.
2. **Layout** dimensions are shown for the work from a surveyor's benchmark or reference point. Show the overall dimensions of the work and the dimensions of the pieces that are to be installed according to this drawing. These dimensions should be tied to the benchmark in order to position the work in the field.
3. **Pieces** and processes are captured and identified in the drawing. For a site plan, call out the buildings, trees, sidewalks, footprint, benchmark, property lines, rocks, rivers, and anything else visible on the plan. Processes include ac-

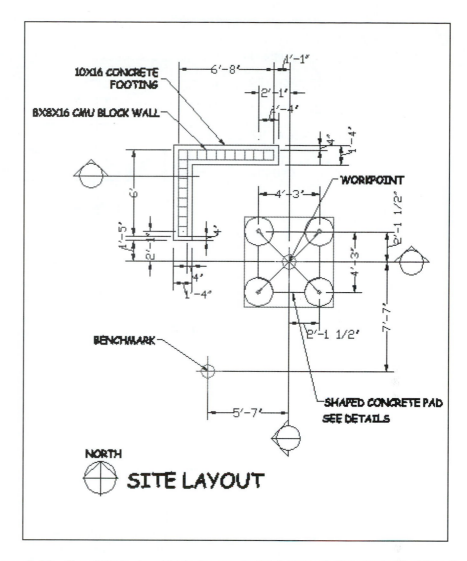

Figure 2-11. The OLPAP checklist helps you to think through the content of the site plan before you draw it.

tions associated with these pieces, like specifications, installation methods, and special instructions.

4. Assembly is shown correctly. For a site plan, assembly includes the relationship of the site features shown on the drawings. They should be in the correct position, with their sequence of installation or the way they are put together clearly referenced.

5. Presentation and the format of the drawing should be clear. There should be a margin, border, and title block with scale, dates, and sheet name. The organization of the sheet, including line weight, lettering, and the position of the information on the page, should be neat, legible, and professional.

Before beginning a sheet, you can also use the OLPAP checklist to think about what you will draft on that sheet and how it will fit onto the paper. For example, Figure 2-12 shows how the same OLPAP checklist helps you to think through the content of a foundation plan. Refer to this figure as you read through the following list:

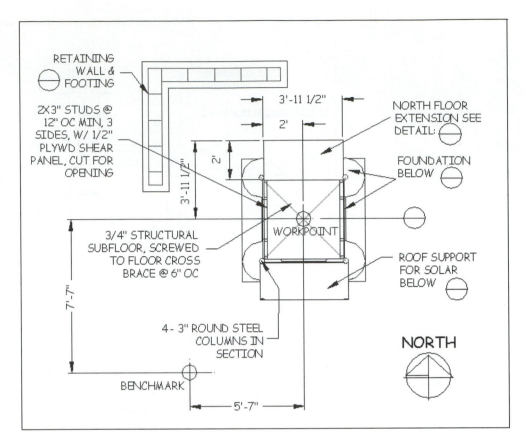

RETAINING WALL & FOOTING

2X3" STUDS @ 12" OC MIN, 3 SIDES, W/ 1/2" PLYWD SHEAR PANEL, CUT FOR OPENING

3'-11 1/2"

2'

3'-11 1/2"

2'

NORTH FLOOR EXTENSION SEE DETAIL:

FOUNDATION BELOW

3/4" STRUCTURAL SUBFLOOR, SCREWED TO FLOOR CROSS BRACE @ 6" OC

WORKPOINT

ROOF SUPPORT FOR SOLAR BELOW

7'-7"

4- 3" ROUND STEEL COLUMNS IN SECTION

NORTH

BENCHMARK

5'-7"

Figure 2-12. The OLPAP checklist also helps you to check the content of a foundation drawing before and after it is drawn.

1. Orient. The drawing should be oriented to the north with an arrow and should show how it fits into the overall set of drawings with a detail number, title, and scale. Orient the workpoint to the benchmark on the site plan. The workpoint is the starting point for all dimensions in the plan.

2. Layout. Provide the dimensions necessary to lay out the pieces shown on the drawings referenced according to the location of the workpoint. For a foundation plan, this includes the components of the walls and anything related to the pieces that are part of the work. The format for the dimensions and how they should appear on the drawings will be discussed later.

3. Pieces and processes. Callouts for all the pieces shown on the drawing should be clearly noted. Include all interior and exterior spaces and all relevant parts of the illustrated assembly. Limit the number of callouts to the specific installations that this plan addresses. For example, you would not call out walkways shown on a site plan unless they were specifically related to the foundation.

4. Assembly. All pieces should be shown in their correct relationships. They should be correctly related and logically positioned. For a plan, include the alignment of objects and other pieces of the general assembly being described by the drawing.

5. Presentation. The drawing should be neat and well laid out to reflect pre-planning, forethought, and a strong management style. Though it does not need to be a work of art, it should look like it was prepared by a construction professional. There should be a margin, a border, and a title block with scale, date, sheet title and your name at a minimum.

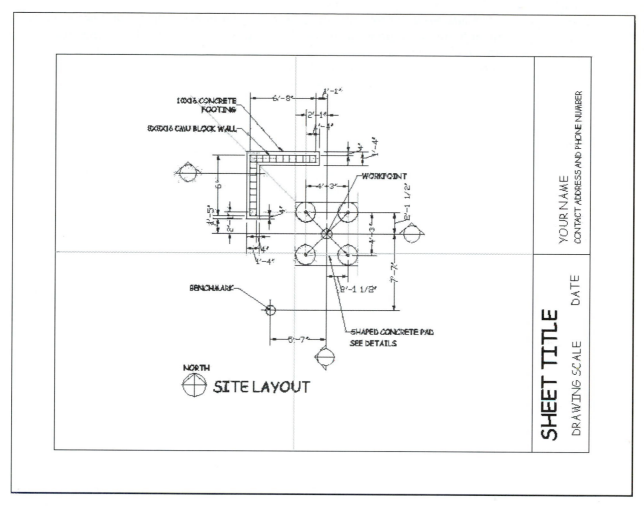

Figure 2-13. When a construction drawing is well laid out, it reflects good planning and forethought. A well-planned sheet gives the impression that it was drawn by someone who knew what he or she was doing.

By thinking through the drawing before you draft it, you can avoid making a plan or elevation so big that it runs off the page or so small that it cannot be understood. As shown in Figure 2-13, good sheet planning means making sure that everything related to the drawing will fit around the image without appearing cluttered or misaligned.

OLPAP and the same kind of planning can be applied to a full set of field drawings. In fact, the key to making sure that a set of drawings works well together, and that all the information necessary for a particular task is available for the construction, is to plan the drawings thoroughly from the start. Using Figure 1-18 to determine the kinds of sheets that might be necessary for a particular project, begin by reviewing the program and the basic requirements of the solution to the problem. Remember, the drawings will represent the solution. The sheets for the schematics will give you a rough idea of what will be necessary for the completed set. The preliminaries are important because, whether they are one sheet or twenty, they will be the base drawings for the engineered set after costs and early specifications have been confirmed. Many architects will use the table of contents to list the types of drawings and kinds of information that must be included on each sheet. Some will even draw a scaled version of the drawings called a "cartoon set" and actually lay out the sheets so that they can calculate the hours it will take to draft each sheet. These cartoons are then adjusted and annotated as new information emerges in the design development process.

Cartoons will probably not be necessary for field drafting, but it is good to keep them in mind if a project is particularly complex. For the field drawings used as examples in this book, most of the planning has already been thought out, but you should understand how to use the basic OLPAP principles and apply them to new sheets or your first field problem.

On the Border

A good way to practice drawing lines with good line weight is to draft the borders and title blocks on the sheets you will need for your field drawings. In practice, you would probably draft a template that you can then reproduce for the other sheets in the set, but drafting the borders and lettering the titles will give you a chance to practice.

Follow the steps in Figure 2-14 to lay out the borders for the base sheets for a small set of field drawings. Try to use just one pencil to draft the different line weights.

1. Start by taping the blank sheet of 11×17 copy paper down to any flat surface. Then use your measuring tape and the rolling parallel ruler to lay out lightly the borderlines. Place a mark about $1/2$" away from all four edges of the sheet. The tools will feel awkward at first, but the point is to practice so you can use them to draft more complicated drawings later.

2. To draw parallel lines, set the edge of the rolling parallel to the edge of the paper and then roll down (or roll across) to the mark placed at the position where you want the lines to be. Be sure to draw a light layout line. You will darken it later.

3. Next add light layout lines for a 1" title block to the right side of the sheet. Divide the 1" title block into rectangles for the title, scale, date, your name, and sheet number.

4. When everything is laid out, punch out the lines of the title block and the borderlines. After you complete the borders and title blocks for each sheet, use two light lines to divide the area within the borders into four equal sections. These lines will act as guides to lay out future drawings.

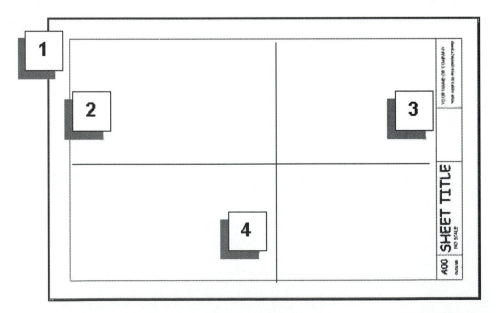

Figure 2-14. Practice your line weight by drafting the borders and title blocks of the sheets you will use in this book.

Construction Lettering

Good lettering is an art. Some might say it is a lost art because it is not commonly found in today's construction drawings. The computer plays a part, although some of it may be because there is little time for hand lettering. For field drafting, however, clear and legible lettering is as important as the lines and symbols on the rest of the drawing. It is used for the callouts and notes that explain the construction, and it includes labels, dimensions, and descriptions of special procedures. For hand lettering, capital letters are easier to print and read. You can develop your own individual lettering style later if you want, but for now you should stick to basic printing and try to be as legible as possible.

In a perfect world, with perfect handwriting, your letters should look like the ones in Figure 2-15. This figure is an illustration of the American Standard Alphabet in its most common architectural form. Note that you should not include italic or slanted letters. Slanted lettering implies a direction, which is distracting and not always appropriate in a construction drawing.

Figure 2-16 shows how to set up guidelines to practice your lettering. You can use a sheet of grid paper, but drawing the lines yourself will help you practice using

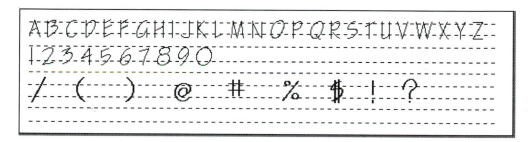

Figure 2-15. Good hand lettering is a dying art that some architects no longer use. For a constructor, your lettering needs only to be quick, clear, and readable.

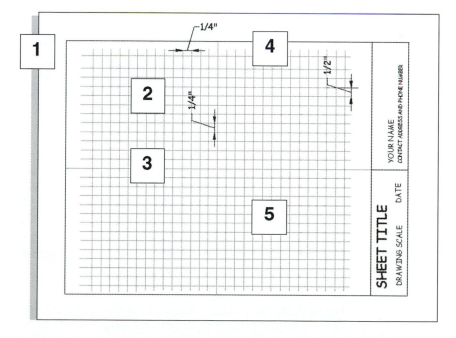

Figure 2-16. Draw a grid of guidelines with your rolling parallel glider to practice your line weight and lettering as well as moving the ruler evenly.

the parallel glider and your pencil to get an even line weight. If you did this again and again, you would probably perfect your own style of lettering. At the very least, you will have a chance to practice using the rolling parallel and a pencil to draft lines.

1. First, tape down a sheet of your bordered paper to a flat surface. Align the rolling parallel ruler with the left borderline of the sheet and roll the ruler to about the center of the paper. Start by drafting a light line with a sharp pencil.

2. Next, use the measuring tape to mark this line vertically with a series of very light marks every $1/4$". You will use these marks to draft rows of parallel horizontal lines as guidelines. As an alternative, you can use two vertical lines, one on each side of the sheet, with $1/4$" marks on both sides to guide your horizontal lines from two points. Keeping your marks parallel and evenly spaced is difficult with this alternative method.

3. The trick is to draft these lines as lightly and as evenly spaced as possible. Remember, the sharper your pencil, the lighter the line. Getting evenly spaced parallel lines is much more difficult, but with practice, it can be done without even thinking about it.

4. Do the same in the opposite direction. Start by picking a horizontal line in the approximate center of the sheet and mark the length of that line into $1/4$" segments. Using the marks on this horizontal line, draft a series of parallel vertical lines to form a grid. When the grid is complete, you should see row after row of consistent line weights in evenly spaced lines.

If you run into trouble keeping the lines parallel, turn the paper over and try it again. It will take time to master the rolling parallel, but once you do, the glider will free you from a drafting board and allow you to draft fairly sophisticated drawings just about anywhere.

Note in Figure 2-17 that it is also possible to use the markings on the vertical edge of your parallel glider. Draw a horizontal line toward the bottom of a blank sheet, then

Figure 2-17. The vertical edge of the rolling parallel glider has a ruler that can be used to space guidelines for your lettering.

move the parallel up $^1/_4$″ using the side of the ruler to note the distance to the next line. It is a little harder to draft a parallel line this way—you have to develop just the right touch—but once you get used to this trick, it can increase your speed and free you from a measuring tape or an architectural scale.

It Takes a Lot of Practice

When you finish the grid, you should have a sheet with a very lightly drafted $^1/_4$″ grid. This grid is a base sheet you can use to help you practice your lettering. As you letter, be aware of the spacing between both the letters and the words. Spacing should appear even for all letters within a word and a little larger, but still equal, for all words in a sentence. Remember, the point is to print clearly and legibly, but also quickly, so you do not need to be artistic unless you feel the need to express yourself.

Use the same pencil to print your name, address, and phone number within the $^1/_4$″ high horizontal lines, starting from the top left of the sheet and filling in every other line. If you want, you can try an old drafting trick illustrated in Figure 2-18. Simply turn the rolling parallel vertical and use it to guide the vertical strokes of your letters. With practice, most people can letter more neatly and quickly using this technique than they can with a free hand.

After you have practiced laying out the grid lines and lettering on a few sheets, your lettering should be good enough to letter in the sheet number, title, and your name and address in the title block of the sheets, as shown in Figure 2-19. Your

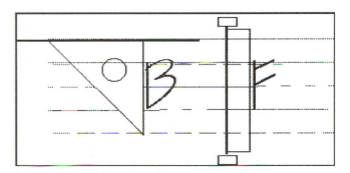

Figure 2-18. You can use a triangle or the rolling parallel glider turned vertically to guide the vertical stroke of your lettering.

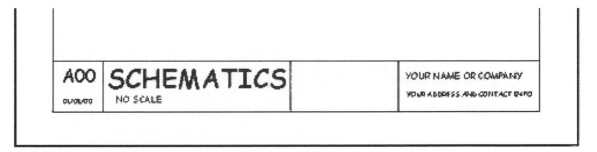

Figure 2-19. Lettering in the title blocks will give workers their first impression of the quality of the information that the drawings contain.

lettering in these title blocks will be the first impression workers will have of the information that the drawings contain.

Lettering well takes a lot of practice. As a constructor, use standard letters. They will clarify your hand by focusing on the consistent vertical and horizontal strokes found in good lettering. But the point here is to be as legible as possible. No one expects you to develop the skills of a traditional architect. In fact, most architects now letter and draft with computers. As a constructor, you do not always have the luxury of a computer when you need to draw something spontaneously in the field. And all that technology is not necessary for most field problems.

Chapter 3

FIELD DRAFTING

The Trainer: A Step-by-Step Example

Of course, the best way to understand how to use this visual approach is to apply the seven steps to a real problem. This will give you the opportunity to practice your line weights and lettering, while giving you a hands-on feel for the construction communications process and the way a set of drawings work together. This book uses a specially designed trainer to walk you through the seven steps and focus interaction and problem solving skills on a common problem. The example includes simple and complex beams, cantilevers, tension and compression rods, and point and distributed foundation loads. It also incorporates many of the fundamental details of both wood and lightweight steel framing, as well as basic heavy steel, masonry, and reinforced concrete construction.

As a result, the building's assembly and finishes will require more than a standardized approach to drawing and detailing a building's construction. In fact, there are no easy answers with this deceptively simple building and the more you work with it, the more you will see the challenges that it presents. This also means there are no standard techniques or any need for special expertise or construction experience. Both the novice and the expert will face the same fundamental challenge: determining the most logically efficient way to build this building while fulfilling all of its programmatic requirements.

Resolving the challenges of this problem will set up the need for questions and discussion to understand its intent and analyze alternate solutions for its design. This interaction will inevitably lead to dead ends and at least some level of frustration because the problem is real. There is no correct answer, and it remains to be seen if any single solution can ever be considered the best possible result.

To complete the field drawings for the trainer, you will therefore have to work through the seven-step process shown in Figure 3-1. You will begin by translating the base requirements as a design concept, document your schematic concept as an engineered set of 2D drawings, add 3D details to explain its assembly, and preconstruct the resulting field drawing to test the accuracy and clarity of the work.

Chapter 3 covers the first three steps of this visual approach to problem solving:

1. Step 1 shows how a vague verbal concept can be reduced to a programmatic diagram of the features that must be included in the final drawings. This step is

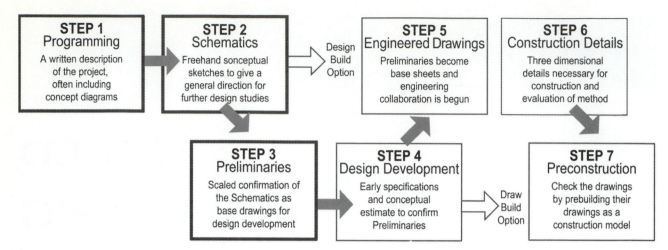

Figure 3-1. Chapter 3 will cover the first three steps in the seven-step visual approach to problem solving. These steps reduce a vague verbal description to a scaled set of drawings that can be used as the basis of the engineered drawings.

important because it generally defines the direction for the schematics drawn in step 2, but it also sets the requirements by which the schematics should be evaluated.

2. The schematics produced in step 2 are rough sketches. Drawn freehand or very roughly to scale, they are conceptual drawings of possible plans, elevations, and sections for the trainer. Their purpose is to resolve the design so that it can be drawn more accurately as the preliminaries.

3. In Step 3, the preliminaries are drawn to scale so that they represent the dimensions of the building. This step is important because it will ensure that all the features in the program and the schematics have been considered.

Step 1: Programming (Defining the Problem)

To draft the construction documents for the trainer, you must first understand the requirements for the building. That's the goal of step 1. A program is a detailed description of the requirements for the project. It can be a combination of written and graphical information, and it includes everything known about the required features or confent of the solution to the problem. The objective of the program is to guide the design of the schematic drawings.

Think about how difficult it is to put together enough information to understand the shape and size of a small building—let alone explain the details of its construction—and you have a sense of what it takes to define what it is that you are trying to solve. It is amazing how many people will try to solve a problem before they fully understand what it is. For example, imagine you are having lunch with the project manager in charge of the construction of a complex of industrial office buildings. The project is about to begin construction in an area with a very high water table and will be spread over several hundred acres. The project manager wants you to design and build a distributed network of communications towers to house the computer equipment that will be used to manage the construction. She calls these buildings trainers because they are intended to guide and instruct the various superintendents and

"Here's what I want you to do: We need six small, simple sustainable computerized 'trainers' to house the distributed servers for the construction information system on this huge project. The job trailer will house the main server with wireless data and telecommunications beamed out to these distributed towers. The computer will share project information, house Web cameras, and maintain current project data. The trainers are like teachers standing in key locations on the jobsite with the latest information and instructions necessary to guide the work.

They should be rugged enough to withstand the high winds of the open site and ground movements from heavy equipment moving around the project. We will also want to move the buildings every few weeks to different locations as the project progresses, so the foundations should adapt to different kinds of terrain. For example, some of them will be placed on the roofs of the new buildings. The first one will go out by the rear gate, near the lower benchmark for the main complex. We need to build a retaining wall for the trainer in that area.

Oh yeah, and I want them to be self-contained and air-conditioned. No external connections for electrical service, plumbing, or mechanical systems should be included. A low-voltage lighting system and battery backup for the computers and the heating and cooling will also be required.

The floor level should be raised about five feet above the ground so that it is out of the mud and we can store equipment under it on a slab. Inside, there should be space for a computer and monitor as well as enough space to roll out drawings and store construction documents. The interior space should be just big enough for a desk and a couple of people to stand. Nothing too spacious.

The raised floor should be open to the north for natural light. The south side is for solar collection, but since there won't be much of a roof, you'll need to put a series of smaller roof panels down the side to increase the solar collection surface area. There should be a ship's ladder and entry door as an access stair from either the west or east, with a 24- to 30-inch operable window on the side opposite the door for ventilation. The door should have some kind of glazing so you can see who is at the door before it is opened. I'm not sure how the door should swing—maybe up?

The frame for each trainer should be very strong, probably steel, so that it can be moved by a crane or forklift into another position in a matter of minutes. When we're through with them, we should be able to deconstruct and pack them into a container for storage in a matter of hours. I would guess the walls should be panelized with hollow cavities and conduit for future wiring. Come to think of it, it would be good to use bright primary colors and put our company's logo and name on them to make them immediately visible on the jobsite and in our aerials.

Put together something by the end of the week so we can get a unit price. I want to have these built on an assembly line. That will be faster and we can control the production quality much better than trying to build them on site.

Any questions? Good, and don't forget your other work."

Figure 3-2. This text represents an oral description of the general requirements for the trainer. It describes a vague concept for a bold new idea and you have to make it work.

managers working throughout the construction site like a practical version of distance learning.

It's a bold idea that deserves the best possible design, and she's picked you as the person to help put it together. She has no idea what the trainers should look like, only a rough idea of the criteria they should meet. Assume that she starts to explain the details of these buildings during lunch and you forgot to bring a pencil. She says something like the conversation in the box in Figure 3-2.

After reading this box, can you visualize the buildings? Do you think you could build them based on her verbal description? You may be surprised at what you still need to know to produce a set of construction drawings for the trainer.

In even the most complex projects, a concept often begins with a casual conversation, usually scribbled down on anything that is available. To the beginning of an idea, more ideas are added, some of them hastily jotted down. Others are carefully researched with clippings and related information attached for future reference.

The result is a casual collection of requirements. In fact, they are often too casual, tricking you into missing a lot of important information that is necessary to bring them to reality. You have to clarify project requirements and make sure that you understand the extent of the work before you put too much time into it.

You could do this the hard way. Ask a few questions, work on it a few days, show her the results, listen to her corrections, do a little more work, ask her again, change what you did, ask more questions, forget some of the answers, and go around and around in a circle until she decides that you may not be worth the trouble and finds someone else to do the job. Worse yet, you could stop bugging her and start guessing based on what you think you remember from her original description. You might then show up in a few weeks with finished drawings that are completely wrong and have to do it all over again. This would be not only a waste of your time, but it would delay the entire project. If you're doing your job, you probably haven't got time to do this project twice (even if they wanted you to try again before they fired you).

What you need is a program to describe fully the problem and the requirements of the solution so that you can get everything completely defined before you begin. Try having someone read the description of the trainer to you again, as if you were still at lunch with the project manager. This time, draw a couple of diagrams of the project as it's being described to begin to get a mental image of what is being said. Use a pen and a scrap of paper or a napkin. If you are sloppy, you may need more than one napkin.

On your napkin, diagram the building as its description is read. Try drawing a plan, elevation, or section. You might also sketch the stair, window, and door if you feel confident enough to locate them. Note that if you don't start with a north arrow to orient yourself (OLPAP), you may get your directions confused as the description is read. Ask questions about the building's design and materials, but remember that the project manager expects you to figure out how to build the trainer. Like most managers, she is going to leave the details to you and just wants the project done right.

The result is a rough diagram of her verbal description. It might be useful to verify spontaneously some of the details that were said, but the real value of the diagram is that you have focused the thinking of more than one individual on a single visual hypothesis. The diagram therefore poses questions that further define the problem but does not yet design the solution. A programmatic diagram is therefore the first step in a visual approach to problem solving because it begins the process with a graphical representation of the key features of the program.

Figure 3-3 is one interpretation of the trainer's description. It has a main frame with four columns that sit on four round foundation pillars and a floor extending off one side of the frame. It is drawn spontaneously with questions like, "What if the solar panels hang from racks off these columns?" or "What if the interior space is like a space capsule, or the cabin of a small boat, efficiently organized so that the solar collectors can support it?" Before the questions, all you knew was that the trainer must be self-contained. After the questions, you will know how small the project manager thinks the inside of the trainer should be and if she really wants it to be totally self-contained.

Now look at your napkin. Did you get all the requirements for the project written down so you understand them? If not, keep asking questions until you feel you have all the information you need to write the program.

What you see as a result of these diagrams is a vague suggestion of physical form, but they are not intended to represent a design. They illustrate one rough interpretation of a building that "sounds" like it fits the initial requirements. From this visual hypothesis, you can ask questions that will continue to define the requirements of the final solution. You will find out what will work and what will not, and you will gather

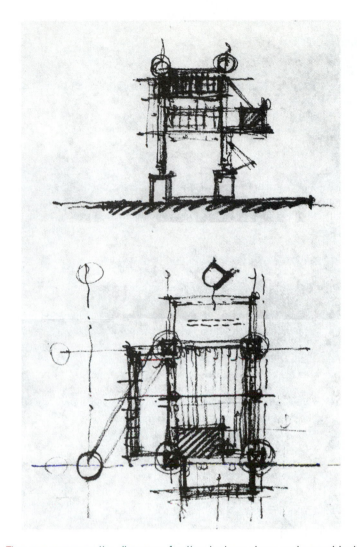

Figure 3-3. The programmatic diagram for the trainer does not need to be artistic.

information that will ultimately be written in the program. The program therefore began with a casual conversation during lunch. You came away from that meeting with a napkin sketch, some notes, and a general idea of what the project manager wants in the final solution.

As a professional, you would follow up that meeting with a memorandum confirming your discussion, like the one shown in Figure 3-4. It describes the general size and shape of the building, a list of the requirements that are to be included in the final solution, and copies of your napkin sketches. The objective is to make sure you understood all the requirements and have all the information you need to begin the schematics.

The project manager may review the memo immediately and either agree with your interpretation or return it to you with comments. She may also ignore your memorandum because she is busy with new problems—until, of course, you call her repeatedly to get her approval to proceed based on the memorandum. This approval is important because there is no use starting schematics until you are absolutely sure what you are trying to accomplish.

15 January 2002

Jane Doe, Project Manager
Upper State Regional Main Assembly Plant, General Aircraft Corporation
Hamdome Engineering and Construction
200 NW Washington Blvd.
Powderhead, New Jersey 54321

Dear Jane:

This memo is to confirm my understanding of the six control towers you would like me to produce for the Upper State Regional Main Assembly project. Per our conversation, each of these trainers is to house computer network equipment and project documentation and be wirelessly linked to servers in the main project trailer.

The buildings have the following program requirements:

1. Design loads for the building will include wind loads of 50 mph.
2. Easily relocatable with a crane and forklift.
3. Deconstructable so it can be stored or moved between projects.
4. Foundation that will adapt to different terrain.
5. Self-contained with solar PV and collectors.
6. Raised floor with open storage underneath.
7. At least one operable window and a skylight.
8. Access stairs to a glazed lockable door.
9. Approximately 20 sq. ft. interior space to include:
   a. Computer, monitor, and peripherals.
   b. Desk or built-in countertop and chair.
   c. Storage for plans and specs.
   d. Conference area.
10. Observation deck.
11. Brightly colored finishes with company logo on the side.

I am also attaching copies of the diagrams we drew during our meeting and the site survey for the area around the rear gate. Please review this material and make any corrections or additions that you would like me to include in the final construction. It is also important to note the location of the first trainer. After your confirmation of this program, I will submit a set of schematics for further approval in preparation for the scaled preliminaries, pricing, and eventual construction drawings and details.

Thank you again for this opportunity and your confidence in my ability to complete this project successfully.

Sincerely,

Robert Goodwind
Building Engineer

Figure 3-4. The program could be a memorandum with copies of the napkin drawings confirming your understanding of the project.

Step 2: The Schematics

Schematics usually include a site plan, floor plans, one or two rough elevations, and a section that shows the heights of the building and the floors. For design professionals, these drawings are often artistic, but as a constructor, you need to draw only enough to confirm the program requirements. For the trainer, a few rough sketches are sufficient; even less would probably be sufficient for most field problems like special formwork, scaffolding, or falsework.

To begin the schematics, you need to have some idea of where the first trainer will be placed so you can work out an initial site plan. The project manager mentioned putting it near the rear gate adjacent to an existing benchmark. There was also mention of a retaining wall. (See Figure 3-2.) The site information and any other existing conditions that will affect the design should be part of the information you received in response to your memorandum.

The schematics are freehand drawings that contain enough information to illustrate at least one way to meet the program requirements. The schematics should expand on the program with visual ideas. These design schemes visually communicate your thoughts so that other members of the project team can see them. In fact, the objective of this step is to generate comments and verify the program. In other words, you want to continue the conversation, perhaps with some off-the-wall suggestions for a solution to find out what the range of possibilities is for the project. These drawings graphically suggest possible directions for the project and get a reaction.

In other words, you use the schematics to test ideas by putting them on the table for comment. In the end, the schematics will be accepted, modified, or completely rejected. If they are accepted, you can proceed directly into scaled preliminaries. If they are modified, you can make changes when you draft the preliminaries. And if they are rejected, you will be able to redraw the schematics with the satisfaction of knowing at least one solution that will not work. Knowing what is not acceptable goes a long way toward understanding what is acceptable.

Most important, all of these drawings should be drawn freehand, without a ruler, to keep the ideas loose and open to input and comment. If you spend a lot of time on the schematics, you will be reluctant to make changes and listen to suggested alternatives. For now, they do not have to be right or perfect, only clear enough to know where they may be wrong.

Figure 3-5 shows a set of schematics with a rough idea of one way to meet the program requirements. The ground level plan shows a retaining wall on the west side to compensate for the slightly sloping terrain. The elevations show four steel columns mounted on four concrete piers for stability. Each of these piers breaks down into a stack of concrete "coins" so they can be deconstructed. The raised floor plan shows a

Multiple Solutions

In practice, it's almost always a good idea to generate multiple solutions to the problem. Generating solutions is often done in sets of three to bracket a clear direction. One idea illustrates an elaborate scheme if money were no object. Another idea is an absolute minimalist approach that barely solves the problem. A third idea could be one that you believe exactly meets the program requirements. The end result is often a combination of all three ideas.

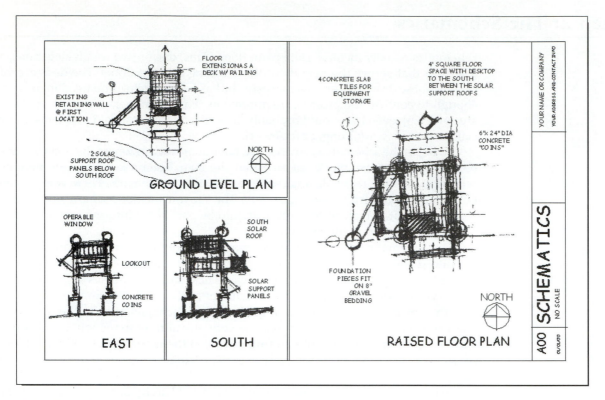

Figure 3-5. The schematic drawings for the trainer illustrate one way to meet the requirements of the program. If they are approved, the preliminaries would represent drafts of this initial concept to scale.

space about 4 feet square under a gable roof, with a floor extension cantilevering from the columns for storage, equipment, and desk space.

As a rule, all the requirements you have from the program should be noted somewhere on the schematics. You should also use the OLPAP checklist to check the content of the drawings. For example, the ground level and raised floor plans should orient the project manager to the site, give overall layout dimensions, and call out pieces and processes like storage areas, stairs, rails, door swings, window placement, workspaces, and possible lift points for moving the structure. Other drawings should suggest roof slopes, ceiling heights, and the general layout of the building.

The schematics suggest a physical form for the building, but they do not really go into any detail. It's obvious at this point that you do not need to know how to build the design and you may not even fully understand the relationships between the plans and elevations or how certain features like the foundation will actually be manufactured. In fact, for most field drawings, including the trainer, a few additional napkin sketches may be enough to clarify a solution immediately and begin the preliminaries. Make sure you get your napkins reviewed, dated, and filed for future reference.

See if you can think of other alternatives that may be better solutions to the program requirements. Be certain to review the memorandum and the existing site conditions carefully. If you can come up with a better alternative, present your idea to a third party and let him or her be the judge. If your idea is better, you are ready to take your idea into preliminaries.

Step 3: The Preliminaries

As shown in Figure 2-2, the preliminaries include a title sheet, index, site plan, floor plans, roof plan, elevations, sections, and a stair plan and section. Because the information shown on these drawings is derived from the approved schematics, the objective of the preliminaries is to draft the schematics to scale to confirm the information shown and verify that everything will fit as anticipated. Almost certainly, corrections will have to be made when the rough sketches are converted to scaled drawings.

Scaled plans, elevations, and sections are called orthographic projections. To understand the relationship of an orthographic projection to a three-dimensional object, it's also important to understand how plans, elevations, and sections relate to each other as a set of construction drawings. These projections communicate information along a two-dimensional plane that could not be shown in any other way.

As you can see in Figure 3-6, imaginary lines extend from the object to the plane of the projection. The object is flattened on this plane into a two-dimensional drawing. The projection is orthographic because the lines are perpendicular and directly proportional to the objects they represent. The lines retain the overall size, shape, and proportion of the object as a 2D drawing.

These projections are important because each is part of the final set of construction drawings. Like the projections shown in Figure 1-10, no single drawing represents the entire three-dimensional object. In other words, you cannot build a building with just a floor plan any more than you can build a building with just one elevation. It takes a set of projections to communicate the shape and size of the total building.

To understand the building, all the drawings must also be read and interpreted at the same time. In the same way that you cannot build a building with just one projection, you cannot draft a set of projections without drafting all the sheets at the same time. To draft a floor plan, you therefore have to draft the elevations and sections. A single sheet cannot be completely drafted by itself. You must draft these drawings

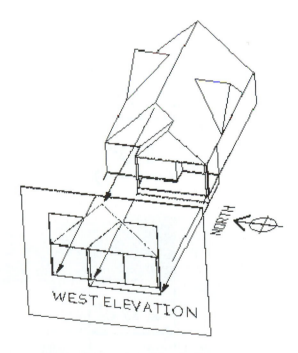

Figure 3-6. *Plans, elevations, and sections are orthographic projections of a three-dimensional object.*

with an inevitable degree of uncertainty. Of course, because so much is unknown, you have to draft these drawings with an inevitable degree of uncertainty.

One factor that makes these projections easier to visualize is a common scale. It's easier to interpret the drawings when they all share the same proportions.

Drafting to Scale

The only tools you need for field drafting are a rolling parallel and a measuring tape or ruler. Thus, drafting a building to scale will take a little practice, partly because all of this is new to you but mainly because, as you can see in Figure 3-7, you will be using a measuring tape instead of a triangular scale like those used by architects and engineers. Some may call this method a macho method of scaled drafting, but it is really a way to get you down to the basics so you can put these drawings together in the field. Of course, an architect or engineer would find this method unnecessarily cumbersome, but as a constructor you will not always have the luxuries of an office and a fully equipped drafting workstation. On a jobsite, with a clipboard and a set of plans rolled out in the dirt, it's much easier to measure an existing condition with a measuring tape and use that same tape to draft the field drawing to scale.

To use a measuring tape as a scale, you need to understand that some fraction of an inch on a construction drawing is equivalent to some full-size physical dimension in the field. For example, $\frac{1}{4}''$ on a drawing might equal 1'0" on a building, or 1'9" on the building would equal $\frac{7}{16}''$ on a ruler. If the scale is $\frac{1}{4}'' = 1'0''$, then $\frac{3}{4}'' = 3'0''$ and $\frac{7}{8}'' = 3'6''$. A building that is 22'4 $\frac{1}{2}''$ square is a little less than $5\frac{5}{8}''$ square on the drawing.

Most floor plans and elevations use a scale of $\frac{1}{4}'' = 1'0''$. Other scales include $\frac{1}{8}''$ = 1'0" for plot plans or floor plans for very large buildings and $\frac{1}{2}'' = 1'0''$ or 1"=1'0" for details. Common engineering scales are 1"=20'0", 1"=40'0", 1"=50'0", and 1"=100'0".

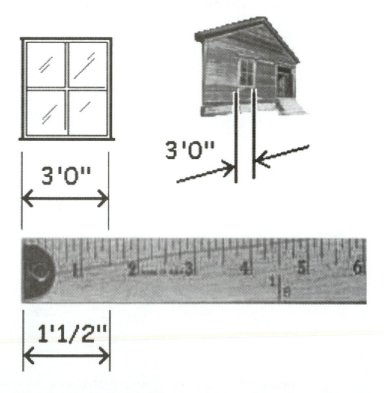

Figure 3-7. Any ruler or measuring tape can be used to scale a drawing. If a $\frac{1}{2}''$ equals 1'0", then three $\frac{1}{2}''$ lengths on the ruler will equal 3'0".

If the scale is 1″ = 20′0″, then $^3/_4$″ will equal 15′ and a 25′ setback for a building would be $1^1/_4$″. At a scale of 1″=50′0″, a 87′0″ long wall would measure just under $1^3/_4$″. Think about it this way: if 1″ = 50′, then $^1/_2$″=25′ and $^1/_4$″ will be about 12.5′. You could also use a calculator, but most of the time you can be accurate enough without one.

Since you are field drafting, don't worry about scaling the drawings precisely. No one in this business measures the drawings in the field unless they absolutely have to and even then, it may be best to get a clarification from the design team. For field drawings, it's necessary only to get the projections into the correct proportions so that the building that is drafted looks like the one being constructed. Even if you took the time to draft these drawings absolutely perfectly, paper stretches, the copy or printing process warps the paper and expands the lines, the sheet gets folded, and no one with experience will be measuring these drawings. As a constructor, the place for perfection is in the construction, not on paper. Be sure the dimensions you give are accurate and the drawing is fairly close to the correct proportion. You will get into dimensioning later.

Laying out Drawings

With this overview of the orthographic projections and scaled drafting, you are now ready to lay out one of the first sheets for the preliminaries. It's important that each sheet is well planned so that it is clear and well organized. The worker's eye should move easily from line to object so that he or she can immediately visualize the information presented.

Use Figure 3-8 as a layout guide and use the OLPAP criteria again as a checklist and leave enough room for dimensions, notes, and details. Remember that important information should stand out when the drawings get to the field. Also think about the

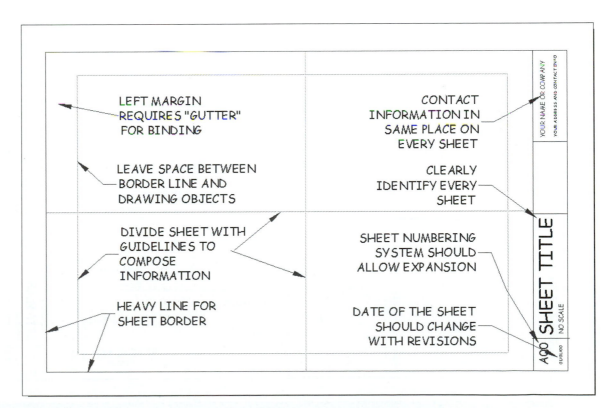

Figure 3-8. Lay out the sheet so that the information can be presented clearly and include plenty of room for notes and dimensions.

way the sheets will be bound together and where the worker's eye will probably go first as he or she flips from page to page. Most believe the right upper side of the sheet should contain the most important information.

Site Plans Are for the Birds

A site plan is an orthographic projection of the building and its site. It's a "bird's eye" view of the building and the property on which it is constructed. It should show the location and orientation of the building from the property lines as well as the size of the property itself.

For most projects, the site plan also gives a "metes and bounds" description for the property lines in relation to a surveyor's monument or benchmark near the site. This description gives the lengths and angles of the property line and is also used for legal purposes. It is based on an exact compass direction from which to align the property lines and a workpoint for the construction.

The site plan in Figure 3-9 shows a base benchmark that sets the height of the ground above sea level and shows the distances from this benchmark to a workpoint on the construction site. The benchmark is set by an engineer according to survey data recorded for the property in the area. It is a reference point used to locate the property lines, setbacks, and the exact location of the building. The workpoint is a site-specific benchmark, usually brought in close to the jobsite so that workers do not have to take measurements continually from the benchmark. For the trainer, the workpoint is centered on the four column locations and will be used in the field to lay out the foundations.

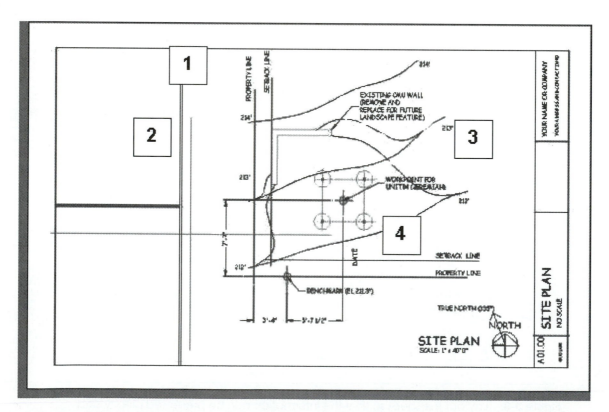

Figure 3-9. The preliminary site plan should be drafted so that it is one of the first sheets in the set of construction drawings.

The sloping ground means that a retaining wall is necessary to provide a flat storage area. The retaining wall for this location will become a permanent part of the total project, so it can be constructed with a continuous foundation and used to enclose a landscaped area after the tower is moved to another location.

To draft the site plan, use the parallel glider, measuring tape, and the sheets you laid out when you practiced the line weights and title block lettering to lightly lay out the content, as shown in Figure 3-9.

1. Site plans should always be oriented so that the top of the sheet is north. A north arrow is necessary to orient the boundaries of the site to a compass direction so it can be laid out in the field.

2. Begin by lightly drafting the site boundaries for the project and the location of the first trainer. The left side of the sheet will be used later for a table of contents, schedules, and general notes. Though not always important for temporary construction buildings, almost every city or county has ordinances for the location of a building on a site. Placement of buildings is governed by setbacks from the property line that are regulated by zoning codes. These laws are passed by local governments to regulate the use of property, the location on the site, and the type of construction.

3. Show existing buildings, trees, and other important natural features and the location of water, sewer, and electrical lines, but do not punch them out. As you can see from the site survey, the trainer is on a lot with three contour lines at 1-foot contour intervals. For large projects, contour intervals are usually shown for every 2 feet of elevation change. Note that you must also assign a "plan north" to orient the floor plan and elevations on the other sheets when the building is not oriented directly to magnetic north.

4. Lay out the footprint of the trainer from the property lines or a benchmark. This footprint must be dimensioned in at least two directions from a surveyor's benchmark near the property line. Setbacks and rights of way, as well as the elevations above sea level of the workpoint and the topographic contour lines, should also be shown where applicable. Note that contour lines also show the elevations for the new grades. These topographic lines represent the direction of the slope of the lot. Sometimes these lines are omitted, even if there is a slope, if the site is very close to flat or the change in elevation is uniform. In these cases, spot elevations are shown as symbols on the plan.

Floor Plans Are Horizontal Sections

Once you finish lightly laying out the site plan, you are ready to begin the floor plans. As shown in Figure 3-10, a floor plan is an orthographic projection of a horizontal section through the building. This horizontal section cuts the building well above the floor line and is the point of origin for the projection. Some say this occurs 3 to 4 feet above the floor, but the height varies depending on what it is that you want to show in the plan view. As a rule, the section should be taken so that the plan shows all doors and windows (even those high off the floor). Whenever possible, it should also look down at the top of stairs or balconies, cabinets, or other features in a particular room.

Like the site plan, a floor plan is a bird's eye or aerial view. It should be oriented so that "plan north" is at the top of the sheet and all geographic references are the same as the site plan. Thus, the north side of the building is on the upper part of the sheet for all plans. When plans are oriented in this way, reading them in the field is simplified because the drawings can be oriented to the north as they are being read.

Two floor plans are necessary for the trainer. One is on the ground plane that shows the storage area and the lower portion of the stair, and the other is for the raised floor showing the main work area and the upper part of the same stair. You do not

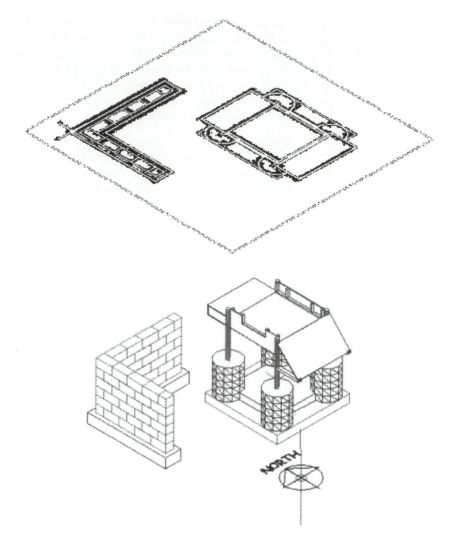

Figure 3-10. Raised floor plan; sheet A3.2 is a horizontal section taken above the floor plane so that it shows the window and door openings that will be provided.

have enough information to detail completely the floor plans in the preliminary drawings, but you can show the overall sizes for these two areas as scaled drawings to confirm the schematics. Because of the program, the schematics show a very tight floor layout. The volume of interior space has to be as small as possible to be self-contained.

The objectives of the preliminaries are to confirm the schematics and to act as the base drawings for the construction documents, so you want to test the scale and proportions of the concept and make sure it is feasible. Begin by drawing the overall dimensions of the trainer and working on the known features. Because this is such a small space, it will be more difficult to get everything to fit, so you have to make sure to be as accurate as possible with your scale.

All the preliminaries must be drawn at the same time because dimensions and perhaps some of the features will change as the drawings progress. If everything is lightly laid out until you are sure it all fits together, it will be a simple matter of punching out all the object lines when the sheets are ready. The idea is to keep things flexible so the information on each sheet can be coordinated and changed as more details are resolved on the other plans, elevations, and section. The floor plans are therefore just part of a series of relationships that need to be evaluated and drafted to make sure everything fits together.

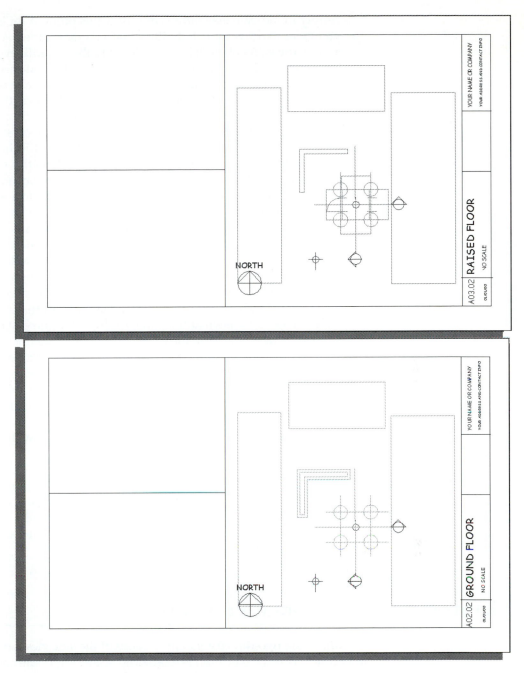

Figure 3-11. The ground and raised floor plans are horizontal sections taken through the building to show the two-dimenisonal relationships of each plan.

Use the parallel glider, measuring tape, and one of the sheets you laid out when you practiced the line weights and lettering for the title block. Remember to lay out the two floor plans lightly, similar to the example shown in Figure 3-11.

1. Use OLPAP again as a checklist to visualize the information that will be required on each of the floor plans. Center the floor plan on the right side of the sheet and position it to allow for dimensions and notes that will surround the plan. Be sure to leave room on the left part of the sheet for future details.
2. Lay out the perimeter of the building with the key features at each level. For the ground level plan, include the open storage area and slab and some of the main features of the foundation. The idea is not to draw too much detail, but

simply to indicate the features lightly at this point. A lot is still unknown, so you want to draw some light lines that you may have to change later. For example, the stairs obviously come down to the ground level, but it is too early to know exactly where they will be. All you can do at this point is to draw a rectangle indicating about where they will be and make adjustments later.

3. Every plan on every sheet should be drafted in exactly the same place from sheet to sheet, including the engineered plans that will come later. This technique helps workers read the plans because their eyes will not have to search for new information as they flip from sheet to sheet. When the plans are aligned, they seem somewhat animated as workers flip from page to page.

4. Use the lightly laid out ground level floor plan to lay out the raised floor plan by tracing over the first plan. You can take the sheets to a window to see the lines through the paper. You can also tape a plan that has been laid out over a blank sheet and use a pencil point to make an "impression" in each corner of the building into the sheet below. (You want to be careful not to punch a hole in the paper.) Once the impression is made, remove the plan and lay out the second floor plan just like the first floor using the impressions to align the two drawings.

5. On the raised floor plan, the exterior walls will be slightly fatter than interior walls because of exterior insulation and siding, but the specifications for this material are not known at this time. At $^{1}/_{4}' = 1'0''$, no one can really tell the difference anyway, so lay all the walls out as if they are about 4" thick. That's just a little less than $^{1}/_{8}''$ on a measuring tape, which is not much room to work with but it gives you a sense of the scale of the drawing compared to the actual 4" visible on the same tape. You will be able to show the actual dimensions and the materials in these walls in one of the details when you know more about them. For now, all you know is that they exist.

6. Once the walls are lightly laid out, you can locate wall openings like windows and doors by drafting a light line at each side of the opening. Lightly show the arcs for the door swings, but do not draw the lines that represent the actual doors. You will do that when you are ready to punch out the drawing. There is not a lot more you can add at this point. Again, you have to wait until all the drawings are blocked out to punch out the walls. For example, the top of the stairs will obviously be at the door and probably be as wide as the door, but their actual construction is not known.

Elevations Are Horizontal Projections

Elevations are two-dimensional projections of the side views of a building. As shown in Figure 3-12, each elevation is referenced according to the compass direction of the projection plane on a site plan. For example, if the projection plane is on the south side of the building, it is the south elevation; if it is on the west side of the building, it is the west elevation; and if it is on the east side, it is the east elevation.

Each elevation works with the other elevations to give a complete three-dimensional picture of the exterior of the building. They are important because they also give floor plans a third dimension. The floor plans give the dimensional relationships along a horizontal two-dimensional plane, while the elevations give the dimensional relationships along a vertical plane. The floor plans therefore depend on the elevations. One must have the other. Both must therefore be drawn simultaneously to be coordinated correctly.

In projects where the exterior treatment is the same on all four sides, it may not be necessary to draft all four elevations at the same scale. In other words, you might draft the entry elevation at $^{1}/_{4}'' = 1'0''$ and the other three elevations at $^{1}/_{8}'' = 1'0''$ if the building is not much different from side to side. For certain buildings, it may not even be

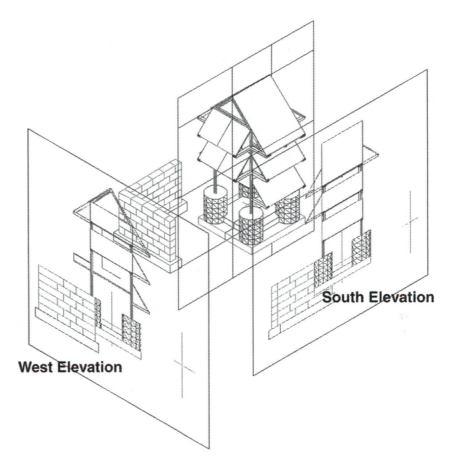

West Elevation

South Elevation

Figure 3-12. Elevations are two-dimensional projections of the building. They work together and with the other drawings to show a three-dimensional image of the building.

Interior Elevations are Projections

Interior elevations show the interior faces of a room. They are shown as if the walls of the room have been unfolded onto the sheet of paper. You should get in the habit of drafting all four elevations of the exterior of a building and all four elevations of the interior of any of its rooms simultaneously.

necessary to draft all four elevations. For others, you may have to include more elevations. The number of elevations you draw will vary with the complexity of the project.

For example, try lightly laying out the elevations for the trainer. One sheet will have the north and east elevations and the other, the south and west elevations. As a rule, these elevations should show the height of the building, the height of the floors, and the location and heights of the windows, doors, and roofs. Also use the OLPAP checklist to plan the kind of information that will be necessary for the elevations, including the retaining wall, entry stairs, outside storage areas, exterior materials, and the racks for the solar panels. Of course, you do not know much about these pieces and may not even use them in the long run, but block them in lightly to see how they fit.

The idea for the preliminary is to get a rough idea of everything so that you can make sure it works. If you do get specific ideas about how items might be put together, you should note them so that you can refer to them later.

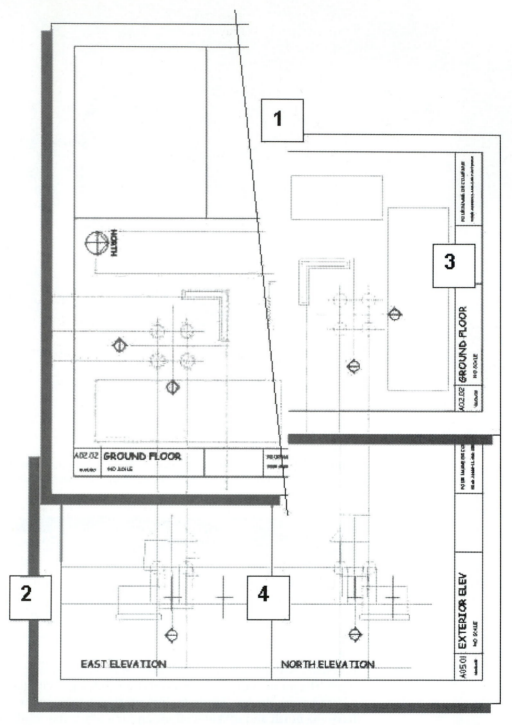

Figure 3-13. To save time and prevent mistakes, the dimensions of many of the main features of the elevations can be projected from the floor plans.

To save time, you can use the floor plans to lay out the two sheets of elevations. As shown in Figure 3-13, this technique is fairly simple.

1. Take a floor plan and tape it above the elevation you are preparing. Orient the floor plans above the elevation so that the side of the building you are drafting faces downward toward the blank sheet. Be sure the sheet is directly over the place on the paper where you intend to draft the elevation. You are facing the elevation of the floor plan that you are projecting, so visualizing the elevation should be fairly easy.

2. Lightly draft the horizontal lines for the floors. Use the parallel glider to project the exterior features from the plan to the elevation. The most important lines in this part of the layout are the finished grade and the floor elevations. The roof elevations will depend on the slope of the roof and the height of the plate for the sloping roof. The top of the plate is the top of the wall that supports the lower part of the roof.

3. When you have one of the elevations lightly laid out, turn the plans to align them with the approximate location for the other elevations. Once the plans are aligned, draw the horizontal lines and continue to project the edges of the features on the plans to the elevations. This drawing will include many of the corresponding dimensions to the elevations and will help you visualize what you are trying to draw. This technique means that you do not have to measure all the lines and will reduce the possibility of error from sheet to sheet.

4. You have to rotate the floor plan for each of the four different elevations. This technique is most useful when there are a lot of features on the plans to transfer to the elevations. The result should be a fairly accurate match of the base dimensions for the drawings. When you are finished, each sheet should have the light lines drafted to scale, with the doors and windows blocked out on the four elevations.

Keep in mind the dimensions and notes that you will need for each of the elevations. Continue to use OLPAP to check the content of the drawings. Again, these are preliminaries so there are still a lot of unknowns.

Sections Are Slices Through the Building

Usually you cut a section through a building in two directions. As shown in one direction in Figure 3-14, it's like taking a knife and slicing the building to show the interior of the building and the vertical relationships of the structure. Depending on the shape of the building, these are referred to as longitudinal sections and cross-sections. Longitudinal sections are usually along the long axis of the building, and the cross-sections are on the shorter or crossing axis.

The purpose of the sections is to show the parts of the building that are not visible in the building's elevations. The section includes the "elevations" of the floors and major components of the foundation and roof. These elevations are different from the exterior elevations of the building because they are measures from a reference point like the benchmark shown in the site plan. The benchmark is both a horizontal and vertical reference for the construction. The benchmark is important because the pieces of the building are thereby referenced from the same point and thus are mathematically related to each other.

For example, the floor-to-floor heights, roof heights, and stair landings are important to show on a section. If they were shown with dimension lines, you would have to show several combinations of dimensions to explain how they are related. Without a common reference point, this could mean a lot of different dimensions going in different directions.

This situation is simplified by using a benchmark set by a surveying engineer as a reference point for all the construction on the site. This benchmark may be outside the property line or difficult to use for a particular part of the project. For this reason, at least one workpoint will also be established close enough to the work and thus be more useful. The location of this workpoint is surveyed directly from the benchmark and provides a common reference for all horizontal and vertical measurements.

For the trainer, the cross-section cuts through the building from east to west. Thus, it cuts through the north and south wall of the building, including the solar panels, the two floor plans, and the roof. The longitudinal section cuts the west and east

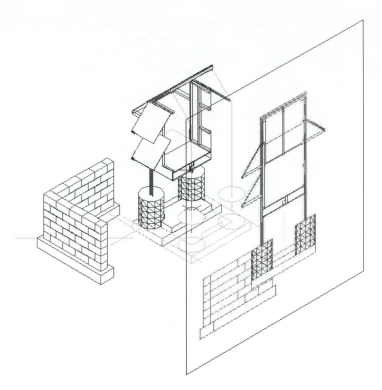

Figure 3-14. A section is a slice through the building to show the vertical relationships of the pieces.

walls from north to south and shows the stair, door and window walls, roof, and the same two floor planes, except in the opposite direction. The reference elevations or vertical heights of the pieces visible in either of these sections should match the heights of the four exterior building elevations.

You can use the same projection techniques to lay out the longitudinal and cross-sections from the floor plan. For example, Figure 3-15 shows a line at the point of the section through the floor plan. This line is used to locate the projection plane of the building and pulls down the dimensions for the section along that line.

1. As you did for the floor plans and elevations, lay out the overall size of the walls and floors before you go into any detail. Use 12" for the thickness of the floors and 4" for the thickness of the walls. The actual widths and the structure of the construction of the walls and floors will be shown in the details later.

2. You do not need to show the details of the structure for the foundation, exterior walls, or roof because again this information is unknown. What is important now is to show that there is a wall or a roof so that its location can be verified before you spend a lot of time detailing its construction. This information will be shown in the details and wall sections later.

3. In fact, at this scale, when a section is cut through the floor and walls, very little detail will be shown even in the engineered drawings. At this small scale, these features can be simply darkened when you punch out the sections to indicate the parts of the building that have been cut by the projection plane. Wall sections and details will clarify the construction of these darkened walls and will minimize the amount of information you have to show in the building sections.

You do not need to show fixtures or features in the rooms exposed by the section unless they have been actually cut by the plane of the section. This kind of information is usually best shown in a finish detail or the interior elevations. The items you

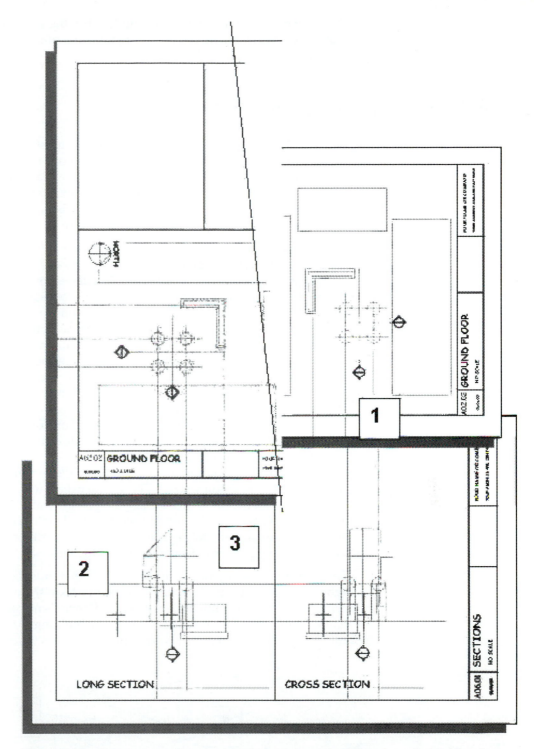

Figure 3-15. You can use the same technique to project lines from the section line through the floor plans onto both the longitudinal sections and cross-sections.

might see in a section are openings beyond, a stair or stairway, or cabinets. Use OLPAP again to check the content of these drawings. You want to orient the workers to what they are looking at, give the layout information you have at this point for the main structure, call out the pieces and processes that will clarify the section, make sure the relationships are assembled correctly, and keep the drawing well planned and readable with good line weight and lettering.

Once complete, review the sections to identify the elements that need to be dimensioned or labeled, but do not punch anything out until you've had a chance to review everything and tie the sheets together.

The Stairs Can Change Everything

The stairs and steps of a building are generally the most important part of the preliminary drawings for any building with more than one floor. In fact, access to stairs and circulation around them often shape the floor plans and dictate the ceiling heights, floor-to-floor elevations, and room dimensions for the building. The parts of the stair, its risers and treads and overall runs and rises, are fixed by certain mathematical relationships. Some of these relationships are shown in Figure 3-16.

1. The riser is the vertical face of a single step on the stair. For a person to use the stairs comfortably, it should be between $6^1/_2$″ to $7^1/_2$″. As a rule, for every set of stairs, there is always one more riser than there are treads.
2. The tread is the horizontal part of the step, the wearing surface of the stairs, and includes the stair nosing. Again, for a person to use the stairs comfortably, it should be within 11″ and 12″. The nosing of the stair is that portion of the tread that extends out over the face of the riser. It is a decorative feature that may also reduce toe and heel marks on the face of the riser.
3. To design a set of stairs, you must balance the rise-and-run ratio of the risers and treads along the nosing. The rise-and-run ratio is the angle of inclination, or slope of the stair. A higher ratio means a steeper stair. As a rule of thumb, use the following formula: 2 risers + 1 tread = 25. For example, two 7″ risers and an 11″ tread equals 25. The closer the result of the formula is to 25, the more likely that the stairs will be comfortable to use.
4. Maximum and minimum dimensions for risers and treads are dictated by code for different building types. These dimensions will vary with the code jurisdiction and use of the stairs. For example, the stairs for the trainer are equipment-access stairs for use as a temporary structure by construction workers. Therefore, they are not regulated as are stairs for more critical uses, like an exit stair coming out of a theater or an auditorium.

The size of the stairs is one of the first details that must be determined after they are lightly laid out. In fact, the room dimension makes the feasibility of stair placement important to the overall design. After all, if there is no room to go up and down the stairs, you might have to redesign the entire building. Although you would not include stairs in the schematic drawings, on some projects you might have to study

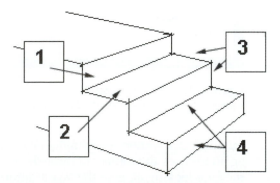

Figure 3-16. The pieces of a stair or set of steps have a mathematical relationship, which means that their placement in a building must be considered carefully.

the size of the stair before you begin the design. This would be a special study that you could reference later if approved for drawing in the preliminaries.

In most cases, it is best to study the stairs after the scaled preliminaries are lightly laid out. First, fitting stairs into a building can be done only after the size of the building and the floor-to-floor dimensions for the stair are known. Second, the drawings are in a state of flux and can be easily adjusted if the stair's design forces changes in the floor plans, elevations, or sections. This adjustment will not be as easy after the preliminaries are completed.

It will not be necessary to detail the stairs fully. Make sure that it generally fits in the preliminaries by drafting an enlarged plan and a section. In fact, it is not necessary to include the sheet with the stair section and plan with the other drawings at this time. This is a design study to determine feasibility and the overall fit of the stairs. Once these details have been determined, detailed plans and sections can be drafted with the engineered drawings and details in steps 5 and 6.

It's important to use a larger scale to draft both the walls surrounding the stairs as well as the stairs themselves. The dimensions of a larger scale will be as accurate as possible and make it easier to spot any "small" problems. The plan and section for the stairs should also be drawn at the same scale. They will show the general profile of the features at the top and bottom of the stairs and make it easier to visualize the fit of the stairs and any possible conflicts.

As an example, the calculations for the trainer stairs are shown in Figure 3-17. The figure also shows how to position the plan and section so you can project lines up or down from one drawing to the other. As you go through the steps, see if you visualize the problem at the top of the stairs. It's a problem that will require some special engineering in step 5.

1. To calculate the most efficient number of risers and treads for the stairs, first determine the total finish floor to finish floor distance. The finish floor is the top surface of the tile, decorative wood flooring, carpet, or other material on top of the subfloor.
2. For the trainer, a concrete pad is at the bottom of the stairs, but the finish floor at the top of the stairs is unknown. For the preliminaries, the subfloor will be assumed to be the finish floor, but this will have to be adjusted when the floor covering is finalized. Thus, the total rise is approximately 5'0", or 60".
3. To calculate the height of the risers, divide the total rise by the number of possible risers. Five risers would therefore be 12" high. Six risers would be 10". Seven risers would be a little less than $8\frac{5}{8}$". A comfortable riser of about 7" would need about 9 risers.
4. You can use the formula 2 risers + 1 tread = 25 to get the length of the tread for the most comfortable stair. A stair for the general public with a $6\frac{3}{4}$" riser would have about an $11\frac{1}{2}$" tread. However, this formula does not work for an access or utility stair. An $8\frac{5}{8}$" riser would have only an 8" tread, not much of a step for a workboot.
5. Once you have the length of one tread, you can calculate the total run because the total run of the stairs is the sum of all treads (without the nosing). It is sometimes referred to simply as the "run." Note in Figure 3-17 that the number of treads is always one less than the total number of risers. For example the eight $11\frac{1}{2}$" treads would have a 92" run, while the seven 8" treads would have a total run of 56", which is quite a difference.

The choice of riser-and-tread combination depends on who will use the stair and the amount of horizontal space available for the stair's total run. For a stair in a residential or commercial building, you want to find the most comfortable run for the most comfortable riser height that will fit in the space available. For the trainer, long treads for workboots and a fairly high riser for fast access are probably best. For example, a 10" riser with a 10" tread is shown in the plans.

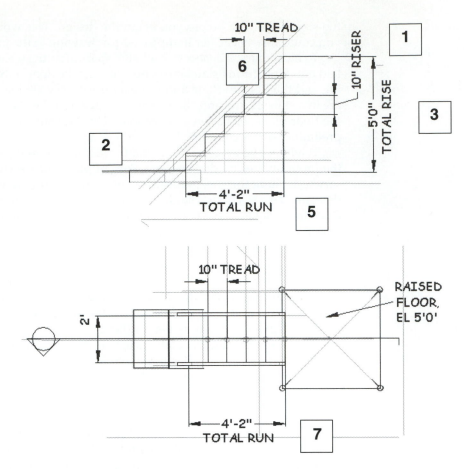

Figure 3-17. The stair for the trainer is outside the building so it can be adapted easily to fit the floor plan. Note how the enlarged stair plan and the section work together to help you quickly determine feasibility.

Every stair has to have a landing at the top and the bottom of the total run. These landings are usually part of the open floor space, but in tight locations like hallways and stairwells, they may have to be added to the total horizontal distance for the stair. As a rule of thumb, the length of the landing equals the width of the stair. For the trainer, the top of the stair uses the raised floor as a landing. The bottom of the stair needs a landing that is a little more than 2 feet long.

Now Tie the Sheets Together

Once the size of the stairs has been determined and everything seems to fit, you can begin to tie the preliminaries together. Tying the drawings together means looking at all the drawings at the same time to make sure they represent the building correctly. Read each sheet to make sure that the drawings correlate with each other and that they have the appropriate references. References are not absolutely critical in the preliminaries because so much is still subject to change. Because these are the base drawings for the full set, however, it is helpful to get these relationships established. For example, the symbols for the section cuts through the building, as well as the labels for the elevations and sections, should be shown on the floor plan.

Use OLPAP to review the entire set and the content of each sheet in the set. Can you visualize how the various images fit together as a set of orthographic projections? Do they describe the shape of the building correctly?

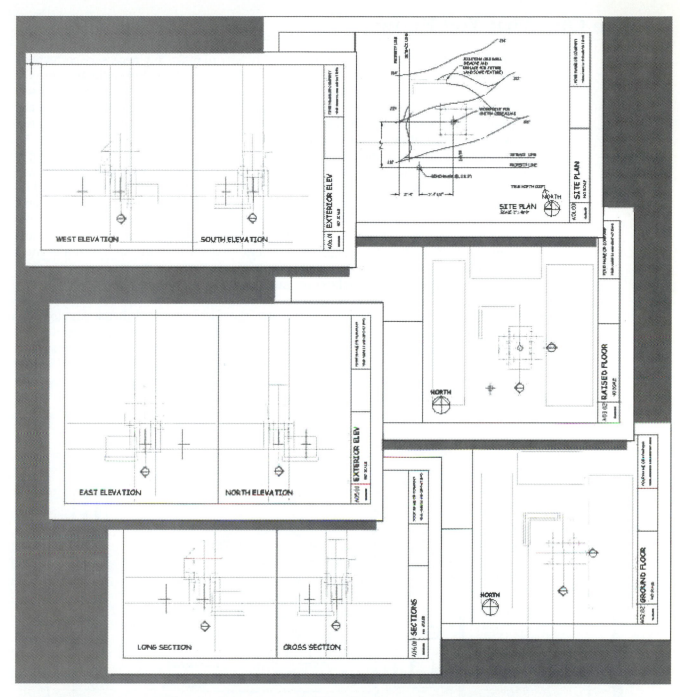

Figure 3-18. Tying the preliminary drawings together means looking at all the sheets at one time to make sure that they work together. Use the OLPAP checklist to make sure you fill in all known details and that you have included the information from steps 1 and 2, the program and the schematics, respectively.

At this point, the objective is simply to make sure everything fits together and that you have covered all the programmatic requirements shown in the schematics. The structure of the building will be clarified once the preliminaries are approved, and many details will change when you start the actual construction drawings. For now, it's important to verify that the schematics work and to determine if you are still on the right track.

Figure 3-18 shows the layouts for preliminary drawings for the trainer. You may have a variation of this design, but the general relationships of the rise and run should be about the same.

Punch Out What You Know

With all the sheets lightly laid out, it is fairly easy to make any necessary corrections to the drawings and to keep them coordinated. This might include adjustment to the site or floor plans based on the stair plan study, or adjustment to the elevations or sections because of a particular window placement or roof configuration. You can make these corrections with darker lines, or you can keep the light layouts until you feel you have everything working together.

Once you are confident that the drawings are coordinated and everything is correct, you are ready to punch out the layout lines and get them ready for dimensioning. The example used in this book is shown in the series of drawings in Figure 3-19. As you darken the lines, be certain to use a sharp pencil and get as even a line weight as you can. Note which lines should be heavier than others and how the worker's eye will move across the paper. Squinting at the sheet to blur the smaller lines will sometimes give you a better feel for how the objects on the sheet will look.

Use OLPAP again to make sure you included all the information you can at this time. It is also important to review the schematics and the program to see if you have forgotten something. Remember, the objective is to confirm all the previous requirements and agreements and to put everything to scale as the preliminaries. Although the preliminaries are base sheets for the engineered drawings, they also serve to finalize input about the design. The objective is to get final approval so that you can proceed to the next step: early specifications and pricing in the design development phase.

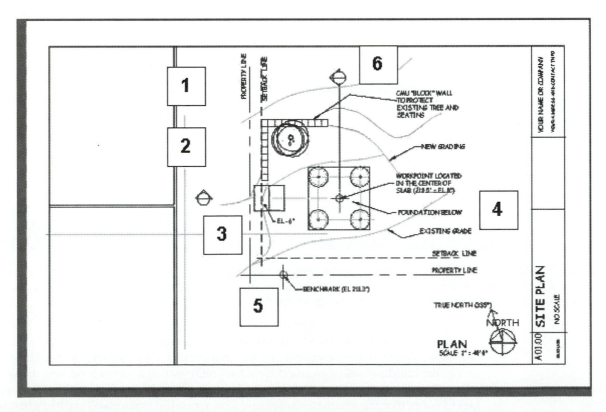

Figure 3-19. Punching out the site plan means darkening the layout lines and clarifying the visual information.

This step-by-step visual approach to problem solving resolves the unknowns. But there are still a lot of unknowns to be finalized. All of them depend on whether the layout is correct or not. Drawing what is known for confirmation and revising according to new input brings you another step closer to understanding what needs to be included in the final drawings. For Figure 3-19:

1. Begin by punching out all the layout lines with the line types shown in Chapter 2. Use a north arrow to orient the building to the Earth. Draft it with a $^3/_4$″ circle and a triangle and letter the word "NORTH" above the point. Darken if desired.

2. The symbol for trees is important to show existing and planned vegetation. This tree has a 6″ diameter trunk, and the cluster of circles describe the diameter of the tree's drip line.

3. The elevation symbol is more like an inverted hockey stick and puck, with the puck located on the top of the surface whose elevation is being annotated. The handle of the stick is where you enter the numerical value of the elevation. The elevation above sea level of different floors, walkways, and curbs should be noted to show changes in height for various parts of the site. Elevations include topographic lines or elevation changes showing the existing shape of the land and new grading.

4. Call out existing and planned walkways, driveways, and other features, including property lines, setbacks, and some of the pieces of the building.

5. Draft a bullet for the benchmark and the workpoint to locate the horizontal location and elevation of the construction. These are usually set by surveyors in the field to make sure the building is in the right place. Draft the bullet with a $^3/_{16}$ or $^1/_4$″ circle and two perpendicular lines, and blacken in the diagonal corners.

6. The symbol for a building section should be shown in the same location as floor plans. Use a $^5/_8$″ diameter circle with an arrow pointing in the direction that the section is facing. There will be two numbers in this symbol. The one on top is the detail number, and the one below is a sheet number.

For Figure 3-20:

1. Use a square to assign room numbers to spaces and reference interior elevations. The box should be about $^3/_8$″ square, with the room number written inside the rectangle and the detail and sheet number for interior elevations (if any) noted near the tip of the triangle pointing in the viewing direction. Locate the square near the center of each room, just below the name of that room.

2. After the floor plans are punched out and before you add symbols and notes, make a copy of the plans. You can use these copies as templates for other drawings. For example, you will need copies of the floor plans for the electrical and mechanical plans of the trainer. Other projects might require floor plans, elevations, or sections for furnishing, equipment, fire sprinklers, and telecommunications layouts. To set up these templates, punch out the floor plans and label the room with just enough information to orient them. Then use a copy machine to create a master sheet for future use.

3. Add standard symbols for sections, details, and other references like interior elevations or stair and cabinet drawings that can be identified at this point.

4. Use symbols at the door and windows to designate door and window types. There is no standard for these symbols. To distinguish them from other symbols, they are sometimes drafted as triangles or hexagons. You usually find an index of symbols used in a drawing near the table of contents.

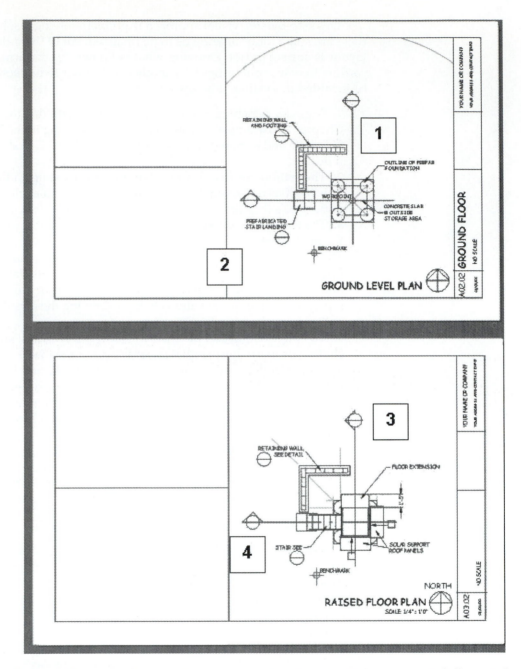

Figure 3-20. Layouts for the floor plans must be coordinated as you punch them out to make sure that the information you need to clarify the preliminaries is represented accurately.

For the trainer, doors and windows use a $^3/_{16}$" square with an alphanumeric designation. For example, use "W-1," "W-2," etc., for windows and "D-1," "D-2," etc., for doors.

For Figure 3-21:

1. A wall section symbol looks just like a building section symbol except that it is a little smaller. Although there are no absolute rules, there is usually no directional arrowhead. Instead, the tail of the symbol acts as a flag that points

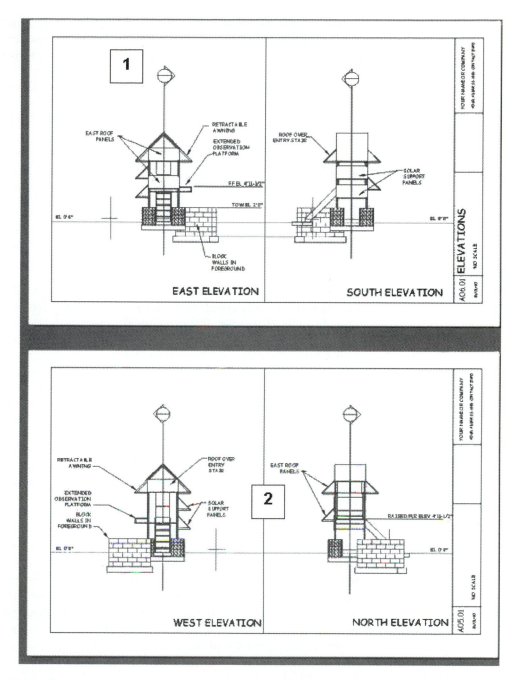

Figure 3-21. Punching out the preliminary drawings means darkening in the lines of the layouts. You can letter some of the titles and notes, but keep in mind that you will be adding dimensions and a lot more information in the next step.

in the direction the wall section takes. There are two numbers in this symbol. The one on top is the detail number, and the one below is a sheet number where you find that detail. For the trainer, use a $1/2''$ diameter circle with a bold flag on the tail.

2. Be sure to label all the known pieces shown as you punch out the layout drawings. Labeling the pieces will clarify the relationships and help to define

whether there are any misunderstandings or corrections that have to be made during the next phase of the development of the drawings.

3. A simple inverted triangle is used to indicate the slope of the roof. The hypotenuse of the triangle follows the same slope as the roof. The vertical leg of the triangle is said to be the rise of the roof. The horizontal leg is the run. The run is always expressed as 12 (because there are 12" to a foot). For the main roof of the trainer, you will use a 12:12 rise and run, or a 45-degree roof.

Dimensioning in Three Dimensions

The reason you draft the building to scale is to get the drawings proportionally correct before you dimension them. After you punch out the drawings, the building shown on the preliminaries should look pretty much like it will when it is built. You will need only to add some dimensions so that the general size of the building can be visualized.

Dimensions are another layer of construction information. In this case, the information is specifically about the location or size of the objects to which the dimensions refer. As such, dimensions are probably the most important information on the drawings and, like everything else, they follow a particular format and standard that is expected by experienced workers in the field.

Most important, a dimension should be placed where it will be most beneficial to the worker who might be looking for it. For example, dimension the location of a retaining wall on the site plan because that is the sheet where the worker will be looking for that information during construction. The footings for that wall are shown on the foundation plan because that is where the worker is most likely to need that information in the field. The dimensions for the height or elevation of a window are shown on the elevations or a section because that is where the worker will expect to find that information. At the same time, the details for the construction of that window would be found in a reference noted in either the section or the framing plan.

You should avoid overdimensioning or repeating dimensions that will not be important for a particular drawing. For example, you would not show the overall dimensions of the building on the elevations. That information is on the floor plans. By the time the worker gets to the elevations, the foundation of the building would have already been completed. Instead, the information shown on an elevation should focus on the heights of the penetrations through the walls or the placement of special finishes or materials visible from the outside. These items cannot be shown easily on the plans.

Fifteen Rules of Dimensioning

1. Draft dimension lines as sharp continuous lines slightly sharper than the object lines.
2. Place dimension numbers above the line.
3. Always use foot and inch marks.
4. Except for finish work, write the dimensions that are less than 1 foot in just inches. Dimensions over 12" should be written in feet and inches.
5. Place overall dimensions outside all other dimensions.
6. When the object to be dimensioned is too small for the dimension to fit between the extension lines, place the number outside the extension line, with an arrow pointing to the dimension line.

7. Windows and doors have symbols that reference them to a door and window schedule. Reference symbols are as important as dimensions because most schedules list the rough openings for that window.
8. As a rule, dimensions for interior walls and partitions are from the face of the stud, not the center of the stud or the face of the finish material. It's hard to center a stud in the field, and the finish material will not be installed when the studs are being framed.
9. Draft the diagonal end marker or the slash at the intersection of the dimension and extension lines so that it clearly shows the extent of the object being dimensioned. Make it heavy enough to stand out.
10. Keep dimensions outside the object and organize them so that shorter dimensions are nested inside the overall dimensions.
11. Nest primary and secondary dimension lines consistently throughout the drawing or about a half an inch apart.
12. Avoid crowding dimensions.
13. Do not touch the object being dimensioned with the extension lines.
14. Do not stack fractions like this: $\frac{1}{2}$. To conserve vertical space and keep your numbers large, use a slash between the numerator and denominator like this: 1/2.
15. Always give the scale of every drawing on a sheet. For sheets with multiple scales, show the scale below the title for the drawing. Scales are important to check a dimension that is not clear. Missing dimensions should be verified.

With these fifteen rules in mind, add the dimensions to the punched out drawings. Figure 3-22 represents the final preliminary drawings. The preliminary drawings can now be submitted for review and comment. Once this review is complete, the design development phase can begin.

Review of Steps 1, 2, and 3

Step 1: The intent of the program is to document the scope of the work and to make sure that there is complete understanding of the requirements for the project prior to beginning the schematics.

Step 2: The schematics are conceptual sketches. They graphically confirm the program requirements with an initial concept in preparation for the preliminaries. For a constructor, the schematics can be drawn on scraps of paper, napkins, envelopes, or anything else that can be filed for future reference.

Step 3: The preliminaries are scaled orthographic projections that show multiple views of the three-dimensional building. They are drawn according to the feedback received after review of the schematics. The objective of the preliminaries is to draw the schematics to scale and make sure everything fits together as drawn. The preliminaries are the base drawings for the engineered drawings.

The preliminaries are incorporated into the final set and function as the base sheets of the engineered drawings. All the sheets in the preliminaries must be drawn at the same time to make sure they are coordinated.

The steps for drafting the preliminaries are the same for any project. First, lightly lay out the plans, elevations, and sections. Once the sheets are roughly laid out, check the fit of critical components like stairs, cabinets, or special equipment and make any necessary adjustments. Use OLPAP as a checklist to be sure that all the information from the program and the schematics is included in the preliminaries. When the

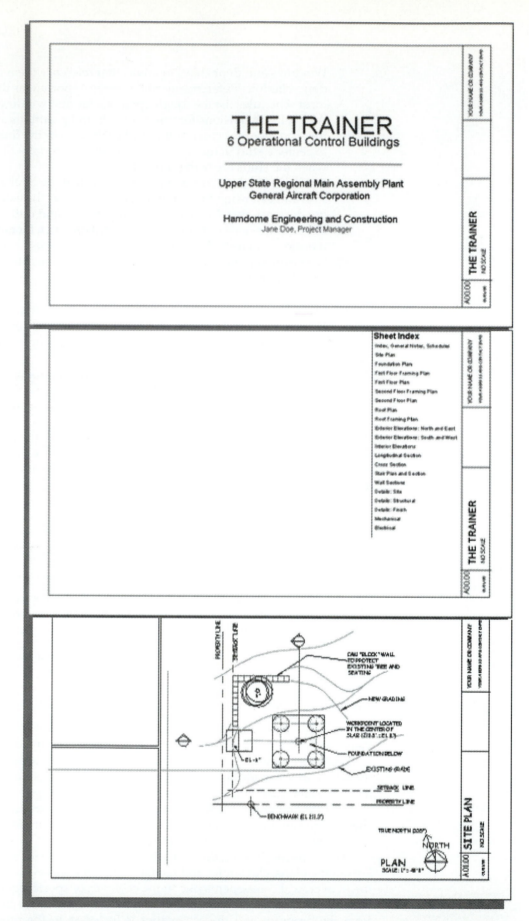

Figure 3-22. Add the dimensions to the drawings after they have been coordinated and punched out. The location of the notes and the dimensions should be coordinated so that the information on the drawings is shown as clearly as possible.

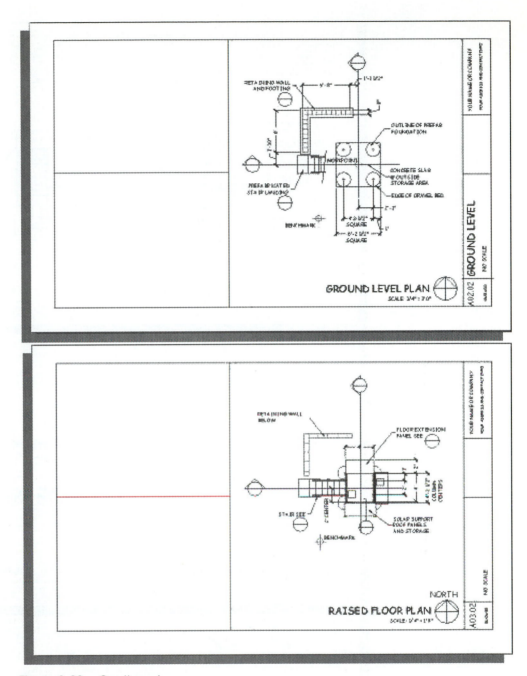

Figure 3-22. Continued

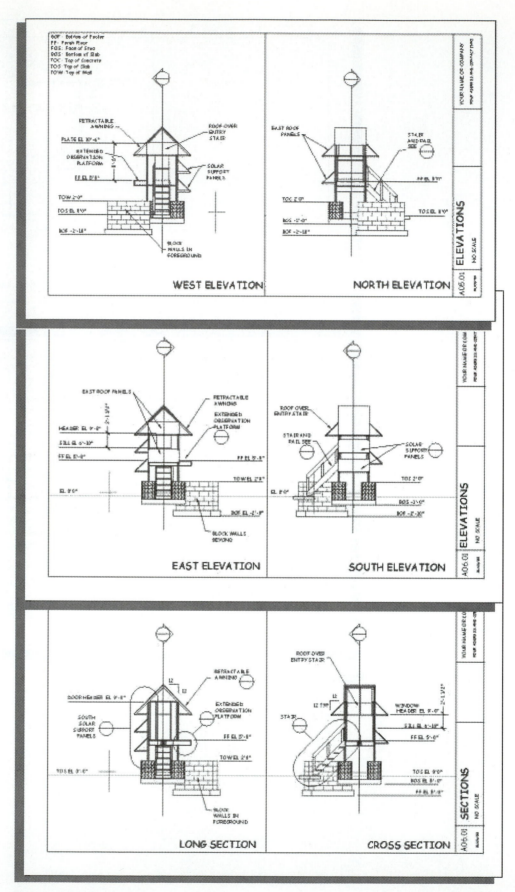

Figure 3-22. Continued

Dimensioning Tips

1. One advantage of working on 11"×17" paper is that you can make copies of these sheets as you go along. Copies can include check sets for markups, evaluation, and pasteups where titles, notes, spreadsheets, or drawings can be cut from other sources and pasted together to make a new sheet. For now, you should practice your lettering, but it's something to keep in mind when you are doing this for real.

2. For the preliminaries, the title, index page, and site plan should be straightforward. Most of the content has been checked with the OLPAP checklist when it was coordinated with the other sheets prior to being punched out. Make sure the title blocks and sheet numbers are added.

3. Note that the end marks or slashes at the intersection of the dimension and extension lines slant in two directions. Use one direction for horizontal dimensions and the opposite direction for vertical dimensions. This technique makes the dimension easier to read. The most important thing is consistency from sheet to sheet.

4. As stated in the dimension rules, the numbers for the dimension should be placed above the dimension line near the center whenever possible. If they don't fit, place them outside the extension lines and draw an extension line to show where they go. These numbers should be approximately $^3/_{16}$" tall, but they will vary with the type of drawing being drafted.

5. A masonry wall will be dimensioned differently from a woodframe wall because of the way the wall is built in the field. Most masonry walls are built from prefabricated blocks or bricks. Since these items come in fixed sizes, the length of the wall will be a module relative to the size of the masonry unit. This is also true of openings in the wall for windows or doors. Masonry dimensions must be written according to the face of the masonry module in the walls. For example, a standard concrete block wall is built to an 8" module because it uses a nominal 8×8×16 inch block. All dimensions must therefore be in increments of 8" to avoid having to cut special block for the wall.

6. Openings in woodframe walls are dimensioned to the centerline of the rough opening for doors and windows, just in case the manufacturer of the window changes. This practice is thought to simplify locating the opening in the field, but in reality it means the carpenter may have to look on another sheet to find the width of the window or door and calculate the position of the studs on either side of the opening to be framed. For this reason, some drafters will give the dimension for the location and the opening on the plans. (This issue will be discussed later with the engineered drawings.)

7. You do not dimension the thickness of the wall or any finish material for a wall on the floor plan. Give the overall length of the wall with the dimension's extension lines aligned to the outside face of the stud, and use a detail to show the components of the actual wall. There is also no need to dimension a concrete block, brick, 2×4, 4×4, or other dimensional material because they are standard sizes and are in the notes.

Dimensioning Tips

8. As a rule of thumb, elevations should also be dimensioned in the way that a worker will work with them in the field. The pieces on an elevation that require installation should be dimensioned and called out. You do not have to show dimensions for the building because they are already in place. This sheet instructs workers what to do with the exterior surface of the structure. Only the items on the face of the building, like ornamental fixtures or trim details, need to be located.

9. Dimensions for vertical elements of the building and the vertical location of details on the walls, should be read from the right side of the page because the sets are usually bound on the left edge of the sheet.

10. Ground level or finish grade should be shown as a heavy border or section line. Floor levels should be shown as hidden lines through the building. The elevations of the floor levels should be labeled with a name, numerical value, and a symbol so they stand out.

11. Sometimes the foundation is shown on the elevations as a hidden line to indicate the depth of the building. This includes the footings, stem walls, and slabs for the building that may be below grade. Use a heavy line to indicate finish grade. It will probably change later when you get more detailed information, but it will most likely be necessary to change only the dimensions and not the actual drawing.

12. The top of the windows is usually the same as the top of the door. Standard doors are 6'8" tall. You will look at door and window details later. At this point, it is just a matter of placement because it is very likely that details will change.

13. Note the elevation and sections of the grade above sea level immediately adjacent to the building in the plane of the section. Also note the finish floor elevations and the elevation of any other vertical elements like window sills.

14. Most of the callouts should have been added when you punched out the drawings, but review the drawings for additional callouts as you add dimensions. Again, these features can't really be shown in detail in the building section, but if something is important, make sure that it is noted.

adjustments are complete, punch out the lines and note and dimension the drawings for approval.

Notes and dimensions should be placed on the drawings so that workers can find the information they need as they are constructing the building. The drawings are your voice in the field so they must be clear, concise, and authoritative to get the work done correctly.

Step 4 begins design development. In this step, the drawings are revised according to feedback received about the preliminaries. Revisions are made to the drawings as required, early specifications are determined, and a conceptual estimate is made to confirm the budget. The preliminaries evolve into engineered drawings as more information is added to their content during step 4.

Chapter 4

THE FIELD DRAWINGS

Almost every field problem starts with a vague description of an idea in a casual conversation. It might begin with a conversation at a lunch meeting, like the one with the project manager in Figure 3-2, or a handwritten memo sitting on your desk on Monday morning. From these loose beginnings, solutions have to move into the field as fast as possible. Some answers are fairly simple to turn around: you can just look at the drawings and specifications. Others take a few phone calls. But a few will be more complex, with a lot of loose ends and possible alternatives. This is where a visual approach to problem solving can help the most. As we've already seen, ideas are written down as a program, schematics give the program life as a collection of rough sketches, and the preliminaries refine the schematics as scaled drawings.

Once the project is drafted to scale, a solution is fairly well defined and it can be analyzed to see if it's financially feasible. At this point you are ready to begin step 4, design development. As shown in Figure 4-1, the objective of this step is to modify the preliminaries to match any additional input about the design, select the major materials as early specifications, and confirm the budget with a conceptual cost estimate in preparation for step 5, the engineered drawings.

Step 4: Design Development Drawings (DDs)

After the preliminaries have been reviewed and approved, you are ready to begin step 4, the design development drawings (DDs). The objective of the DDs is to make sure that the drawings are correct. This step includes three tasks: revising the preliminaries based on review comments, selecting early specifications for pricing and detailing, and completing a conceptual estimate to confirm the budget.

Revising the preliminaries

Revisions to the preliminaries incorporate changes, make clarifications, or add new requirements. These changes come from checking the drawings against the schematics

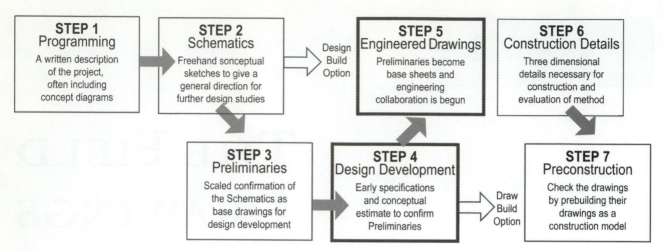

Figure 4-1. Steps 4 and 5 are covered in Chapter 4. These steps finalize the design and confirm financial feasibility for the engineered drawings.

and the original program requirements and can include anything from simple corrections like spelling, confused wording, or incorrect dimensions, to more complex details like adjustments to the dimension of rooms, modification to roof lines, changes to window or door locations, or the addition of missing information.

Misinterpretations of the size and shape of the building should be minimal if the program and schematics were clearly interpreted. In other words, if the schematics followed the program accurately and have already been approved, you should have to make only a few minor adjustments. If you've made an error or incorrect assumption and major changes have to be made, however, there's not much you can do at this point except to apologize and make the changes.

At the same time, if a change occurred in the program or someone thought of something to add to the schematics after they were approved, be certain to note the additional work in a memorandum to document your time, especially if the change is so great that you have to redraw the preliminaries and resubmit them for another review. But all changes should be noted because sometimes even the simplest new requirements have a major impact on your schedule for the completion of the project.

Whatever adjustments need to be made should require only minor changes to the preliminary drawings using an eraser and a few new lines. You do not want to have to redraw the drawings, unless modifications are extensive. That's why it is so important to make sure the drawings are well planned and there is plenty of room to incorporate additional information as it comes in.

The objective of this part of the DDs is to get the drawings in their final format for pricing. These drawings are graphic representations of what should be a clear understanding of the layout of the building. There are still many unknowns about the building's construction, but the basic design should be set. There should be enough information to think through some of the materials, calculate a conceptual estimate, and confirm the budget.

Selecting early specifications

Once the preliminaries have been revised, you need to research and outline some of the major specifications for the building. These specifications are necessary so that you can make certain basic assumptions about the major materials you anticipate using in the construction. Different types of materials will affect how the building is to be constructed. These specifications are important because they benchmark the cost estimate. Whether these exact materials are ultimately used in the building or not, they establish a base price for changes. In other words, new specifications will be for materials that will either cost less, cost more, or be about the same as the original.

There are many kinds of roofing to choose from for this building. You could arbitrarily select one of these and proceed into the engineered drawings. No matter how many people review and agree to your initial decision, you will probably have to change the roofing to something else later if it was inappropriate or too costly. Of course, it's best to take the time to discuss the alternatives and specify the most accurate choice possible to avoid making too many changes to the drawings later.

If too many changes come in the engineering or detailing, or worse yet after the drawings are complete or into construction, it could mean a lot of redrafting and wasted time. It could also set up the possibility of an error in the drawings because any change has to be coordinated on all the sheets in the set at the same time.

You do not want to spend a lot of time, however, writing lengthy specifications or generate a lot of needless paperwork. Computer programs can write volumes of specifications automatically from master databases. These computerized specifications may be useful to defend (or enforce) construction contracts, but they have little value in field drafting. For example, for the trainer the important specifications are for the structural materials, exterior surfaces, mechanical equipment, weatherproofing, doors, windows, and roofing. In a more detailed project, you might also be concerned with interior finishes, special equipment, appliances, lighting and plumbing fixtures, hardware, stair railings, shelving, or anything else that might affect the cost of the building. But such a lengthy list is pretty rare for a field problem.

A quick way to find information on alternate materials is to use the World Wide Web. For example, Figure 4-2 is a screen shot of Sweets.com—just one of many construction portals that are now appearing on the Web. These sites are sometimes referred to as "vortals," or as an industry-specific portal, or as a Web site. Sweets.com acts as an index of material suppliers and specifications similar to its well-known catalog. It provides product information, specifications, and even CAD drawings for constructors.

Once you are logged onto the site, you can search the Sweets database by product type, manufacturer name, trade name, or CSI division. For example, a search for "roofing" under product types turned up more than 125 companies with almost 600 pages of information. A narrower search for "metal roofing" came up with more than fifty companies and 120 pages of information. Figure 4-3 shows the partial result of a search for "corrugated roofing," which turned up more than twenty companies and fifty pages of specifications. Individual companies can be contacted through Sweets or their listed 800 numbers to finalize pricing. You can also look them up at their own sites and make direct contact with their sales department.

Almost all manufacturers and suppliers now have their own Web sites, most with detailed information about their products, as well as contact addresses that will save you time getting unit prices. A good way to find a manufacturer is through a search engine like AskJeeves.com or a directory like Yahoo.com.

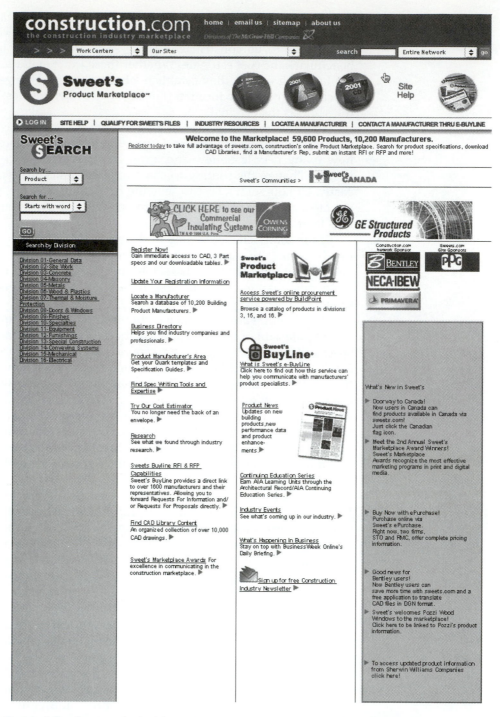

Figure 4-2. Screen shot of Sweets.com, a construction materials portal that allows you to search for alternate materials and specifications.

Sweet's Group   Back To Top

Return to the Flexospan page on Sweet's Online
Visit the Flexospan WEB site.
Send an e-mail to Flexospan

FLEXOSPAN

ROOF AND WALL PANELS
PRODUCT CLASSIFICATION: 07410
SWEET'S CATALOG CODE: 07410/FLE

FLEXOSPAN
253 Railroad Street
Sandy Lake, PA 16145
Tel: (724) 376-7221
Toll-Free: (800) 245-0396
Fax: (724) 376-3964
E-mail: sales@flexospan.com
Web site: www.flexospan.com

CORRUGATED 7/8"

Corrugated 2.67" x 7/8" is a traditional industrial and commercial exposed fastener roofing and siding panel. Corrugated 2.67" x 7/8" is available in 26 gauge through 18 gauge in bare G-90 Galvanized or Galvalume. Corrugated 2.67" x 7/8" is also available in G-90 Galvanized with a Silicone Polyester, 70% Kynar or "Flexshield" paint finishes.

Corrugated 2.67" x 7/8" is available in the 29" width only in 24 gauge through 20 gauge Stainless Steel, Types 304 and 316.

Corrugated 2.67" x 7/8" may be used with a liner panel or with draped vinyl faced fiberglass insulation to achieve various "R" values.

The minimum recommended roof pitch for Corrugated 2.67" x 7/8" is 1" : 12". Corrugated 2.67" x 7/8" may be factory curved.

SPECIFICATIONS FOR FLEXOSPAN ROOFING AND SIDING PANELS

1.0 - WORK SCOPE:
Furnish the metal wall or roofing system with related accessories as outlined in these specifications and drawings where applicable. Material will be furnished by FLEXOSPAN, Sandy Lake, PA. All other manufacturers shall be approved by the architect prior to bid date.

2.0 - MATERIALS:
Materials furnished under this section shall be as follows:

2.1 Exterior Panel shall be manufactured from _____ (26, 24, 22, 20, 18 Gauge G-90 Galvanized Steel), (26, 24, 22, 20, 18 Gauge Galvalume) or (24, 22, 20 Gauge Stainless Steel).

2.2 Exterior Panel Finish: Exterior panels shall be finished with _____ (Silicone Polyester), (70% Kynar), (Flexshield) or (Unpainted). Color to be selected from Manufacturer's Standards.

2.3 Fastening of Exterior Panels:
A. Panels shall be attached with No. 14 self-tapping screws when attached directly to structural steel.

B. When used in conjunction with "FL-24" liner panel and subgirt system, panels shall be attached to the subgirt with a No. 14 x 3/4" self-tapping sheet metal screw.

C. When used with a painted panel, fastener heads and washers shall be color coated the same color as the panel. All fasteners shall have a bonded metal and neoprene washer.

2.4 Flashings: All flashings shall be the same gauge and finish as the adjacent panels.

3.0 - ERECTION OF PANELS:
3.1 No metal panels shall be erected if structural steel is not aligned to the tolerances of the A.I.S.C. Code of Standard Practice, Section 7. It will be the responsibility of the contractor to examine this alignment before erection of panels.

3.2 Panels shall be erected from left to right unless otherwise specified.

4.0 - QUALIFICATIONS:
4.1 Due to the inherent tolerances of the base metal any flat surface panels could have some "Oil Canning." This is not a basis for rejection of the product.

4.2 Products and Specifications are subject to change without prior notice.

CORRUGATED 1/2"

Corrugated 2.67" x 1/2" is a traditional industrial and commercial exposed fastener roofing and siding panel. Corrugated 2.67" x 1/2" is available in 26 gauge through 18 gauge in bare G-90 Galvanized or Galvalume. Corrugated 2.67" x 1/2" is also available in G-90 Galvanized with a Silicone Polyester, 70% Kynar or "Flexshield" paint finishes.

Corrugated 2.67" x 1/2" is available in the 34" width only in 24 gauge through 20 gauge Stainless Steel, Types 304 and 316.

Corrugated 2.67" x 1/2" may be used with a liner panel or with draped vinyl faced fiberglass insulation to achieve various "R" values.

The minimum recommended roof pitch for Corrugated 2.67" x 1/2" is 1" : 12".

Corrugated 2.67" x 1/2" may be factory curved.

SPECIFICATIONS FOR FLEXOSPAN ROOFING AND SIDING PANELS

1.0 - WORK SCOPE:
Furnish the metal wall or roofing system with related accessories as outlined in these specifications and drawings where applicable. Material will be furnished by FLEXOSPAN, Sandy Lake, PA. All other manufacturers shall be approved by the architect prior to bid date.

2.0 - MATERIALS:
Materials furnished under this section shall be as follows:

2.1 Exterior Panel shall be manufactured from _____ (26, 24, 22, 20, 18 Gauge G-90 Galvanized Steel), (26, 24, 22, 20, 18 Gauge Galvalume) or (24, 22, 20 Gauge Stainless Steel).

2.2 Exterior Panel Finish: Exterior panels shall be finished with _____ (Silicone Polyester), (70% Kynar), (Flexshield) or (Unpainted). Color to be selected from Manufacturer's Standards.

2.3 Fastening of Exterior Panels:
A. Panels shall be attached with No. 14 self-tapping screws when attached directly to structural steel.

B. When used in conjunction with "FL-24" liner panel and subgirt system, panels shall be attached to the subgirt with a No. 14 x 3/4" self-tapping sheet metal screw.

C. When used with a painted panel, fastener heads and washers shall be color coated the same color as the panel. All fasteners shall have a bonded metal and neoprene washer.

2.4 Flashings: All flashings shall be the same gauge and finish as the adjacent panels.

3.0 - ERECTION OF PANELS:
3.1 No metal panels shall be erected if structural steel is not aligned to the tolerances of the A.I.S.C. Code of Standard Practice, Section 7. It will be the responsibility of the contractor to examine this alignment before erection of panels.

3.2 Panels shall be erected from left to right unless otherwise specified.

4.0 - QUALIFICATIONS:
4.1 Due to the inherent tolerances of the base metal any flat surface panels could have some "Oil Canning." This is not a basis for rejection of the product.

4.2 Products and Specifications are subject to change without prior notice.

Figure 4-3.   A page full of specifications is the result of a search for corrugated metal roofing.

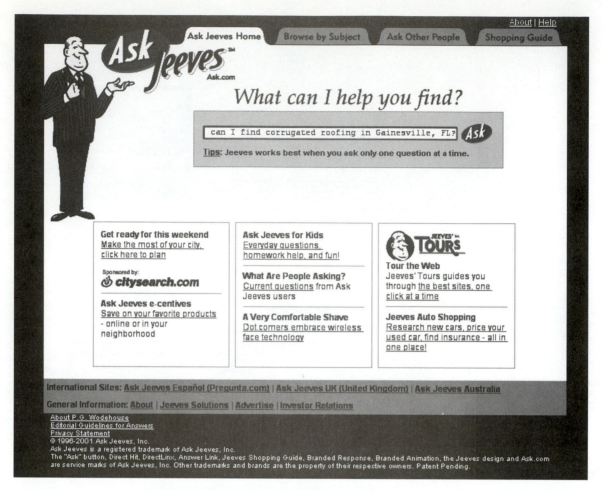

Figure 4-4. The AskJeeves.com search engine allows you to search for a particular kind of metal roofing using a question worded in English.

AskJeeves.com (see Figure 4-4) allows you to ask a question in English that will lead you to a number of possible answers. For example, in Figure 4-5, the results of the question Where can I find corrugated roofing in Gainesville, Florida? leads to the name and address for local distributors of roofing, including links to a map, driving instructions, and even a link to check the background of the suppliers in the area.

As an option, Yahoo.com has a series of directory links that begins with their business and economy section. In that directory is a companies link that will lead you to more information about particular types of companies. In the Business directory is also a business-to-business link that goes to a construction heading. Under the construction heading is a link to thermal and moisture protection, then roofing, and finally metal roofing. The route to the information is a bit long, so if you are trying to find something specific, you might want to stick to a search engine. Yahoo's search engine is Google.com, and their search link takes you right to that site.

As you can see in Figure 4-6, the advantage of Yahoo.com is that it allows you to browse broad categories and inform yourself of many different possible suppliers and types of roofing. To use directories, however, you have to understand what you are looking for. It also doesn't hurt to have a few hours experience on the site, and the best way to gain experience is to practice.

Begin the research by listing all the materials needed for the trainer, including details like the skylight, photovoltaic system, windows, roofing, and siding. The list does

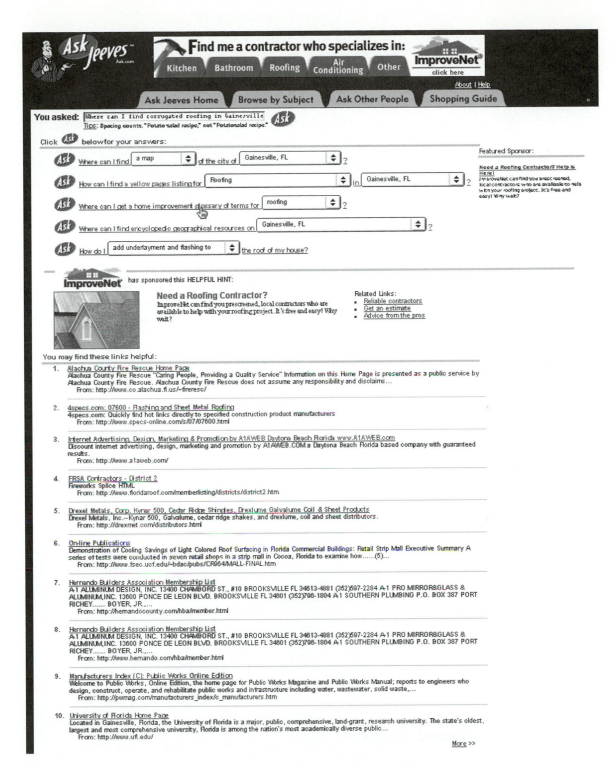

Figure 4-5. The result of the search at AskJeeves.com brings you to a list of possible suppliers. The site allows you to click a link to learn the telephone number of the supplier, get a map or directions, or do a quick background check to help you make a choice.

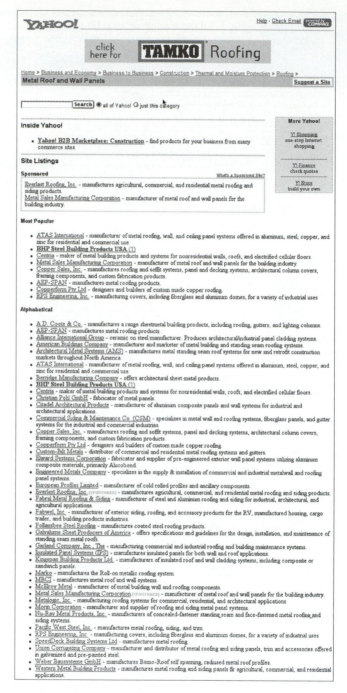

Figure 4-6. Yahoo.com does broad category searches that are good for generalized information.

not need to include common construction materials like steel, wood, concrete, and masonry. The common materials are well known and can be quickly priced using estimating manuals or bids from subcontractors. The materials and equipment unique to each particular building are the items that will need to be specified carefully. As you find the material you want, write down the name of the product; the name, address, and phone number of the manufacturer; and the CSI specification number. You can also bookmark or add the Web address to your favorites menu in your browser for later reference.

With the Web, you can bookmark different alternatives and send pages to other team members for review. When you're ready with the final selection, all you have to

CONCEPTUAL ESTIMATE					
Description	Total	Units	x	Unit cost	Total
Site work	200	sq ft	x	$ 5	$ 1,000
CMU wall	75	sq ft	x	$ 8	$ 600
Footing @ wall	2	cu yd	x	$ 100	$ 200
Concrete slab	1	cu yd	x	$ 100	$ 100
Gravel base	1	cu yd	x	$ 50	$ 50
Precast foundation	20	pieces	x	$ 20	$ 400
Steel columns	80	lin ft	x	$ 6	$ 480
Raised floor / walls	16	sq ft	x	$ 45	$ 720
Floor extension	8	sq ft	x	$ 45	$ 360
Solar support panels	8	sq ft	x	$ 15	$ 120
Main roof and entry	30	sq ft	x	$ 15	$ 450
Stair	8	lin ft	x	$ 75	$ 600
Solar electric	1	lump		$ 1,000	$ 1,000
Solar mechanical	1	lump		$ 1,000	$ 1,000
Miscellaneous	1	lump		$ 500	$ 500
Total Cost (Budget)					$ 7,580

Figure 4-7. Component-based conceptual estimates are thought to be more accurate than lump-sum or cost-per-square-foot calculations.

do is print the Web pages. (You can add marginal notes with pricing information.) A stack of Web printouts, a few e-mails, and a couple of phone calls should give you all the information you need to start a conceptual estimate.

A conceptual estimate

Once the outline specifications are defined, you need to prepare a conceptual estimate of the cost of the construction to verify the budget. If the price is underbudget, you might want to add more during the design development phase. If the price is right on budget, you are ready to proceed. And if your price is over, it's a good time to let everyone know so they can either cut back on the program or find more money. Of course, with the trainer, the budget is unknown, so this is the first time the project can be evaluated for financial feasibility.

A conceptual estimate is so named because you do not have enough information to calculate fully all the material and labor. After all, none of the finishes or structural framing have even been drawn or detailed. In a normal building, you can usually give a fairly accurate estimate based on the square footage of the building. To do so, two factors must be considered: the cost per square foot and the total square feet of the building. The total estimated cost is then simply a multiplication of these two factors. The formula looks like this: estimated cost = total square feet × cost per square foot.

The total square feet of the building is an area takeoff that you can do from the scaled preliminaries. As a rule, use the dimensions to the outside perimeter of the walls to make these calculations and adjust the price for the square footage of overhangs and outside decks. The cost per square foot can be found in estimating manuals, but these references include generalized numbers and are not always of value in every location. These costs can be calibrated to a particular location by contacting any good contractor, lumberyard salesperson, or realtor. These professionals will have a thorough understanding of the average cost of construction for their market area.

All of this is not going to be that easy for the trainer however. First, it is only about 20 square feet. Even at $100 per square foot, it's fairly clear this will cost more than $2,000 to build. Second, it will be very difficult to get an exact number because there is no direct comparison from which to base its construction. The trainer is, to say the least, an unusual building. Although there are some telephone equipment buildings that are similar to the purpose of this building, none are both relocatable and easy to deconstruct.

As shown in Figure 4-7, one way to increase the accuracy of any estimate is to itemize the cost and unit or square footage for different parts of the building and total them as list of "definitive" numbers. The result remains a conceptual estimate, but because each of the building's components is taken into consideration, confidence in the number is increased. You have a separate cost per square foot for several components of the construction rather than a single lump sum for the total. The general idea is that the more information you include, the closer your number will be to the actual price. At least your estimate will be derived from a closer examination of the various parts of the building.

The DDs Wrap Everything up for the Engineered Drawings

Figure 4-8 illustrates how the DDs in step 4 refine the preliminaries. This refinement should include mostly minor adjustments to the schematics that came to light as the project was drafted to scale.

Once the drawings are revised, outline specifications and a conceptual cost estimate can be completed. The specifications include suggestions for the materials that will be shown in the engineered drawings and later details. These specifications will act as benchmarks when materials change later during engineering and analysis.

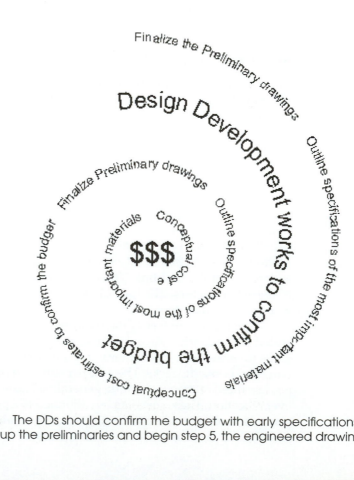

Figure 4-8. The DDs should confirm the budget with early specifications so that you can wrap up the preliminaries and begin step 5, the engineered drawings.

With these specifications, conceptual cost estimates can be prepared. These estimates are a reality check to verify the budget and make sure everyone is in agreement before beginning the larger portion of the work. You want the input of as many people as possible. Consultants cost money, however, so be sure that cost is also in the budget.

This is the last point of input for the owner or, in this case, the project manager. From the DDs onward, the dimensions and materials of the building must be clearly established or confusion will inevitably develop. Any future change may mean redrawing the preliminaries and starting all over again, a point that should be made clear as you proceed into step 5. The engineered drawings broaden the size of the team and are critical to the success of the project. In other words, when step 4 is completed and approved, the design phase is over. Along with steps 1, 2, and 3, this step finalized the shape and size of the building. Its dimensions, specifications, and costs have now been defined and you have phased documents to show that it meets the program requirements. You have a paper trail of the interactions and communications that have occurred in the form of submitted and revised drawings. Many of the drawings will be markups with specific notes and new instructions. It's only a matter of putting together the drawings and details necessary to construct the building.

Step 5 therefore begins the engineered drawing phase of this visual problem solving process. In this step, the structure of the trainer, from foundation to roof, will be completed. If you have the expertise available, it would also be possible to engineer the solar power system and the HVAC system and to integrate them with the structure. Both require innovative approaches to a design that would support the habitable space of the trainer, and the topic will not be covered in this book.

Step 5: The Engineered Drawings

Refer again to Figure 2-2. Step 5 involves two courses of action. The first is to finalize the site, floor, and roof plans as well as the exterior elevations and sections. These drawings must be substantially complete before you can begin to study the structure of the building. Changes and modifications will continue to be made as more engineering details are generated, but you want to make sure the drawings represent all the information you have up to this time, before you begin the bulk of the work in step 5.

Once these drawings are ready, the following new sheets can be added to the set:

1. The foundation plan.
2. The first floor or ground level framing plan.
3. The raised floor framing plan.
4. The roof framing plan.
5. Enlarged floor plans and wall sections.

Note that four of these drawings are structural drawings, and the fifth can be drawn only when the structural drawings are substantially complete. For the trainer, the structural drawings will be interleaved with the drawings that have already been completed. On a large building, however, all these sheets might be produced by an outside consultant and attached as a separate part of the set. When this occurs, the base drawings are coordinated with the engineered information when they are submitted for review and of course can be done with any number of other consultants. For example, both mechanical and electrical engineers could also be preparing separate drawings, all of which would have to be coordinated with the main set and each other.

With the addition of the structural sheets comes the beginning of documenting the structure integral to the assembly of the building. Up to this time, almost nothing was considered about how the building would actually fit together. In this step, many of the details for the construction will have to be planned so that you can draw the structural plans and the enlarged plans and sections. Many of these details will include items that will not be drafted at this point but should be noted in the margins of the drawings or on separate sheets of paper so they can be referenced in step 6. Saving the details until the next step will allow you to think through all of them at one time and to put them into the full set of drawings in the most logical order for the construction.

The second course of action for step 5 is to distribute the preliminary drawings to engineers and consultants and begin to generate input and discussion about the best way to put the building together. This process will refine the information on the current drawings and allow you to transform the preliminaries into a set of engineered drawings.

Most construction professionals would agree that the more input you can get from engineers, consultants, and workers, the more you will maximize the quality of the final drawings and minimize risks and the possibility of error. Of course, engineers and consultants want to be paid, so you can get only as much input as you can afford. The quality of the drawings will thus depend greatly on the amount of money available to invest in outside services.

For most field problems, this kind of coordination may not include much more than a couple of faxes and a few telephone conversations with a structural engineer, carpenter, mason, and a steel fabricator. But for more complex problems, coordination of the consultants and engineers is the heart of the entire process and will include long meetings, analysis of alternative schemes, value engineering, and careful collaboration.

To start these interactions, you will need to make a few assumptions about the structural layout. Some of these assumptions were made in the preliminaries. For example, with the trainer, early requirements for portability and deconstruction made the structure an integral part of the design. At this point, any major variations in its foundations will directly affect the way it is designed. The idea for the stacked precast concrete piers grew out of the program requirements. There are alternatives, of course, but these should really have been evaluated early in the problem solving process. A change now may mean resubmitting the drawings as preliminaries and running through the DDs again to make sure everyone is in agreement. Redesign and resubmittals are not unusual, and any time a better idea comes along, the entire project team should look at it. Some of the process may have to be repeated, perhaps starting again with the schematics.

Redesign usually means not enough time was spent examining the alternatives during the preliminaries, but even a well-thought-out design will mean changes to the early drawings as the structure is developed. For example, Figure 4-9 shows how the elevation of the grade around the trainer affects the elevation or height of the foundation walls, the size and depth of the footings, and the construction of the stair. These elevations will vary from location to location, so they will need to be reconsidered to make sure that they can adapt to various installations.

In most buildings, the foundation will affect the size of rooms shown in the floor plan, the finishes, and the installation of equipment or cabinets. For example, consider an exterior wall for a bathroom with a partial height retaining wall, like that shown in Figure 4-10. When the grade is above the finish floor, the foundation wall intrudes into the room. Depending on what is on the wall, the obstruction that is created in the room could be turned into a shelf, hidden behind a cabinet, or simply be the reason to install a thicker wall. If this obstruction affects standard fixtures like bathtubs and water closets, each alternative will change the size of the room, first, because of the actual placement of the fixture and second, because of the supply, waste, and vent pipes that must service it.

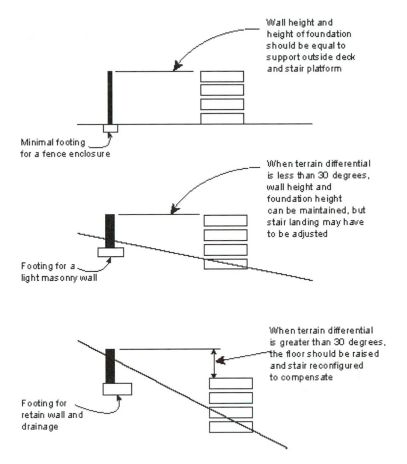

Wall height and height of foundation should be equal to support outside deck and stair platform

Minimal footing for a fence enclosure

When terrain differential is less than 30 degrees, wall height and foundation height can be maintained, but stair landing may have to be adjusted

Footing for a light masonry wall

When terrain differential is greater than 30 degrees, the floor should be raised and stair reconfigured to compensate

Footing for retain wall and drainage

Figure 4-9. Variables related to the way the foundation sits on different kinds of terrain will dictate the overall flexibility that must be built into the trainer foundation.

The Sheets Must Work Together

Drafting the foundation and framing drawing is a lot like drafting the orthographic projections for the preliminaries. All must be drawn at the same time. You have to lay out all the structural plans lightly and think through the entire assembly, sheet by sheet, all the way to the roof, before you can go back and confidently punch them out and tie them together with the preliminary drawings.

This holistic coordination is important because the floor plans, exterior elevations, and sections that have already been completed will be informed by what you do with the engineering. For example, in a woodframe building with a crawlspace, like the one shown in Figure 4-11, you have to determine the elevation of the finished grade from the height of the finished floor, and vice versa, because the height of the foundation wall is set by the height of the ground around the building. In turn, the first floor framing sits on the foundation wall and the finish floor sits on the framing. Even the bottom of the footing is therefore determined by how these dimensions will relate to each other. One variable literally builds on another, and a change in any of them can change the original floor plan.

When a change occurs, you have to rethink the actual dimensions as you work through the foundation and framing plans and adjust all the drawings that are

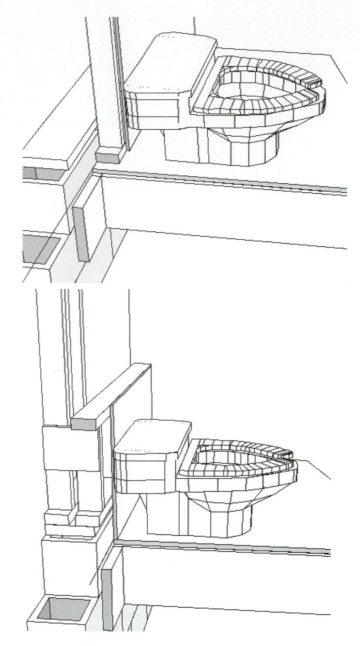

Figure 4-10. Different foundations will mean that the framing for the floor will change, and the position of objects in the room will have to accommodate the variations.

affected, even though you completed the scaled floor plan in the preliminaries. This may also include reevaluating the specifications and recalculating the conceptual estimates. For most changes, redrafting is not necessary. You can make minor adjustments by simply changing the dimensions. However, any change in the base drawings should be communicated to all the members of the project team for review. Even the most insignificant dimension often turns out to be critical to someone in some unpredictable way.

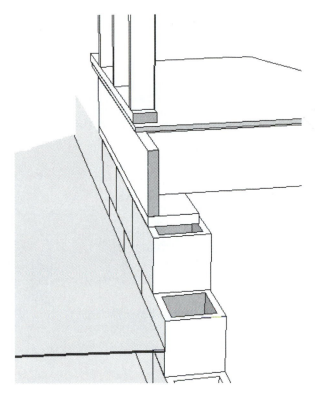

Figure 4-11. The finish grade, height of a foundation wall, and the floor framing all fit together to set the height of the finish floor.

Soils and Foundations

A foundation's design must take into account the type of soil, weight of the structure, and climatic characteristics. The type of soil determines bearing capacity. Bearing capacity is the total weight that the ground can take before the weight of the building compresses or laterally displaces the dirt. Hard clay can potentially carry more weight than soft sand because of lateral displacement. At the same time, the clay can be expansive, which means that it could push up on the foundation when it is wet. To get good bearing for the foundation, it is therefore important to remove the organic topsoil from the construction area and set the foundation on well-compacted or a stable undisturbed soil called natural grade (NG).

One of the purposes of a good foundation is to eliminate settlement and "heaving," or the lifting of the building's structure by the soil. If the soil is "soft," or so unstable that a normal foundation cannot avoid these problems, special pilings or caissons might have to be used to mitigate the problem.

If the building has to be located on old fill or the soil conditions are poor, an engineer should be consulted for the foundation design. Soil engineers measure bearing capacity in pounds per square inch. Using the bearing capacity given in a soil report, structural engineers can size the foundation and reinforce it to compensate for field conditions.

The concrete block wall next to the trainer uses continuous reinforcing called rebar. The reinforcing is continuous because the rebar in the footing runs continuously for the length of the footing. Thus, the footing will act as a single structural unit. Because it is often impossible to install one long piece of rebar, shorter pieces are bent and spliced to go around corners.

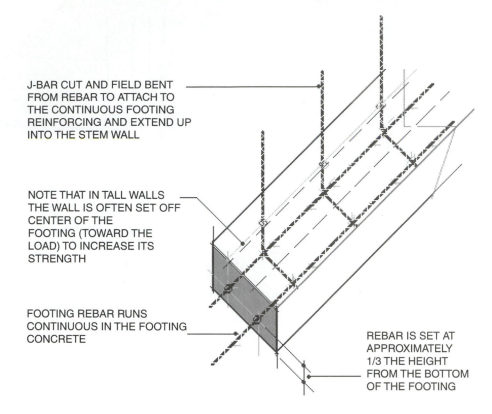

J-BAR CUT AND FIELD BENT FROM REBAR TO ATTACH TO THE CONTINUOUS FOOTING REINFORCING AND EXTEND UP INTO THE STEM WALL

NOTE THAT IN TALL WALLS THE WALL IS OFTEN SET OFF CENTER OF THE FOOTING (TOWARD THE LOAD) TO INCREASE ITS STRENGTH

FOOTING REBAR RUNS CONTINUOUS IN THE FOOTING CONCRETE

REBAR IS SET AT APPROXIMATELY 1/3 THE HEIGHT FROM THE BOTTOM OF THE FOOTING

Figure 4-12. The reinforcing in a footing is made up of continuous rebar and bent vertical pieces called J-bars.

For a large building, tons of reinforcing will be necessary and an engineer must calculate its design and placement. But for most small retaining walls or simple, single-story buildings, the reinforcing is fairly standard. In Figure 4-12, for example, the poured-in-place concrete footings for the trainer retaining wall would use two continuous #4 rebar. J-bars would then extend up from the footing to provide a splice point on which to tie the vertical reinforcing for the masonry stem wall. The bottom legs of the J-bars are tied to the continuous rebar in the footing. Note that the site survey indicates the elevation change for the grade around this wall is not more than a couple of feet of soil. Figure 4-9 showed how the foundation design will change with the grade. As the load on the wall increases, the structural design for the wall will also increase. A structural engineer should design any freestanding retaining wall with a retaining load of more than a foot or two high.

Reinforcing a Concrete Block Foundation Wall

The concrete block masonry stem wall raises the elevation of the bearing from the floor framing and brings it down to the concrete footing so that the load can be distributed to the soil. The stem wall is designed to support the soil behind the wall, the wall itself, and anything that might be set on it in the future. Stem walls can also be made from wood, concrete, or other types of masonry like brick or tilt-up panels.

As you can see in Figure 4-13, there are hollow cells in the concrete blocks to lighten their weight and allow the placement of reinforcing. Masons insert reinforcing in these cells and fill them with grout. Grout is a cement mixture that strengthens

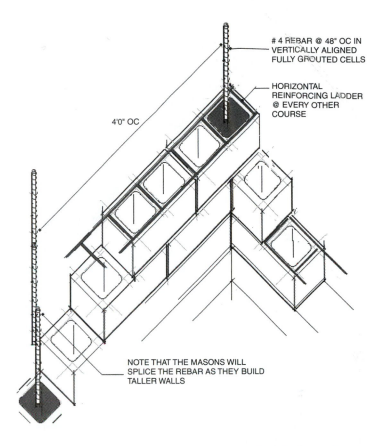

4 REBAR @ 48" OC IN
VERTICALLY ALIGNED
FULLY GROUTED CELLS

HORIZONTAL
REINFORCING LADDER
@ EVERY OTHER
COURSE

4'0" OC

NOTE THAT THE MASONS WILL
SPLICE THE REBAR AS THEY BUILD
TALLER WALLS

Figure 4-13. Reinforcing for the concrete block involves both vertical and horizontal rebar, which is embedded in a finer mix of concrete called grout.

the wall by making it solid. The steel reinforcing is the same rebar used in the footing. It is usually placed in the corners and in some of the vertically aligned alternate cells of the wall. For a heavily reinforced wall, rebar can be placed in every vertical cavity.

This reinforcing also attaches to the J-bars coming out of the footing. Once aligned, the footing, J-bar, and vertical rebar form columns within the wall because the hollow cells in the wall align vertically as they are being constructed. The vertical wall rebar is lapped and spliced to the J-bar coming out of the footing. Masons continue to lap and splice pieces of vertical rebar by tying them together with wires as they build the wall.

Horizontal reinforcing is made from heavy gauge welded wire and comes in two basic shapes. One is a "ladder," where the "rungs" of the ladder sit in the mortar of the joints that hold the wall together. The other is a horizontal truss, where the diagonals of the truss cross from one mortared side of the wall to the other. Horizontal reinforcing is lapped to strengthen the connections between various lengths and run in alternate courses of the wall. In a heavily reinforced wall, horizontal reinforcing can be placed in every course, or bond beams can be used to strengthen the wall.

Figure 4-14 shows another form of horizontal reinforcing in a concrete block wall. This reinforcing is a bond for horizontal strength or a lintel beam to carry loads across an opening in the wall. Masons build these beams in the field using U-shaped concrete blocks fitted in a row of block. When in place, these open blocks create a hollow horizontal space that can be filled with rebar and grout. Bond beams are used as a continuous course around the foundation to strengthen the wall against lateral forces. In a retaining wall, they are coupled with the grouted vertical reinforcing to form a surprisingly strong net of reinforced concrete. For maximum strength, every cell of the masonry units can be filled with grout and rebar.

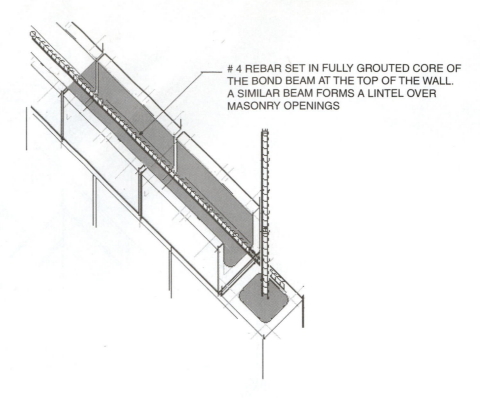

— # 4 REBAR SET IN FULLY GROUTED CORE OF
THE BOND BEAM AT THE TOP OF THE WALL.
A SIMILAR BEAM FORMS A LINTEL OVER
MASONRY OPENINGS

Figure 4-14. Bond beams are concrete blocks that are open at the top. Once in place, rebar can be inserted in the U-shaped cavity so that concrete can be poured into the cavity.

A steel angle or precast concrete beam is commonly used as a lintel to replace a bond beam over an opening in the wall. Steel lintels are sometimes used to support the bond beam while the grout is curing. When the opening is large or specially shaped, falsework can also be used to support the bond beams temporarily.

It's important to note again that, because of the standard dimensions of masonry units, the overall size of the wall and the locations of openings are critical to the way the wall is constructed. A concrete block wall should be built in increments of 8". Any opening in the wall should conform to the same 8" module. If the openings do not, the masons will have to cut the block to match nonstandard dimensions. This work will raise the cost and weaken the integrity of the wall.

Three Types of Foundations for the Trainer

Of course, the trainer's structure must be designed according to the principles of foundation design, but the program requirements for relocation and deconstruction mean that overall design will require something more than a traditional foundation. For the main tower, there will be minor variations as it is moved from location to location.

Except for the permanent retaining wall at the location used as the example in this book, any concrete that is poured in place will be difficult to relocate when the trainer needs to be moved. For the same reason, heavy foundation members like large reinforced footings and walls will require special labor and equipment to deconstruct and reinstall.

1. T-foundations are combinations of stem walls and spread footings. They support continuous loads like the weight of a row of floor joists. The stem of the T is usually a concrete or masonry wall. With a deep footing, the height of the wall can be increased to create enough headroom for a basement.

2. Prefabricated concrete slab can be used as the stair landing. The landing should be set on a gravel base, with anchor bolts provided for the stringer. Concrete slabs distribute floor loads across a broad surface of soil. Use slabs where soil conditions are soft or where the types of loads will vary across the floor.

3. Crushed rock is often used under a concrete slab to level the natural grade, distribute the load, and provide drainage under the slab.

4. Bearing pads take a point load from a column above and distribute the weight over the soil under the pad. In some buildings, these pads are column loads that carry the weight of the floors and the roof, including special fixtures or equipment inside the building.

The foundation for the trainer must also support the weight of the building on different kinds of surfaces, while protecting its contents against lateral wind loads and vibration from heavy equipment operating in the area. The design of the concrete coins and other foundation features will compensate for the varying terrain and these operational and structural requirements.

Figure 4-15 shows the suggested design for one version of the trainer's foundation and three kinds of foundations used to distribute the loads imposed by a building. The first type of foundation is a standard continuous footing and stem wall, like that discussed in the sections above. This footing must carry the weight of the wall, plus the weight of the soil that the wall is retaining. There is also the possibility of using the wall to support an observation deck or visitor area in the future.

For the relatively minor variation in the elevation of the soil shown on the site survey, this wall will not need to be extremely strong, although it will have to be heavily reinforced because of the potential for impact or additional lateral loading. If the height of the soil behind the wall were higher, or if the soil were subject to a lot of moisture, a drainage system and cast-in-place concrete wall might have to be substituted for the concrete block.

The sizes for the footing, rebar, and wall reinforcing must be finalized before you begin the construction details. Obviously, the retaining wall cannot be relocated once the trainer is moved, so it would probably be incorporated into the permanent site work for the main project. If this were a real project, the engineering for the wall and its design would be the responsibility of the project's design team, although there are many situations where the wall might be constructed as a temporary installation in a long-term construction project. For this example, however, it's important only to understand how the wall is constructed and how to draft it into a set of field drawings.

The second type of foundation is a slab on grade. The principle behind a concrete slab is to spread the weight of distributed loads over a broad surface area of the soil. The thickness and reinforcing for the slab depends on the weight of those loads and the relative stability of the soil.

One of the slabs for the trainer will be placed under the tower to provide open storage for equipment like generators and pumps. This installation is straightforward, except that this slab has an additional requirement: it must be portable. For this reason, the foundation design uses a set of four precast concrete slabs set on a gravel bed. These slabs distribute the load of equipment stored on them and are removable so that they can be stored when not in use. The shape of these precast slabs also acts as a spacer to reinforce the four piers supporting the steel columns and the main steel frame for the tower. The reinforcing and details for the slab will be drawn in step 6.

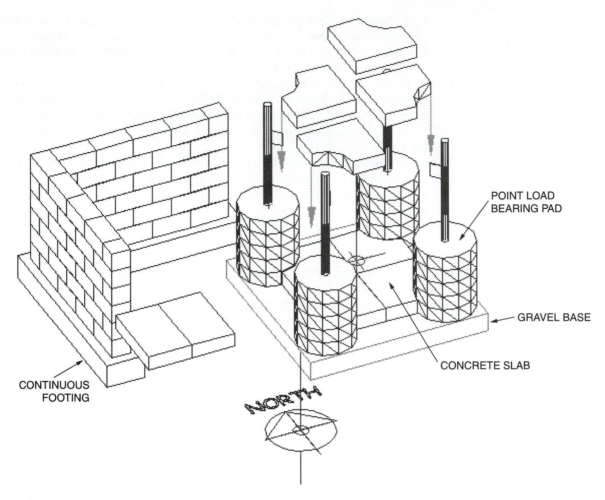

POINT LOAD
BEARING PAD

GRAVEL BASE

CONCRETE SLAB

CONTINUOUS
FOOTING

NORTH

Figure 4-15. Three different kinds of foundations are used for the example in this book: continuous footing, concrete slab, and point load bearing pad.

The second slab is the concrete pad at the base of the stair. This slab has to support the lower half of the stair as well as a landing for the stair. It too will be portable and bedded in a gravel base. Except for the fact that the stair bolts into this slab, the actual construction for this slab would not be much more than a sidewalk. The inserts for the bolts and the reinforcing for the slab will be detailed in step 6.

The third type of foundation is a point load footing. Point load bearing pads differ from continuous wall footings because they transfer the weight of the trainer to the soil through four isolated points. Each footing carries approximately one-fourth of the total live and dead load of the trainer. Live loads include people, furniture, and equipment that can be moved around. Dead loads are fixed in place and cannot move because they are part of the structure or a fixture or piece of equipment that has been attached permanently to the structure.

The surface area of the ground under the footing must be able to support the weight of the tower. The footing must have a large surface area in soft soil and spread its load more evenly or have a smaller bearing pad for denser soil, which does not require as much surface area. For the trainer, a relatively broad set of pads is used to compensate for almost any soil condition.

The preliminaries showed that the bearing pads are composed of a stack of precast concrete coins. Like the precast slabs, the weight of each coin must be small enough for one or two people to remove and replace them for different installations. In addition, the coins must be bolted together to act as a counterweight against the movement of the tower in windy conditions. The collective weight of the piers will hold the trainer down in the wind and stabilize it from uplift and lateral loads. The combined weight of the concrete coins without the weight of the rest of the tower is approximately 1 ton.

The steel frame is attached to a steel insert cast into the coins, but the exact detail of the attachment and how the coins link together will not be finalized until the foundations are detailed in step 6. Of course, the reinforcing and attachments must be confirmed after the structure has been substantially engineered and detailed.

The Foundation Plan

The foundation shown in the initial layouts of the engineered drawings is really a hypothesis. It is a suggestion for one possible design that needs to be tested with further discussion and study. The idea is to write these ideas on paper so that you can gather input from others and perhaps find a better solution. Modifications will occur, so it is important to illustrate the basic idea so that it is clearly understood.

Because it is a hypothesis, it is possible to show this design to a consultant as a schematic plan. It would be difficult, however, to coordinate the dimensions and provide accurate layouts to calculate loading without continual reference to the preliminary drawings. For this reason, transfer the perimeter of the trainer onto a new sheet of paper to start the foundation plan. (See Figure 4-16.) Getting the plan in the same place on all the sheets is important again because it allows workers to flip through the construction drawings and visualize the information as it builds from sheet to sheet.

At this point, you want to trace lightly the layout of the foundations for the trainer, making some logical assumptions (educated guesses) for the sizes of the footings. Since everything is subject to change and so much of the rest of the building is unknown, the foundation plan will almost certainly be refined as more information becomes available. This information is also the kind you would get from a good structural engineer.

Like the preliminaries, all the structural plans have to be drawn at one time, which is true of any set of engineered drawings. There is so much information that has to work together as a system that it would be impossible to complete one part of the drawings and proceed to the next. This is especially important when you consider the interface between the foundation plan and the floor framing systems, which includes the framing for the main part of the trainer. Given the program requirements for this project, it is fairly certain that the framing for this building will not be standard. It is important, however, to understand how conventional buildings are framed.

To begin the foundation plan, tape the ground level plan to any flat surface and then tape the blank sheet for the foundation plan over it. Lightly trace the perimeter of the ground plan onto the blank sheet for the foundation plan. This process will position the foundation plan in exactly the same place as the other plans and make it easier for workers to orient themselves as they flip from sheet to sheet.

1. With the perimeter of the plan outlined on the sheet for the foundation plan, draft the stem wall and footing in plan view. The footing is centered and extends out from the face of the wall in both directions.

2. Now lightly draft a single line around the perimeter of the slab on grade at the south wing.

3. The elevations of the footing, the top of the wall, and the slab have to be determined in the building elevations and wall sections. Of course, this vertical information will not be available until you can coordinate these details with each particular sheet. For now, add symbols for wall sections in the same three places shown on the floor plans, elevations, and sections.

Don't worry about all the details or completing the parts of the foundation plans that still need to be defined. Make notes of what you need to know. You will go back and punch out the entire set as soon as you finalize the framing plans.

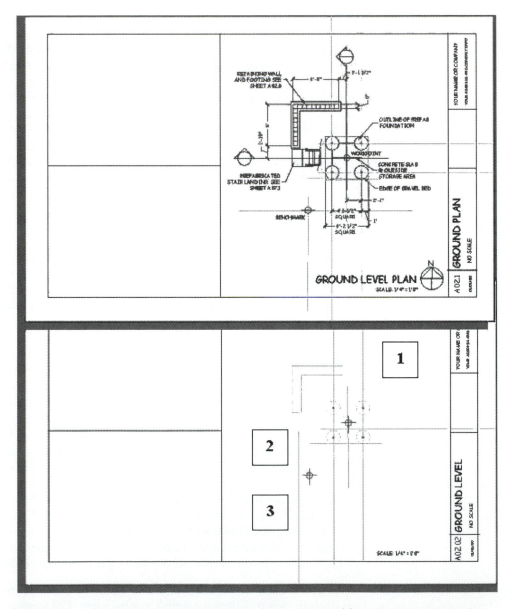

Figure 4-16. Once the outline of the foundation is traced from the floor plan, align the sheets so that you can project the dimensions from the floor plan and draw the foundation plan.

Traditional Wood-Framing Systems

The material for the structural system of a traditional building can be steel, masonry, precast or cast-in-place concrete, lightweight steel, or standard wood-framing. Each framing system has its advantages and disadvantages, given the loads and the shape of the structure.

The most popular form of framing continues to be woodframe construction, but lightweight steel framing is becoming increasingly competitive and has its own distinct advantages. There are two conventional methods for both types of framing: balloon framing, often used where ceilings are tall or weather is a factor during construction, and platform or western framing, which is more common today because it allows rapid and efficient assembly.

As shown in Figure 4-17, balloon framing is an older form of wood-framing. As its name implies, the idea behind balloon framing is to build the shell of the building

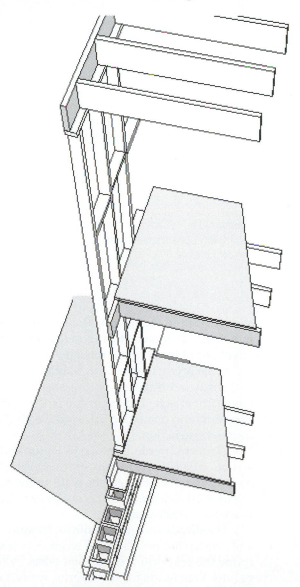

Figure 4-17. Balloon framing uses continuous exterior studs for the outside walls to enclose the building before interior floors and walls are added.

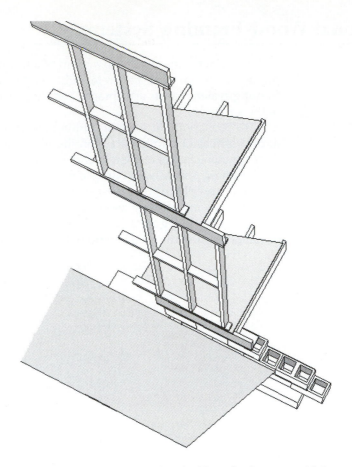

Figure 4-18. Platform framing uses shorter stud lengths to support intermediate floors and then uses those floors as platforms on which to lay out and frame the walls for the next level.

and then fill in the interior floors and walls, including all the exterior walls and the roof. The advantage of balloon framing is that you can enclose a space immediately to get out of the weather quickly. This advantage is critical in winter construction.

Some argue that balloon framing also allows you to create a more tightly sealed and insulated building with a structural envelope that has fewer exterior seams. Floors are attached to the inside of the studs of the balloon frame, allowing the exterior studs and insulation to be installed without the break you would find in platform frame construction.

Platform framing, shown in Figure 4-18, differs from balloon framing because it is more efficient and usually quicker to erect. Each floor in the system is used as a platform from which to erect the walls of the next floor. Workers can assemble the building in sequence and they do not have to build scaffolding or temporary supports to work on certain areas.

The disadvantage of platform framing is that it takes more construction material and sets up the possibility of weather penetration. The amount of material it takes to frame the platform is somewhat offset by the fact that this kind of framing does not require long studs for the exterior walls. Long wooden studs are becoming increasingly difficult to find because so little native growth remains available for construction. The potential for weather penetration is reduced with modern sheathing and sealants; nevertheless, the exterior skin of the building is broken by floor penetrations.

In both types of woodframe construction, the walls in the floor plans use the same framing technique. Exterior studs can vary from 2×4 to 2×6 or even 2×8, depending on the structural loads and the thickness of the wall required for insulation or mechanical equipment like ductwork or plumbing. These studs are almost always spaced at 16″ on center (OC). When 2×6 or 2×8 studs are used, however, spacing is usually increased to as much as 24″ OC. This wider spacing is possible because of the heavier wood.

When the studs are spaced at 16″ and 24″ OC, standard 4×8 foot sheets of sheathing, plywood, or sheetrock can be applied to the walls in even modules. This allows the joints of this material to abut each other on a common stud. Increasing the spacing beyond 24″ OC or using a different spacing pattern is not practical because these interior and exterior finish materials can be more difficult to apply.

A single bottom plate and a double top plate frame the studs in these walls. These horizontal members are usually made out of the same material as the studs. Carpenters build these walls flat on the plywood floor decking, with just one top plate for each wall. When the walls are tilted up and set in place, the second top plate is attached so that it laps across the intersections of the walls to tie the walls together. Once the walls are in place, drywall and other wall finish materials can be attached to the studs. To make this easier, corners and intersections have traditionally used the three-stud detail as shown in Figure 4-18. However, corner clips are now commonly used to support the interior finish panels.

Wood and Lumber

Wood is one of the oldest and most widely used construction materials. Because it varies with species and moisture content, the American Lumber Standards group grades wood for construction. There are three categories of graded lumber: heavy timbers for beams, stringers and columns; framing materials for joists and decks; and boards for sheathing and general siding. A grading stamp on the lumber identifies its origin, grade, and moisture content. Obviously, it's important to specify and use the correct grade of material for its application in the structure of a building.

As shown in Figure 4-19, lumber in the United States comes in standard sizes and is available in increments of 2 feet, usually starting with 8-foot lengths. The mill cut size of lumber is called out according to its nominal size—or what used to be the actual size of milled wood when trees were plentiful. For example, a 2×4 is called a 2×4, but its actual dimensions are slightly less than $1\frac{1}{2}″ \times 3\frac{1}{2}″$. To make sure everything fits in a detail, draft lumber at its actual size and call it out in your notes at its nominal size. Also note that there are no inch marks (″) after either the 2 or the 4 in the 2×4 callout. If you use inch marks (like 2″ × 4″), these sizes would be interpreted as the actual sizes to be installed. It would be like asking workers in the field to take a larger piece of material, say, a 6×6, and cut it down to exactly 2″ × 4″. Exact dimensions like these are more often found in cabinets or boat building.

Engineered wood can now be substituted for milled lumber in various applications. These composite materials are usually more stable and of higher quality than standard lumber. They are also often lighter and easier to handle. Three of the more common engineered woods are glue-laminated beams (called glu-lams), plywood, and pressure treated lumber. (See Figure 4-20.)

Glu-lam is a manufactured material made up of layers of wood glued together under high pressure. The advantage of glu-lams is that thinner strips of wood can be used to fabricate large beams. These smaller pieces are specially selected for uniform grain and species and are processed to reduced moisture. They are trimmed to standard sizes for joining. Glu-lams can also be manufactured for extremely long spans, arching or curved spans, chambered or prestressed beams, and other special struc-

Nominal sizes	Actual size
2x4	1-1/2" x 3-1/2"
2x6	1-1/2" x 5-1/2"
2x8	1-1/2" x 7-1/4"
2x10	1-1/2" x 9-1/4"
2x12	1-1/2" x 11-1/4"
4x4	3-1/2" x 3-1/2"
4x6	3-1/2" x 5-1/2"
4x8	3-1/2" x 7-1/4"
4x10	3-1/2" x 9-1/4"
4x12	3-1/2" x 11-1/4"
6x6	5-1/2" x 5-1/2"
6x8	5-1/2" x 7-1/4"
6x10	5-1/2" x 9-1/4"
6x12	5-1/2" x 11-1/4"

Figure 4-19. Nominal and actual sizes of milled lumber.

tural specifications. They come in various sizes and depths, in increments of $1\frac{1}{2}$". Because factories manufacture them to a specific size, draft them and call them out according to their exact dimensions. A glu-lam beam that is the same size as a 6×8 on the drawings is noted as a "$5\frac{1}{2}$" × $7\frac{1}{2}$" glu-lam."

The second kind of engineered material is plywood. Plywood is a manufactured material made up of cross-grain layers of veneered wood. These veneered plies are glued together under high pressure. The grains of the layers are perpendicular to each other to strengthen their resistance to bending. For this reason, plywood always has an odd number of plies, and the face-ply on both sides of the sheet run in the same direction.

Plywood comes in standard sheets of 4'0" × 8'0" but can be special ordered in 10'0" or 12'0" lengths. The thickness varies in $\frac{1}{8}$" increments and can be found in sheet thicknesses of $\frac{1}{4}$" through greater than 2" for special structures. The most common sizes are $\frac{5}{8}$" or $\frac{3}{4}$" for subfloors and decking, $\frac{1}{2}$" for roof sheathing, and $\frac{1}{4}$" or $\frac{3}{8}$" for exterior siding.

Plywood varies in strength and purpose, depending on the species of plies, face veneer, type of glue, and edge treatment. It is especially resistant to shearing stress and can be water resistant. It is an inexpensive and efficient use of rare woods like birch, maple, oak, and other hardwoods. There are many different grades and finishes of plywood, depending on the quality and type of face material.

The third pressure treated material that is becoming increasingly common is chemically treated wood. For example, pressure treated materials like Douglas fir pressure treated (DFPT) are part of a group of chemically altered woods on the market for special purposes like moisture control or insect resistance. Most of this material has been treated with insecticides to prevent decay and infestation. Scraps and dust from these materials are toxic and should be handled with care.

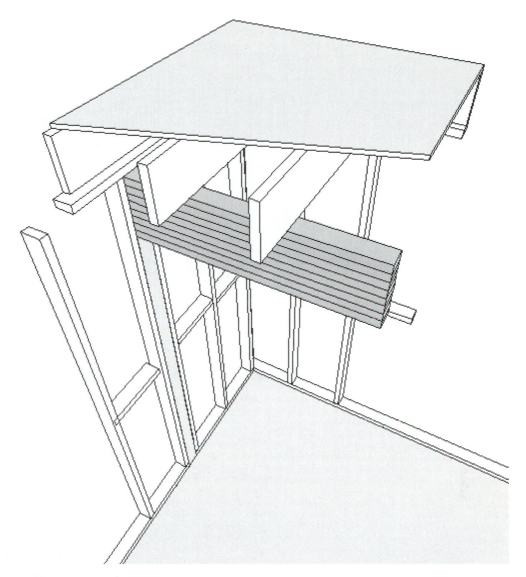

Figure 4-20. Engineered wood like glu-lam beams, plywood, and pressure-treated woods integrate seamlessly into standard wood framing.

Lightweight Steel Framing

An increasingly popular framing system uses lightweight galvanized steel extrusions. The system is designed to replace lumber or be integrated into wood-framing and includes common shapes that are $3^1/_2''$ and $5^1/_2''$ wide to match nominal lumber sizes, as well as studs that are 2″, 4″, and 6″ wide. They come in varying thicknesses of steel called gauges and can be extremely strong when required. The shapes also include structural steel C-shaped joists of varying depths.

Figure 4-21 shows a typical lightweight steel stud framing system. The pieces of this system are nearly identical to those found in a wood-framing system and use all the same nomenclature, including platform and balloon framing. In this case, however, balloon framing seems to be more common because of the engineered properties of the material. This makes drafting the base plans, elevations, and sections quite simple because none of the drawings require special callouts or knowledge to use.

Figure 4-21. Lightweight steel framing is becoming a popular alternative to wood-framing systems.

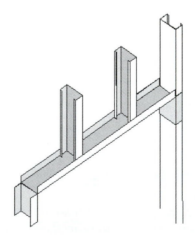

Figure 4-22. The flanges of the horizontal members in a lightweight steel framing system are clipped and then bent down to be screwed onto the studs.

The walls have a top and bottom track to hold the studs in place. The studs are welded or screwed to the top and bottom track through the side flanges of the extrusion or attached with metal angle clips to the base of the track. A strap is used to tie the top of the walls together, so there is no need for a second top track similar to the top plate in wood-framing. A boxed header is used for openings in bearing walls. Steel beams or heavier gauged steel joists are used as headers in larger openings. Figure 4-22 shows the more typical nonbearing header in a lightweight steel wall. Installers cut the flanges of the track and bend it to fit over the jambs on each side of the frame.

Although the advantages of steel framing may or may not be lower cost, it is clear that steel studs can be a better value in many cases, as you can see in the following list:

1. There is a significant reduction in jobsite waste because material can be ordered cut to length and prepunched for mechanical and electrical lines.

2. Steel studs are relatively quick and easy to install because the pieces are spot welded or screwed together and manufactured to relatively close tolerances and uniform quality.

3. The framing system can be deconstructed and reconstructed, which means it has a great deal of design flexibility. These features might also be important to the programmatic requirements for the trainer.

4. The material is easily recycled and readily salvaged because it does not require sorting or the separation of nails and other hidden fasteners.

5. The materials are impervious to insects and galvanized to prevent corrosion; however, they must be sealed carefully to prevent condensation and contact with pipes or electrical wiring.

6. Most important, metal studs are not combustible, making them mandatory in certain fire districts and for building types where there is a risk of fire danger to the general public, including almost all mid- and high-rise buildings, commercial buildings, large public spaces, auditoriums, hotels, and hospitals.

Framing the Trainer

Of course, framing the trainer to fit the program requirements is not as straightforward as a choice between platform or balloon framing using wood or lightweight steel members. Even though the initial layout on the foundation plan shows four footings that could support column loads from several different kinds of structural systems, standard framing techniques will not be practical.

As shown in Figure 4-23, a traditional foundation with standard joists and studs might work for a one-time installation, but it would be too cumbersome to be moved from location to location on one jobsite or for multiple reconstructions. Even if the pieces were screwed together so they could be reassembled, wood or lightweight steel framing members are not designed for repeated reuse and would break down and lose stability after one or two installations. In addition, deconstruction and storage would take a long time and be fairly inefficient, with a high probability of lost or damaged pieces, especially around old fastener penetrations.

The program also requires that the trainer be relocatable. In fact, it might be moved several times in the first project and reused in subsequent projects for several years. The program purpose is to make the on-line database or reference materials available for project-specific training and instruction throughout the jobsite. One tower might be located near a laser control point during sitework and excavation, shifted to a crane control position during foundations, or lifted from one floor to another as the building is constructed.

The programmatic requirements for this kind of movement means the building needs to be strong enough to be lifted regularly from place to place and at the same time be broken down and packaged in a container for long-term storage. These requirements are what a value engineer would call the basic or critical functions that need to be met by the frame's engineering. One way to do this is to design the tower around a very strong skeletal steel frame. As illustrated in Figure 4-24, the steel frame must be able to carry the weight of the roof, walls, floors, and stairs so that these loads

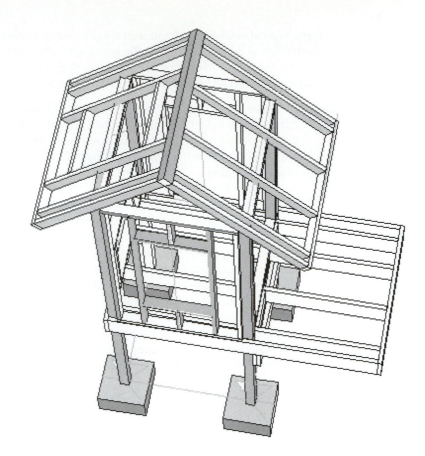

Figure 4-23. A traditional platform framing system for this project would not fulfill the program requirements.

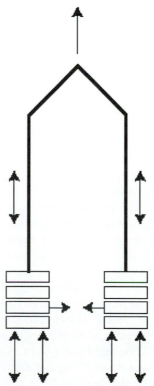

Figure 4-24. The steel frame for the building must be able to lift and support its own weight.

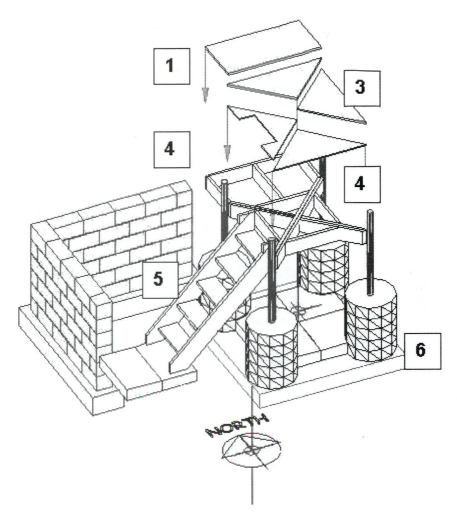

Figure 4-25. The X-joist that supports the floor and stair also braces the main structural steel frame when it is lifted and moved to different locations.

can be supported by the foundation when the building is at "rest." At the same time, the frame must be able to lift the weight of the foundation, floors, walls, and equipment when the building is moved to another position.

This frame can be internal or external to the building envelope, but it seems likely that connections and adjustments would be facilitated by having as much of the frame as possible outside the building's envelope. This position increases interior square footage and means that connections and equipment could be accessed for service or adjustment without going into the habitable portion of the trainer.

The steel columns must be bolted to the concrete foundation to support both uplift and lateral loads. If the four columns are built in two pieces, a platform framing technique similar to that found in traditional systems can be used to build first one level and then the next. The lower part of the frame can be supported by half the columns and at the same time act as a scaffold to build the upper part of the frame and the roof. (See Figure 4-25.)

The X-joists are shown in the figure to span diagonally from column to column and act as the primary members of a moment frame. The idea is to keep these columns spread out during lifting and supporting the weight of the raised floor. The X-joists must also support the stair and brace the frame against twisting and racking under lateral and vibration loads. Once bolted to the steel frame, four triangular floor panels can be screwed to the X-frame to strengthen the assembly against horizontal shear. This technique allows workers to erect the lower part of the columns to support the raised floor and use the floor as a platform to erect the columns for the roof.

The floor extension will require further study. One idea is to cantilever the floor framing from the main floor, but this would mean a heavier floor structure with more joists and a lot more weight. An alternative might be to hang the floor extension from the roof rafters, but this cannot be determined until the roof is laid out and studied. For now, the floor can be lightly drafted in, but like everything else at this stage, it is subject to coordination and change as the complete structure is finalized.

1. The framing for the floor extension is 2×8 Douglas fir pressure treated (DFPT). The joists are attached to the main floor frame but are suspended from the roof support structure above.

2. The stair is probably best made out of a pressure treated wood so that it can be modified quickly for different installations. Whenever DFPT is specified, write a clear note on the drawings about the precautions for cutting, handling, and disposing of this material during construction. Also be aware of the danger they pose for children and for food contamination.

3. Structural plywood floor panels act to stabilize torsion about the central axis. They are screwed to the crossing joists at 6″ OC. The plywood for these panels and the floor extension should be marine grade exterior plywood in case they get wet during reconstruction.

4. Note the four floor headers at approximately midspan of the X-joists. They support the floor extension, stair stringers, and any equipment that might be attached below the floor frame.

5. The stair stringers and treads are shown as part of the floor framing system, but they are drawn in detail on a separate sheet. It is important only to show the relative position of the stringers to the floor framing on the floor framing plans.

This foundation system is the same that was lightly laid out in the foundation plans drawn in Figure 4-16. Now that you have at least one idea about how the floor might be constructed you can lightly draw your design for the raised floor plan as shown in Figure 4-26. Again, keep the drawings aligned by using one of the other plans to trace the perimeter of the framing plan.

Use light lines to lay out everything you know about the framing. Keep in mind that many details and relationships will have to be coordinated as the structural system is finalized. Many unknowns cannot be resolved until the entire frame of the building is roughly laid out. For now, it's important to think through the floor framing and its relation to the foundation, then proceed immediately to the walls that will sit on the floor. Write notes in the margins or on separate drawings to remind you of items that will have to be looked at and coordinated later, including the support for the floor extension, attachment of the stair, attachments to the concrete foundations, and how the X-joists will be mated to the columns themselves.

Again place a blank sheet of 11″×17″ paper over the raised plan and lightly trace the perimeter of the walls to locate the structural pieces in the same position on the sheet as the other plans. Once the perimeter of the foundation is drafted on the blank sheet, remove the underlying sheet and lightly draft the columns, slab, and bearing pads below. Now it's a simple matter of visualizing a plan of the framing over the foundation walls. Use your circle template to draw each of the four columns and then lightly draft two crossing layout lines from center to center and lay out the rest of the floor joists.

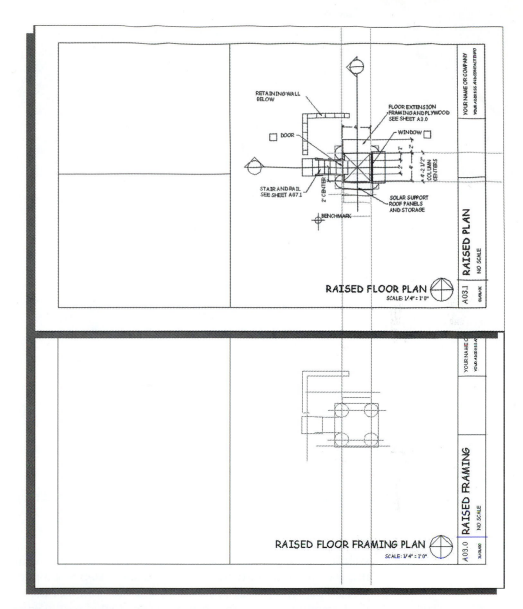

Figure 4-26. Lay out the raised floor plan and the framing plan so that they are in the same location on each sheet. Lightly lay out the X-frame and the four columns of the steel frame, and proceed immediately to the next sheet.

The Wall Framing for the Trainer

One way to frame the wall for the trainer is to use 2" galvanized lightweight steel studs with a 2" rigid insulated board inserted in the wall cavity. The reduced weight will cut down the total weight of the trainer for the lifts and make it easier to take the building apart in panelized sections. The problem with a standard lightweight steel system is that the studs and tracks are not designed for continual reuse. Thus, an unconventional framing system will have to be engineered once the framing is determined.

Whatever wall framing method is used for these walls, it should not change the floor plan that has been drawn. There may be changes to some of the dimensions, but how the wall is constructed should affect only the wall sections that will be drawn

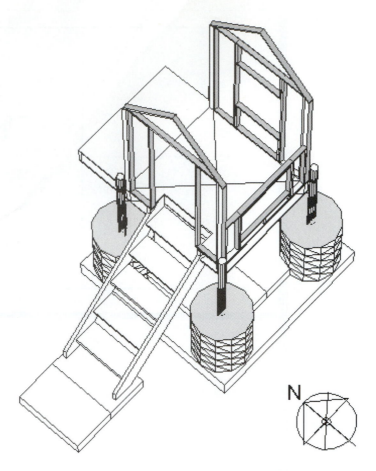

N

Figure 4-27. The nonbearing wall framing system should be panelized for deconstruction but rigid enough to support the door, window, and storage units that will be attached to it.

later in this step. This does not preclude looking into new and innovative solutions. It is only a reminder that, because you are in step 5 of a particular design, a framing system that completely rethinks the current design of the trainer should go back to the beginning of the process and be reevaluated by the entire design team as a new schematic design. If approved, it could then be studied again in a new preliminary and DD review.

Three walls must be framed. (See Figure 4-27.) The walls on the east and west elevations are 6'0" tall from the finished floor to the top of the top plate or track. Above the top plate is the gabled end of the roof. This triangular face frames an opening that can be either glass or solid. It might also be used as a vent to extract air from the upper part of the habitable space. Remember, both computer equipment and humans generate a tremendous amount of heat.

One idea might be to fabricate the pieces of this wall as individual units so that they can be assembled as prefabricated wall panels. If lightweight steel studs are used, $^1/_2$" plywood shear panels can be screwed to the outside surface to strengthen both the wall panel and the steel frame. The inside face of the walls might then have $^1/_4$" pegboard screwed to the studs as a finish surface. The wall surfaces can then sandwich the rigid insulation or be filled with rigid polyurethane foam insulation after they are assembled.

Figure 4-28 shows the west wall with a door centered over the stair that extends partially into the room to provide more clearance for a person's head when he or she

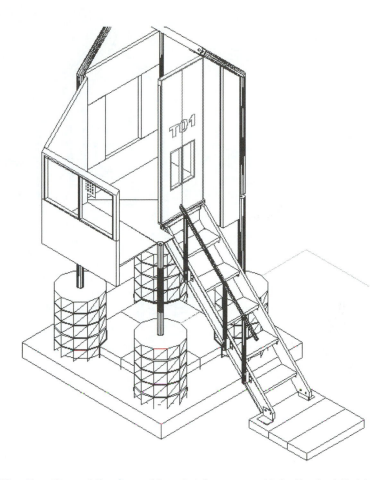

Figure 4-28. The door at the top of the stair is recessed into the habitable space to provide headroom for the stair.

is walking up the stair. This solution is chosen in the book's example to resolve the headroom problem discovered in the preliminaries. How the frame around the door works with the stair and the interior portion of the room is not known and really cannot be figured out until the roof framing is studied. Again, you have to suspend a complete understanding until you have a better idea of what is feasible for the entire structural system.

The east wall frames a rectangular casement window centered in the wall. The exact size of the window would have been defined in the early specifications of the DDs. The window should be set high enough off the finished floor to allow the placement of a baseboard and possibly an electrical or mechanical fixture. This arrangement would also keep the fixture out of the way in a tight space so it is less likely to be damaged by equipment placed on the floor.

The south wall is a partial height bulkhead wall with access to a countertop and storage cabinet. This cabinet was shown first in the schematics and later in the preliminaries, but it has not been studied. The size of the opening and the way the cabinet will be installed in the wall have not been detailed. This is yet another unknown that has to wait its turn in the problem solving process. One idea, shown in Figure 4-29, is to hang the cabinet from the wall using heavy gauge steel studs, but the steel studs would have to support a great deal of load in cantilever. Another solution is to build the counter and the storage as a complete unit that might be inserted into the wall and hung from the rafters. You will need to make a note of possible solutions that must be studied more carefully after the roof has been laid out.

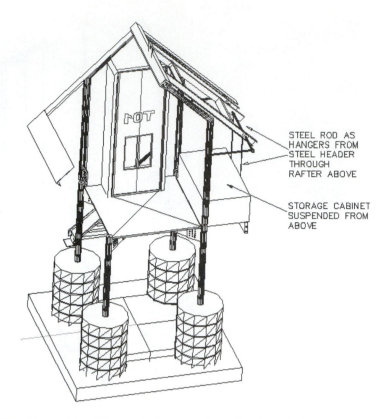

STEEL ROD AS
HANGERS FROM
STEEL HEADER
THROUGH
RAFTER ABOVE

STORAGE CABINET
SUSPENDED FROM
ABOVE

Figure 4-29. The cabinets in the trainer can be attached to heavy steel studs or suspended from ceiling rafters.

The north side of the space has a floor extension that must support the floor loads and the walls on the north side of the trainer. We know from the building section that the ceiling height in this area is very low, so the kind of loading will be restricted to equipment storage or seating. These walls need to be shown on the floor plans, but their exact size cannot be determined until the roof structure is studied. You will therefore have to study the placement of the walls as well as how the floor is supported as you study the roof framing.

Almost anything that you decide to do with these walls will affect the existing floor plans for these spaces. Be sure to draft them lightly until the entire structural system is understood. Any changes made at this stage will probably have to be changed again as more details are determined. It might even be better to write marginal notes and leave everything until all the sheets are ready to be punched out at the same time. Don't forget to come back and make those changes later.

It should be fairly clear now that, like the preliminaries, the two-dimensional sheets of the engineered drawings must be drafted simultaneously to make sure they are coordinated and that they communicate correctly the construction of the three-dimensional object they are representing. You are not drafting sheets in a set of drawings. Instead, you will use those sheets and the drawings to think through the entire structural system. All the drawings remain in a state of flux, constantly changing as new problems and solutions are discovered. This visual approach to problem solving should therefore illustrate how important the drawings are to finding and communicating the unknowns. Without them, the problems would just spin forever in the mind of each individual team member and never find a point at which they can be focused for collaboration.

Roof Framing for the Trainer

As illustrated in Figure 4-30, there are four different roofs in the preliminaries for the trainer. The west roof over the entry door protects the door against the weather and afternoon sun. The position of this roof needs to be studied carefully because its location may make it difficult for the door to open outward. This problem is not obvious from the plan or elevation, but it is fairly noticeable after studying the section. It might be resolved in the design of the door or the design of the roof later in this phase. For example the door could roll up instead of swing out, or the roof might be attached to the door itself so that it moves with the door. This is an example of a detail problem to keep in mind as the roof framing evolves.

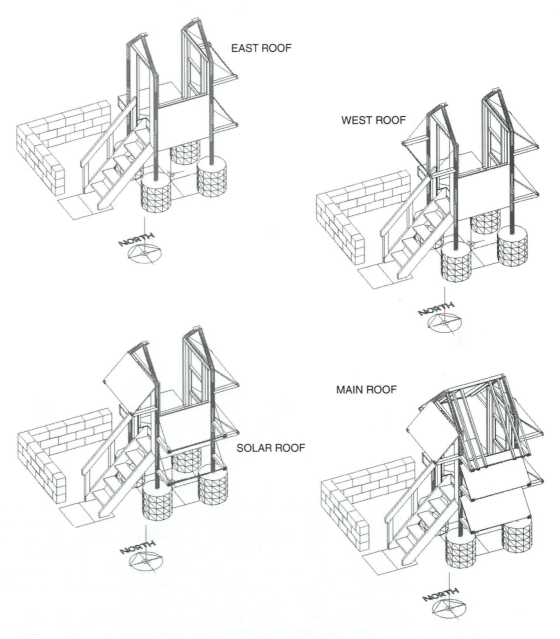

Figure 4-30. The roofs of the trainer provide protection from the weather, support for the skylight, floor extensions, and support for solar panels.

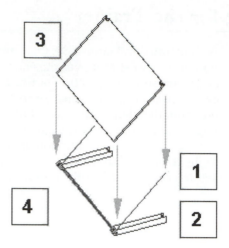

Figure 4-31. One way to detail the racks for the solar equipment is to hang the panel from the main frame of the trainer.

The north roof has an operable skylight to add ventilation to the habitable space. The specifications for the manufacturer, size, and installation were completed with the materials research in the DD phase. One idea is to cantilever the roof rafters out to support the floor extension. To brace the rafters for the cantilever, you could use a header beam, like the traditional framing system shown in Figure 4-23. Another idea is to support the floor with knee braces back to the columns of the frame below the floor. A third idea is to hang the floor from the rafters, similar to hanging something from the wire structure of a coat hanger. As shown in Figure 4-30, the sloping portion of the hanger has a horizontal compression member that supports the weight of the load. This solution seems to have the greatest potential for both the uplift and gravity loads with the lightest weight structure and is the one studied in the sample details for this book. Any other ideas could also be explored; remember, however, to detail them carefully so they can be evaluated for cost and ease of construction.

The south roofs include the main roof and two solar support panels hanging from the vertical frame. These secondary panels have been added to take advantage of the southern exposure and provide more surface area for the solar collectors. The photovoltaic panels are mounted to the main roof with clips, per the manufacturer's recommendation. This feature will be detailed in the next step. The hot air and water collectors for heating system are mounted to the solar support panels, as shown in Figure 4-31. These sloping panels are designed more as equipment racks than roofs. In other words, though they should remain waterproof, they are installed more to support the environmental systems above their surface than to protect habitable space under them.

The preliminaries also show two roofs on the east elevation. The upper roof provides protection from the sun and the weather for the casement window. The lower roof was added to act as a radiator to dissipate heat collected by the air-conditioning system and could be hung like the solar support panels. The design of the heating, ventilation, and air-conditioning (HVAC) system is not known at this time, but it will include the same basic components as any other cooling system: a condenser, heat exchanger, and pump. One idea is to use this lower roof panel as a convective heat exchanger. Of course, this idea needs a lot of study and will involve coordination with a mechanical engineer or meetings with an air-conditioning technician.

The details for the solar support panels will be drawn in step 6; however, their general construction should be studied to make sure they are feasible and you can go ahead with the structural plans. Figure 4-31 shows the structure of the solar support panels, which includes:

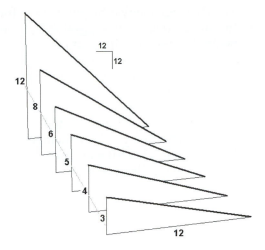

Figure 4-32. The slope or pitch of the roof is shown vertically proportional to twelve horizontal units of measure.

1. A tension member along the 45-degree angle of the roof slope. This steel angle is bolted to the steel column.
2. A horizontal compression arm holding the panel away from the building. This compression arm is threaded into the center of the vertical steel column and attached to the end of the tension members. The threaded tension member arm can then be adjusted to fine-tune the slope of the plywood.
3. A piece of $^3/_4$″ plywood screwed to the tension members. Roofing can then be applied to the top surface before making any necessary penetrations and attaching equipment to the top or underside of each panel.
4. A horizontal steel rod, perpendicular to the compression arms, that ties the two arms together and supports the long end of the plywood panel.

Note that all the roofs have the same 12:12 or 45-degree pitch roof. As shown in Figure 4-32, the slope of a roof is measured according to the proportions of its vertical dimension and 12. This measurement can be 12 inches, 12 feet, or any other unit as long as the same units are used for the vertical measurement.

As shown in Figure 4-33, you cannot lay out a lot for the roof plan except perhaps the perimeter of the roof, the ridge beam, and some suggestions for rafter placement. One thing to keep in mind is that the rafters on the north side of the main roof must be spaced to support the skylight selected during DDs. These are the same rafters that support the floor extension, although precisely how this might be done remains to be studied and detailed. The rafters on the south side will probably be evenly spaced to support the photovoltaic solar collectors. The retaining wall and the stair are shown for reference, but you do not need to include a lot of detail or information because these features are not the subject of the drawing.

To start the roof plan, again place a blank sheet of 11″×17″ paper over the raised plan and lightly trace the perimeter of the walls to locate the structure in the same position on the sheet as you did for the other plans.

1. Once the perimeter of the foundation is drafted on the blank sheet, remove the underlying sheet and lightly draft the columns, slab, and bearing pads below. Now it's a simple matter of visualizing a plan for the framing over the walls of the raised floor.
2. Lightly draft the layout lines for the center of all four columns. Then use your circle template to lightly draw the four columns. Add lines for the ridge beam and the rafters.

There are many different ways to frame almost any part of the trainer. The objective at this point is to suggest at least one structural system as a possible solution to begin discussions with your consultants. Notes in the margins of the drawings or in your files might even suggest other alternatives for the same roof. The result of your conversations might be that you were totally wrong or that some adjustments might have to be made to your initial assumption. With experience, you may even know exactly what needs to be done and simply have to confirm your assumptions with an outside consultant. What is important is that you have some ideas for the roof's construction and that you have them lightly laid out for further discussion. The lines are lightly laid out so that they can be changed or adjusted according to whatever comes to light in your discussions.

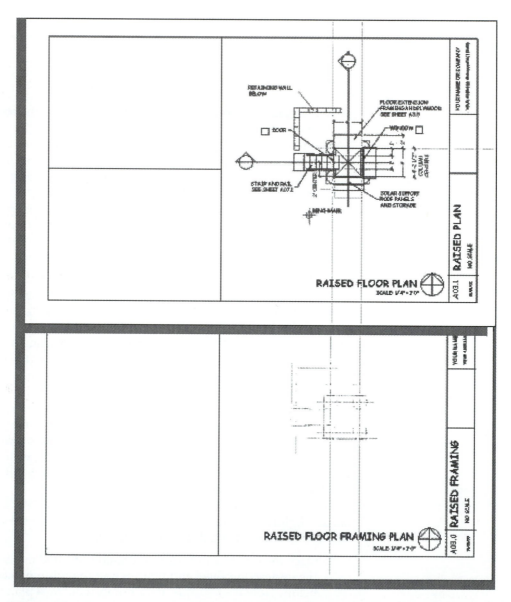

Figure 4-33. The layout for the roof plan should be located in the same place on this sheet as on the other plans. More details will be added as you get more input from outside consultants.

Wall Sections

Of course, your thoughts are a bit fragmented at this point. You know basically how the foundation works and have some idea of the floor framing system and how it might affect the walls surrounding the trainer's habitable space. The roofs are more complex, however. You have some understanding of how the solar racks might be supported and generally how the stairs might be constructed, but everything needs a lot more thought.

You can clarify your thoughts by slicing the building open. An example is shown in Figure 4-34. This was done in the preliminaries with the longitudinal sections and cross-sections, but it can also be done with wall sections drawn at a larger scale to show more detail. A wall section is a detailed drawing taken from the foundation to the roof. When you cut a wall section, the entire structure must be studied at the same time. With it, you can look first at the overall vertical relationship of the floors and then the detail of the individual structural elements and how they fit together.

A wall section resolves several unknowns because you must also study how the proposed structure affects the plans, elevations, and sections that have already been drawn to see the vertical relationships. In other words, as you lay out the wall sections, you will have to make adjustments to both the structural layouts and the other drawings in the set. It's important to remain flexible as you make these adjustments so that you can incorporate changes that will occur as you continue to evaluate the feasibility of the structure.

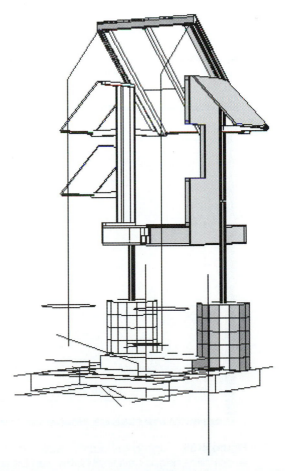

Figure 4-34. A wall section is a detail that cuts through the entire building, from the roof to the foundation.

These sections begin by identifying where they will occur on the plans. Once located on the plans, a wall section symbol is added to the all the plans, elevations, and sections. Be sure the wall section symbol is shown in the same place on every sheet of the plans and elevations. For the building sections, draw a detail bubble and a circle or oval around that portion of the building where the section occurs. Once you have the location of the section identified on all the existing sheets, you begin the wall section by lightly laying out what you know about the vertical relationships for that wall.

For the trainer, the floor-to-floor height is fairly well established so you can lightly lay out the wall sections in order to study some of the structural details. See Figure 4-35. You know how most of the pieces in the foundation plan fit together and

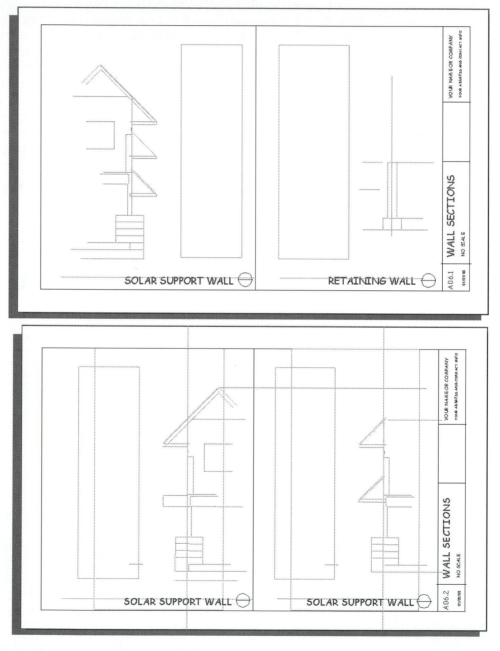

Figure 4-35. Lightly lay out the wall sections with the information that you know. The exact dimensions and final notes can be added or changed as you get more information.

have a general idea of how to frame the raised floor and walls. The height and pitch of the roof are fairly well established, though its structure should probably be the first item to be studied in detail.

Of course, you will not be able to detail the exact construction, but it is time to start addressing how it might be done. In other words, although the structural details are going to be drawn in step 6, you need to look at the layout drawings that you have completed to see if you have a fairly good idea of how the building should actually be put together.

You'll add more information as you proceed with the other related sheets, make more notes of items to analyze, add more details that explain your final solution, and make decisions on the best way to go about the eventual construction. All this will take time. For now, you have to suspend your total understanding of the details so you can explore as many possible solutions to particular areas of the structure before making that final decision.

Remember, you are visually resolving these details by identifying them graphically, drafting them for analysis, and then using the drawing to think through your solutions. Even though you do not know the details of the building, there are several wall sections you can draw and a good deal of information that you can use to work progressively through each of these relationships until you have the entire building in your mind.

The objective at this point is to set up the relationships for analysis. Again, it is important to leave details open for change as you refine your structural assumptions. Figure 4-36 is an example of a partially completed wall section. Notice how it shows the details of the structure in a reduced scale. You can see that the wall sections will

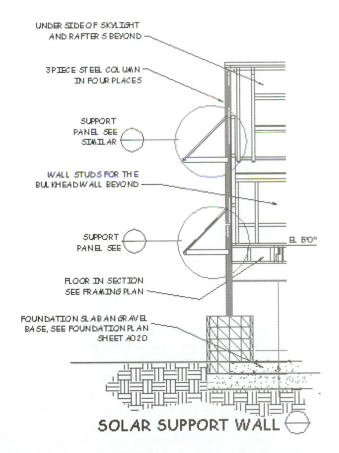

Figure 4-36. The section can be drafted on the same sheet or as a separate study to get feedback on the final construction details. The detail references must be added after they are drawn in the next chapter.

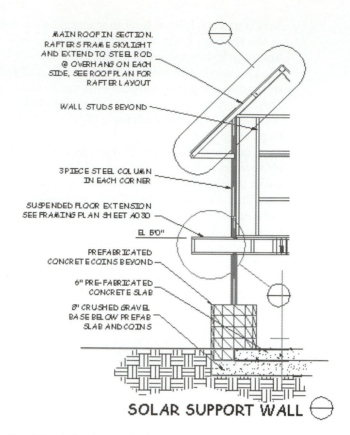

MAIN ROOF IN SECTION.
RAFTERS FRAME SKYLIGHT
AND EXTEND TO STEEL ROD
@ OVERHANG ON EACH
SIDE, SEE ROOF PLAN FOR
RAFTER LAYOUT

WALL STUDS BEYOND

3 PIECE STEEL COLUMN
IN EACH CORNER

SUSPENDED FLOOR EXTENSION
SEE FRAMING PLAN SHEET A030

EL 5'0"

PREFABRICATED
CONCRETE COINS BEYOND

6" PRE-FABRICATED
CONCRETE SLAB

8" CRUSHED GRAVEL
BASE BELOW PREFAB
SLAB AND COINS

SOLAR SUPPORT WALL

Figure 4-37. The idea is to show what you do know and fill in the blanks about what you need to know to complete the construction drawings.

show how the framing sits on the foundation, and you can see the vertical alignment of the floor and roof framing.

Figure 4-37 is another example of a partially completed wall section. Some architects draw these sections on separate sheets of paper to analyze the structure and prepare for meetings with their consultants. With a computer, it would then be quite easy to revise the wall section after it has been reviewed and cut and paste it into the final set. For hand-drawn field drawings, the process is straightforward. It's simply a matter of putting down what you know and thinking through the best way to build what you do not know.

Even though you haven't determined the exact sizes for the reinforcing for the foundation, you do know the elevation of the grade around the wall and the location and relationship of the gravel base and concrete slab. You also know that there is a stack of prefabricated concrete coins under each of four columns. These coins act as the column bearing pads. You have not confirmed the diameter of the columns or the coins, but you can draw them in lightly for later clarification. In fact, some of these assumptions were punched out in earlier steps, but every sheet in the entire set is subject to change as different pieces in the assembly are understood and coordinated.

Sizes for these pieces can be drawn within a few inches of their eventual size. Dimensions can be adjusted later or clarified with a larger detail. At a scale of $1/2'' = 1' 0''$, a 3" difference between one footing width and another is $1/8''$ on paper. No one is expected to scale the drawings at this point. Some details are still unknown. The idea is to work through the unknowns, using the drawings to test ideas and come to tentative conclusions that can be confirmed as you continue to study the details of the construction.

Drawings as a Way of Thinking

At this point, you need to get some feedback on the structural layouts that you have completed. On a big job, the project architect, or job captain, might actually distribute the lightly laid out sheets to the engineers to use for their analysis and drawings. They would then return the completed drawings to the architect so the sheets can be coordinated with the rest of the drawings. Of course, with computers, drawings are now sent as CAD files, drafted by the engineers on their own computers, and then returned via e-mail for incorporation into the main set.

On a smaller job, much of this coordination is probably more likely to be done with a fax machine and a few telephone calls. Sometimes a quick face to face meeting will resolve all the problems in a simple project, and you will walk away with everything you need to continue. Be certain to record important decisions made at the meeting in a memo to summarize what was said and document where the information on the drawings may have originated.

For very small buildings, like a simple house or commercial building, the structural review may be so standard that it requires no direct input. For example, a homebuilder might use standard tables and reference material found in books and catalogs to complete the specifications for a structural design. In these cases, the structural layout might be incorporated as a refinement of the preliminaries. All that would be needed are a few callouts, notes, and details on the floor plans and sections of the base drawings, with no need for an entirely different set of engineered drawings.

For most field drawings, you'll probably be hard pressed to find someone to review your drawings simply because everyone would be busy with their own work on the main project. Even the simplest structures may require a licensed professional, however, to review the drawings and do the calculations if for no other reason than to get a building permit. Even if no one is available to give you feedback, the structural layouts will help you think through the structural system. Once you have a clear idea of how to proceed, you will need only to punch out your drawings and add your notes and dimensions.

Tie the Drawings Together and Punch Them Out

When the foundation and framing plans are lightly laid out, use them to update the floor plans, elevations, and sections that were the result of the DDs. Look at all the sheets as a single set of drawings. You have to incorporate whatever input you received or found in tables regarding the structural sizes and constructibility of your ideas. This includes all the revisions that may have come from outside sources. For a large building, revisions may come in the form of reviews by special consultants, architects, engineers, and construction managers. But for most field projects, input from experienced workers and subcontractors are probably all that is necessary. No matter what the source, outside input on your ideas is invaluable when construction begins because it gives you an immediate collaborator to turn to for advice if the construction has a problem in the field.

With this input, you can also finalize the engineered sheets and cross-check them to make sure they are coordinated before you proceed to detailing in step 6. In step 6, you will draft the details of the building's assembly and finalize the dimensions and callouts on the full set of field drawings. You will not be able to draft everything necessary to complete these drawings and will have to suspend full resolution of exact dimensions. You will draft only what you know. Your assumptions are defined enough to punch out the drawings, but some of the details may still need to be studied. For now, use the wall sections and any sketches you've made of various structural conditions to guide your updates to the current drawings. The drawings therefore continue to be the focus of ongoing conversations because the final notes and details must be drawn and checked in the last steps.

In the layouts for the structural drawings for the version of the trainer shown in Figure 4-37, the coins act as bearing pads for the columns. These are also reflected on the framing and floor plans, and on the elevations and sections. You know there is a column in the center of the round bearing pads that carries the load from the roof. Both the pads and the columns are shown, but it is only after all these sheets are tied together as a single set of drawings that someone can look at them as a structural system and begin to calculate the sizes that will ultimately have to be used for the actual construction.

Use the OLPAP checklist to determine what might need to be completed from sheet to sheet. The OLPAP checklist should remind you to make sure that all the plans are marked clearly and coordinated correctly with the new structural information. This includes orienting the sheets with titles and detail references, adding dimensions for the layout, calling out all the pieces and processes of the assembly, and making sure every sheet is coordinated with the other. It also includes detail bubbles for details that need to be drawn, north arrows, titles, scales, and the dimensions that are important to each level of completion. Also, be sure that the building section and wall section symbols are located in the same place from sheet to sheet, which will give the drawings a uniformity that is important for a cohesive set.

Figure 4-38 shows other items that can be added to the rest of the engineered drawings, including notes and lines for the doors, windows, and the roof openings; all the notes for the framing plans necessary to explain the framing; callouts for the materials and reinforcing for the foundation, walls, sill plate and anchors; and the sizes and spacing for the joists, subfloor, and studs.

Summary of Steps 1 to 5

In step 1, a written program puts ideas on paper. Verbal descriptions evolve into a list of written requirements that must be met for the project to be successful. This includes some early conceptual diagrams to clarify relationships that may not be fully understood. On a large project, the program can be crucial to the final design and might even include some form of early value engineering. For most field projects, a program is nothing more than a memorandum of a conversation. It documents the scope of the work and clarifies expectations prior to beginning the work.

In step 2, the schematics are drawn as at least one freehand illustration of a solution to the program. The purpose of the schematics is to suggest a physical form that can be discussed for further refinement. They are loosely drawn concepts intended to clarify the requirements of the program. For a large project, they can involve elaborate illustrations and models. For field drafting, however, they may include only a simple sketch to think through the program requirements and suggest a three-dimensional form.

In step 3, the preliminaries refine the schematics as a set of scaled drawings. These two-dimensional drawings are a series of orthographic projections taken from the three-dimensional object and are the plans, elevations, and sections necessary to explain the building. They are the base sheets of the final drawings that will be used in the field. They finalize the design and begin the engineered drawings that will be necessary to complete the construction.

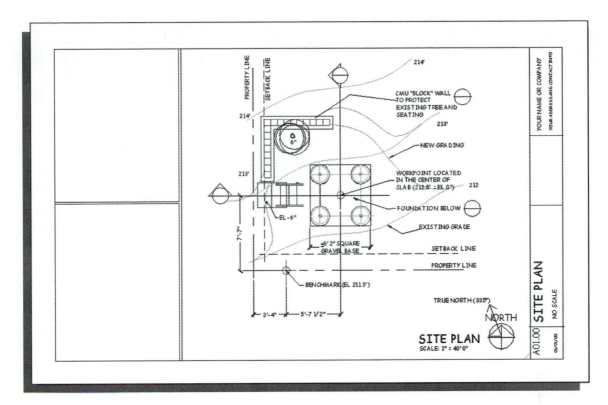

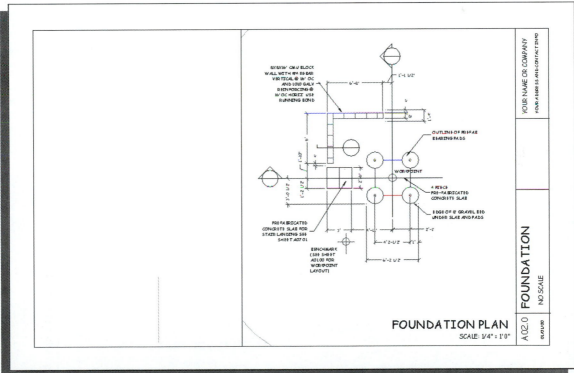

Figure 4-38. Once the engineered drawings have been coordinated, the drawings should be updated and coordinated with the lightly laid out engineered plans and wall sections. All the drawings should be punched out to get them ready for the details.

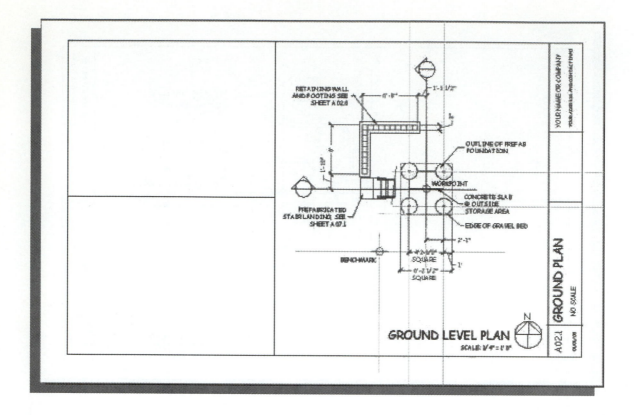

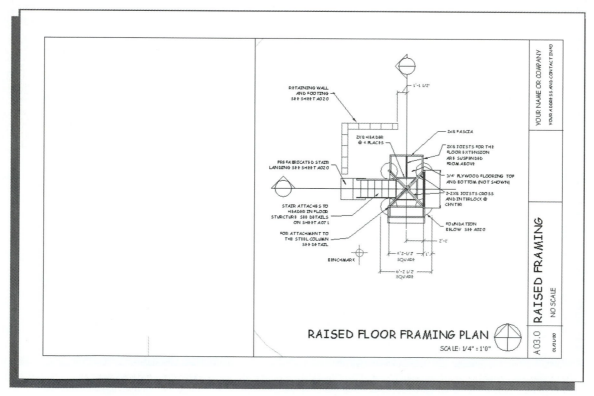

Figure 4-38. Continued.

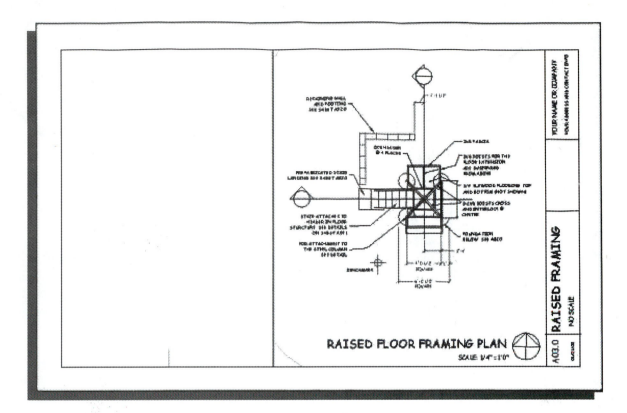

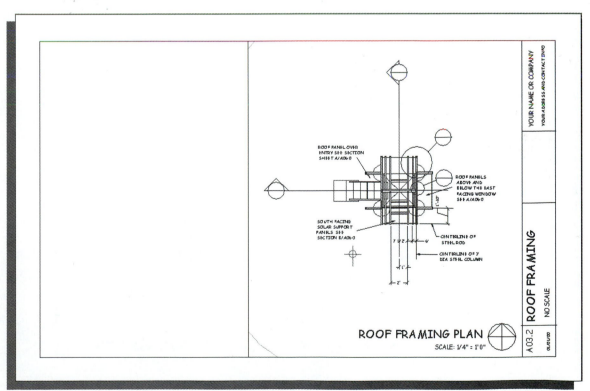

Figure 4-38. Continued.

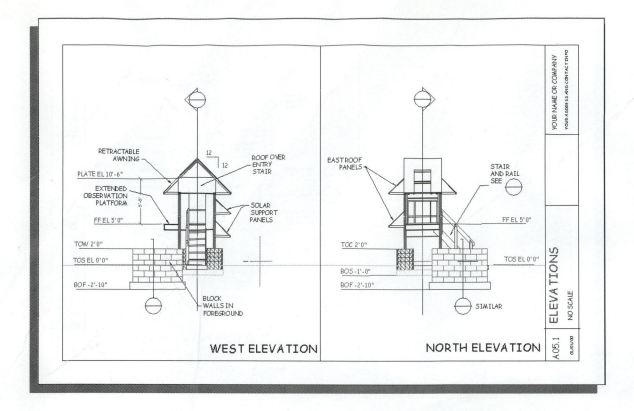

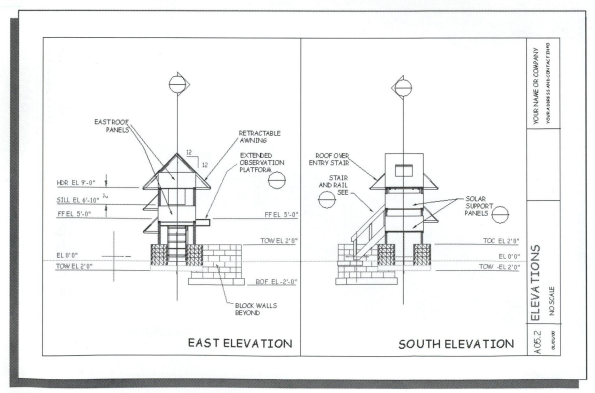

Figure 4-38. Continued.

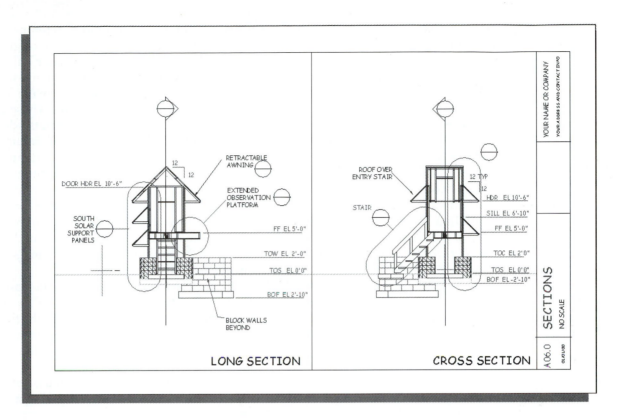

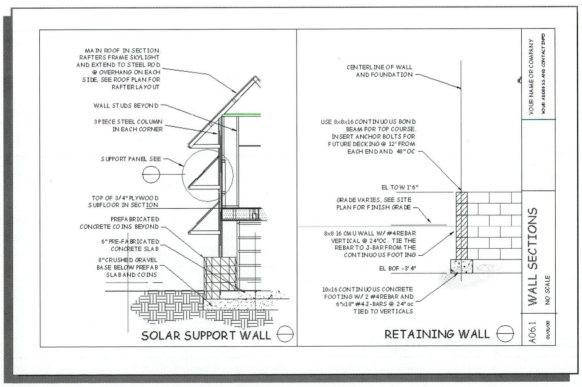

Figure 4-38. Continued.

In step 4, the DDs or design development drawings refine the preliminaries with corrections or design revisions. These might include changes to the original program or the schematics, but more than likely they will focus on minor adjustments that come to light after the project is drafted to scale. Once these changes are made, outline specification and a conceptual cost estimate can be completed. The specifications suggest materials that will be included in the cost estimates. These estimates are a reality check to call attention to the cost that is represented in the documents up to this point. Once the DDs are complete, the design should be finalized and ready for the engineered documents. Transition to the next step is important because you do not want to spend a lot of time and money engineering something that might change again.

In step 5, you look specifically at the foundation and structural frame for the building. The structure will affect the layout of all aspects of the building. For example, a foundation wall can reduce the size of a room or affect any number of mechanical or electrical systems. The structural frame for the building includes column sizes or whether these columns are inside or outside the finished spaces.

To engineer a building, you "build it on paper" by using the lower level plan to lay out lightly the foundation plan and then using the foundation plan to lay out lightly the lower level framing plan. The floor plans are then used to lay out the floor framing. The roof plan is used to engineer the roof framing. Each plan therefore builds on another, and details or problems are noted for further study. All the drawings are lightly drawn until everything can be coordinated as a single set.

Once the structural plans are laid out, wall sections are taken through the critical elevations of the building. These wall sections look at the vertical and horizontal relationships of the structure from the foundation to the roof. Like the building elevations, longitudinal sections, and cross-sections in the earlier phases, wall sections add a third dimension. This time, however, they are specifically intended to study the feasibility of the structure. Wall sections are also drawn at a large scale so the structural details can be coordinated.

Once the wall sections and the structural plans are understood, the original plans, elevations, and sections can be updated with new information and with input from outside consultants and engineers. The structural drawings are coordinated with the main set so they can be issued to outside consultants for their review and assistance in finalizing the information shown. The idea is to prepare them as a single, lightly laid out set for circulation and further input and refinement. This input can be an ongoing and continuous interaction with outside advisors, or it can be formalized as a review set of structural assumptions shown in the structural plans and wall sections. How this is handled will depend on the complexity of the project and the availability of the consultants. For a large project, these consultants may actually draw the drawings. For field drawings, a couple of site meetings with subcontractors and other specialists may be all that is required to know you're on the right track and you can begin to punch out the final drawings.

What to Expect in Step 6

Once the overall structural scheme shown on the structural drawings has been finalized, all you have to do is make sure that all the current information is posted to the final set. In some cases, this might involve redrawing a plan, elevation, or section, but in most cases, only specific sizes and exact configurations will need to be noted as the details are drawn in step 6. In the next step, it's only a matter of drafting the construction details necessary to build the building.

It should be clear by now that completing these drawings is a process. You do not have everything you need to finish all the notes on every sheet, so you take the drawings as far as you can go in each step. In each step, the drawings are the result of a series of ongoing conversations. They are the media for communications with workers, subcontractors, consultants, and engineers. Questions are asked in meetings, on the telephone, and in writing via e-mail or fax, and the results of these communications are recorded on the drawings themselves. They are usually checked again by the consultants to make sure everything was understood correctly. For a particularly difficult detail or unusual situation, the process might go through several iterations of exchanges and adjustments before you are ready to continue with the next step.

The complexity of putting together a set of construction drawings for a large building means that everything cannot be resolved before you begin the next step. Combinations of complete and incomplete information begin to mix together. As you can imagine by looking at the unknowns in this simple set of field drawings for the trainer, it takes a great deal of skill and experience to deal with these unknowns in a full-size building.

When handling the unknowns is done correctly, the documents will reflect the quality of the interactions and exchanges that occurred to complete the drawings. When the drawings are not clear or have missing information, errors, and contradictions, it means someone failed to follow up on a change or did not bother to coordinate the two-dimensional sheets as a single set of construction information. The result will be an increased need for clarifications, incorrect installations, delays in the schedule, and conflict. Poor drawings then lead to a frustrating and contentious construction experience on the jobsite.

Chapter 5

CONSTRUCTION DETAILS IN 3D

Step 6: Questions and Detailed Answers

Sometimes the engineering drawings produced in step 6 can end with as many questions as answers. The answers are the lines, notes, and dimensions drawn on the sheets of drawings that have been completed at the end of step 5. They include the general size and shape of the trainer, the location of doors and windows, and the basic construction materials and structural relationships of items like the stair and the retaining wall. This information is clarified by the wall sections and structural layouts. Some sketches were drawn of details showing how the different materials could be put together.

The questions are the blank detail references and marginal notes on the sheets that have been completed. Resolving these questions is the focus of step 6. For the trainer, the floor extension from the rafters may have been considered a good idea by all the people who looked at it, but a lot needs to be understood before the floor and wall can be constructed. In fact, you can find the rafters, tension rods, and compression arms on almost every sheet of the engineered drawings, but the details of how the pieces fit together are not understood. The wall sections show how the cantilevered rafters support the floor, but the details of the attachment of the floor to the tension rod, or the attachment of the same rod to the rafter, have not been shown. These details must still be resolved.

Other questions also need to be answered. For example, the mounting brackets for the solar panels on the south elevation, or the handrails to the stairs, or the way the window sits in the wall, all need to be studied so that workers in the field know how to put the building together. These questions cannot be asked until the structural system and kinds of materials to be used in the construction are fully understood. Attention now turns to particular construction concerns to resolve the inherent problems and to provide some detailed answers.

In Figure 5-1, step 6 is shown as the phase where you will answer all these questions and make certain everything in the entire building fits together. You will draw an enlarged detail for as many parts of the construction as time will allow. For most typical buildings or field drawings, this will not be more than a couple of special conditions. For the trainer, it will include as many details as you have time for, but certainly not more than those necessary to explain the construction to the prefabricators and manufacturers for the concrete coins, stairs, steel, and wall panels.

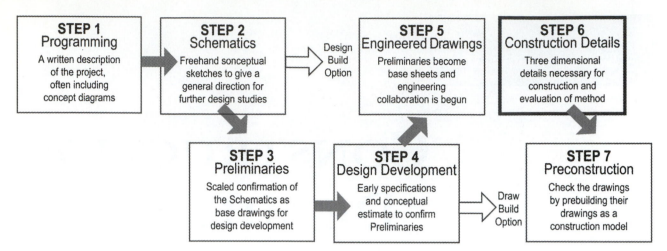

Figure 5-1. In step 6, the construction details are studied and drafted for final construction. This step is the most important in the visual problem solving process because it addresses the actual assembly of the building.

The information in these details is fundamental to the construction of the building and will ultimately affect everything that has been drawn to this point. You will have to coordinate the details with the full set of drawings to make sure there are no conflicts. This includes adjusting dimensions, making sure callouts and references are consistent, and adding the appropriate notes to guide workers to the new information you are providing.

Most of these changes will occur because this is the first opportunity you will have to study the construction. Using a larger scale to draft a detail will mean that you have more opportunity to see how all the details fit together. Other changes will occur because of misinterpretations in the two-dimensional plans, elevations, and sections already drawn. For example, the door of the trainer will hit the west roof if it swings out over the steps, which is a detail problem that needs to be studied. The resulting solution will affect the raised floor plan, west elevation, cross-section, wall section, and stair plan and section.

The Error-Prone Two Dimensions

The work you completed in the first five steps depended on your ability to shift mentally from a three-dimensional object to a collection of two-dimensional drawings, and back again. As you can see in Figure 5-2, this process can be like a house of mirrors, with the shape of the physical form described in a series of seemingly unrelated two-dimensional surfaces.

When the object is complex, the challenge is to visualize the object and translate its assembly to and from a flat piece of paper. The two-dimensional plans, elevations, and sections represent three-dimensional physical form, but it is easy to miss the relationships from drawing to drawing because so much of the object has to be held in memory as it is either drafted or visualized for construction from the 2D drawings. These drawings are collections of two-dimensional projections, where the plans describe the horizontal plane, and the sections and elevations define the vertical relationships. The ability to visualize all the drawings as a single object is critical to drafting and interpreting correctly the information that they contain.

Figure 5-2. The orthographic projections that describe the three-dimensional form can be like a house of mirrors requiring careful visualization.

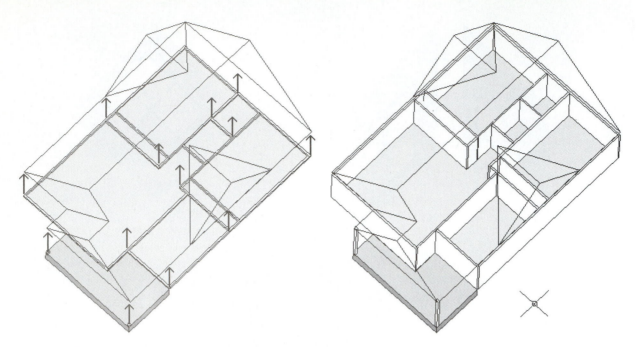

Figure 5-3. The difficulty of visualizing a set of two-dimensional drawings reduces most of the architecture we see to simple extrusions. These are simple two-dimensional drawings that can be understood easily, priced quickly, and constructed efficiently.

The challenge of drafting in two dimensions is in the ability to draw more than one sheet at a time. In a building like the trainer, this is a matter of visually transferring the physical form to several sheets of drawings at the same time. In a complex building, where several people are drawing different sheets simultaneously, this transfer takes careful coordination. When this is done well, the drawings that result will need little clarification. In practice, however, both drafting and interpretation are error prone and often result in a set of drawings that is not coordinated and full of errors and omissions. Much of this occurs simply because of the challenge of gradually resolving so many unknowns as the drawings evolve, but the difficulty of drafting a three-dimensional object on multiple sheets of drawings at the same time also presents a challenge.

Switching from dimension to dimension is a skill that even experienced architects and engineers find challenging. In fact, many would argue that this is the reason most buildings are simple vertical extrusions of two-dimensional plans, as shown in Figure 5-3. The complexity of drafting 2D drawings of 3D objects makes many designers—and builders—shy away from anything that appears too complicated.

When drawing a detail for a complex assembly, it's often impossible to simplify the solution by creating a two-dimensional extrusion. Instead, a good deal of time must be spent carefully thinking through the three-dimensional context of the problem and translating the resulting solution to a series of 2D drawings. This is especially challenging when drawing an enlarged detail, first, because the context of the detail almost always involves several components from different parts of the set of drawings and, second, because any detail should be confined to as clear an illustration of the solution as possible. After all, that's the purpose of the detail. Shifting from three to two dimensions therefore sets up the possibility of error and complicates the problem solving potential of a field drawing.

Avoiding the Visualization Shift by Drawing Details in 3D

One way to avoid this shift is to simply draw the detail in three dimensions. Three-dimensional drawings eliminate the need to visualize two dimensions and can be much more descriptive in the field for those who cannot read blueprints. They are also easier to draw because the information that might normally be found on several different sheets is found in one drawing.

Simple perspective

Figure 5-4 shows three kinds of 3D drawings that you can use to communicate the shape of a building: a simple perspective, an isometric, and an axonometric. A simple perspective is probably most useful for visualizing the general design of a building. As shown in Figure 5-5, it has a horizon and one or more vanishing points. As the vanishing points are moved along the horizon, the position of the viewer moves left or right, or closer or farther from the object. The horizontal lines of the building in the drawing are said to diminish toward the horizon at different angles. At the same time, vertical elements on the building appear to be spaced closer together when the vanishing points are closer together.

A simple perspective drawing can be deceptive because it is based on the geometric relationships of the drawing and not on the object itself. For example, a vanishing point close to the middle of the horizon has lines that can diminish much more sharply

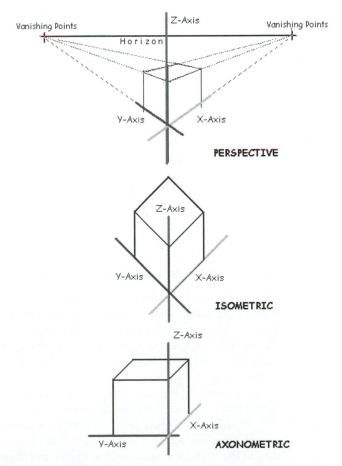

Figure 5-4. There are three basic types of three-dimensional drawings: perspective, isometric, and axonometric.

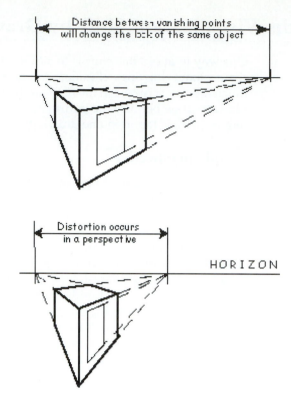

Distance between vanishing points
will change the look of the same object

Distortion occurs
in a perspective

HORIZON

Figure 5-5. Perspectives are difficult to use in construction because the placement of vanishing points results in distortion.

than they would appear on the actual building. A perspective can be precisely laid out, but skilled artists can adjust the illusion of the position of these elements to make a building look dramatically different than it would appear when fully constructed.

For this reason, hand-drawn perspectives are not always useful in construction. The diminishing horizontal lines mean that objects along the surface that are in perspective may appear to be drawn to scale when they are not. Exact scale and correct proportions are important to construction drawings because objects that appear in the drawing must be correlated correctly so that they appear to fit together as they are drawn. A quick perspective can be enlightening to a client or worker in the field, however. As you will see later in this chapter, once you can draw a box in perspective, you can draw almost anything to fit inside it.

An isometric is a scaled three-dimensional drawing

The most useful 3D drawing for construction is an isometric. Isometrics are simple to draw. They can be important tools for helping you think through and understand a particular construction detail because, by definition, they represent more than one side of the assembly at the same time. You can see the problem from three different sides at the same time. They also represent clearly the proportional relationships and how the pieces of the detail fit together, primarily because they are scaled drawings and therefore represent accurately the placement of the shapes of the pieces in the assembly. But distortion is also reduced by the use of a consistent set of three parallel lines on three fixed axes.

As shown in Figure 5-6, isometrics are built from three lines. These three lines are parallel to three axes. A vertical line describes all vertical edges, and two angled lines define the two dimensions of the visible horizontal planes. These angled lines are usually drawn at either 30 or 45 degrees. The most important fact about an isometric is that, depending on the orientation, every horizontal and vertical line in the object will be

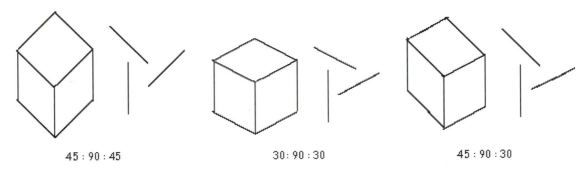

45 : 90 : 45   30 : 90 : 30   45 : 90 : 30

Figure 5-6. The Cartesian coordinates are plotted along each axis using equal units of measurement. Every object in the system therefore has an address, and scaled objects can be located in three dimensions.

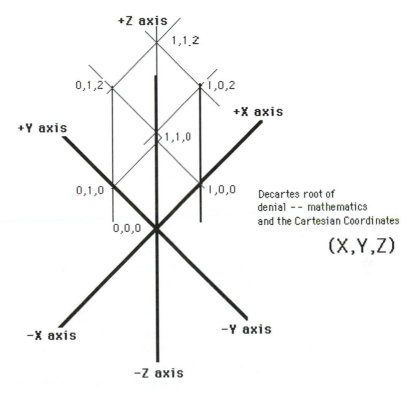

Figure 5-7. Every isometric has three axes represented by three lines. The edges of the object are parallel to one of these three lines.

parallel to one of these angled lines. Also important is that each of these lines can be divided into units so that the objects they represent can be measured and proportionally scaled. These measurements are possible because of the Cartesian coordinate system.

The Cartesian coordinate system: This three-dimensional coordinate system was created in the seventeenth century by René Descartes. Figure 5-7 shows how Descartes used three lines as the primary axes. By dividing the lines into equal units, any point or line can be located and scaled precisely in three-dimensional space.

The three axes of the Cartesian system are X, Y, and Z. Each axis is divided into equal units in both positive and negative directions. Using these units as coordinates, any point within three-dimensional space has a three-axis address denoted by its Cartesian coordinates. These coordinates follow an X, Y, Z order, where the values of X, Y, and Z are the negative or positive values for the position on a point along each axis.

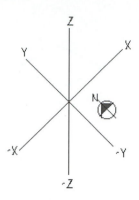

Figure 5-8. The Cartesian coordinate system allots units along three lines to locate objects in three-dimensional space.

In Figure 5-8, for example, 1,1,0 would be a point in space on the X-Y plane at a distance of positive Y = 1, positive X = 1, and Z = 0. A rectangular box standing on one edge has eight corners with eight different addresses: 0,0,0; 1,0,0; 1,1,0; 0,1,0; 1,1,0; 1,0,2; 1,1,2; 0,1,2. The line between each one of these corners also has its own address. For example, 0,0,0 to 0,1,0 is a line, as is 1,1,2 to 1,0,2.

The Cartesian system also has three planes defined by these axes: X-Y, X-Z, and Y-Z. The sides of any object can therefore be located within the coordinate system. For example, 0,1,2; 1,1,2; 1,0,2; and 0,0,2 describe a plane parallel to the X-Y plane with a Z coordinate two units above it.

The X-Y plane is the two-dimensional plane used to draft any plan. Construction drawings are two-dimensional because they have only two coordinates, X and Y. All lines and points lay flat on this plane when they are viewed from above. As shown in Figure 5-9, there is no third coordinate to the X-Y plane because an object needs to have a Z value to rise above the X-Y plane. In other words, you would add a Z coordinate to define the three-dimensional object. Figure 5-10, for example, adds the third dimension (and the third Z coordinate) to the plan and elevation of the simple building.

The X-Z or the Y-Z planes are the planes on which the elevations and sections are drawn. They are two-dimensional because, even though they lie in a vertical plane, the projection itself is plotted flat onto the plane. Any point on one of these planes therefore has a two-dimensional X, Z, or Y, Z coordinate.

To orient the X-Z or Y-Z planes to a set of drawings for a building, the positive Y direction is always north. The east elevation of the building is on the Y-Z plane viewed from the positive X axis, while the west elevation is on the Y-Z plane viewed from the negative X-axis. The south elevation faces the X-Z plane viewed from the negative Y axis, and the north elevation is on the X-Z plane viewed from the positive Y-axis. These elevations are two-dimensional drawings projected onto these vertical planes and measured along their two axes.

A Cartesian cube: It might be easier to understand the Cartesian system when you see it built as a three-dimensional model from three two-dimensional planes. You can see in Figure 5-11 that each of these planes has two axes and a compass direction that relates to the orientation of the construction drawings. When the axes are divided using the same units of measurement, objects can be located according to their coordinates.

For example, an index card that represents the X-Y plane has a positive Y-axis that is oriented toward the top of the page, or north. The positive X-axis is oriented to the right, or east. The negative X-axis is oriented to the left, or west, and the negative Y-axis is oriented to the south. These axes divide the plane into four quadrants. All floor plans are drawn in this plane.

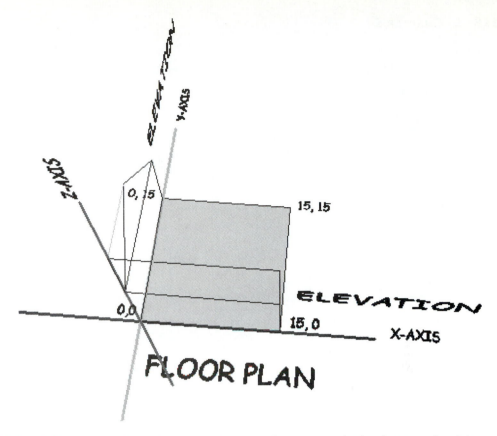

Figure 5-9. All two-dimensional drawings are drawn on a single plane, and points and lines on the plane have two Cartesian coordinates.

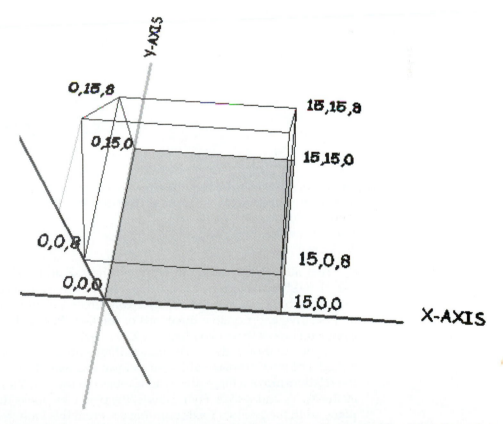

Figure 5-10. An isometric adds a third Cartesian coordinate and the third dimension to the plans and elevations.

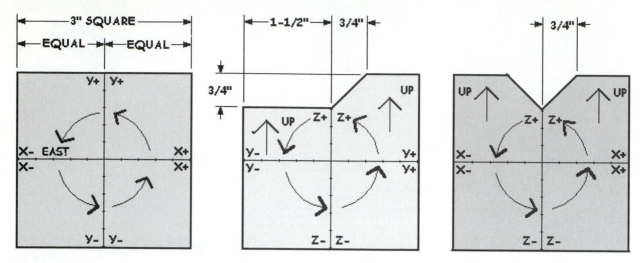

Figure 5-11. Each of the three two-dimensional planes of the Cartesian system has two axes, two specific compass orientations, and two rotational directions.

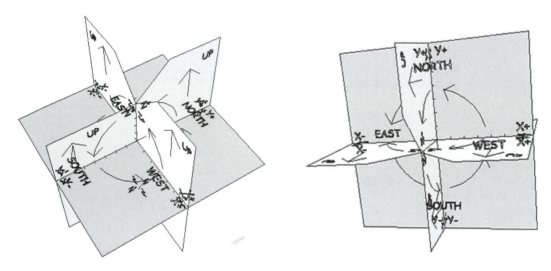

Figure 5-12. When the planes are cut out and fit together, they make up the Cartesian coordinate system. Each plane has its own orientation, and any object can be scaled and located within three-dimensional space.

Two more index cards can represent the X-Z and Y-Z planes. An arrow on the Y-Z plane shows which way is up: this is the positive Z direction. Each plane has two axes, with both positive and negative coordinates, positive and negative quadrants, and positive and negative directions of rotation. Plans, elevations, and sections are drawn on one of these two planes: X-Z and Y-Z.

If you cut these index cards so they fit together as shown in Figure 5-12, you have a model of the Cartesian cube. You can use this model to obtain a hands-on feel for the relationship of a three-dimensional object to the X-Y, Y-Z, and X-Z planes, as well as the X-, Y-, and Z-axes. For example, the plan view looks directly down on the X-Y plane, with the positive Y-axis pointing up. From this view, the Z-axis is said to be "in your face." The notches fit together to fit your nose and mouth as you look down at

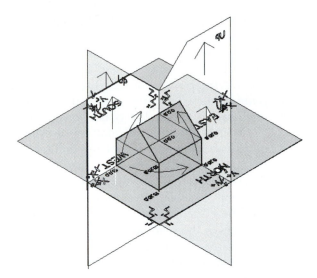

Figure 5-13. In the Cartesian coordinate system, a 45-90-45 degree isometric occurs when your viewpoint is equidistant along all three axes.

the X-Y plane. From the plan view, the positive X-axis is to the east. As you turn the cube to view an elevation projected onto the Y-Z plane, the right side of the cube is the east elevation and the left side is the west elevation. The north and south elevations are projected onto either side of the X-Z axis.

As you look at the cube, your particular point of view is a viewpoint in the Cartesian system. Every viewpoint is a point in space and has a corresponding target, or point of focus, for that view. Both the viewpoint and the target have their own Cartesian coordinates. Moving along a line between the viewpoint and the target is the same as zooming in closer or farther from the target.

Back to the isometric: When the X and Y coordinates of the viewpoint are the same and the target of the viewpoint is 0,0,0, any object in the Cartesian system will appear as an isometric. For example, a building would have three-dimensional coordinates that can be plotted along the X-, Y-, and Z-axes. If one corner of the building is set at 0,0,0, the coordinates of the isometric would look like those shown in Figure 5-13.

Note how all the lines of the building parallel the X-, Y-, or Z-axis, and each corner and line on the drawing has a set of descriptive Cartesian coordinates. These coordinates are expressed as X, Y, Z. For example, the four bottom corners of the base of the building are 0,0,0; 15',0,0; 15',15',0; and 0,15',0, as they were in Figure 5-10.

Given that the positive Y-axis is always north, the viewpoint that makes this illustration an isometric is in the southwest quadrant of the X-Y plane. The coordinates of this viewpoint are along a line where the values of X and Y are equal and the target of the view is 0,0,0. In this case, the viewpoint is elevated in the positive Z-direction, but an isometric can be drawn with any value of Z, as long as the X- and Y-values are the same. When the Z-coordinate is the same as the X- and Y-coordinates, the axes of the isometric will appear as the 45-degree lines shown in Figure 5-7. For example, the viewpoint of Figure 5-13 could be 10,10,10 or 100,100,100.

Once you understand the principles of the Cartesian coordinate system and the position of the viewpoint for any isometric, you can use the same three parallel lines to draw an isometric of almost any object. As soon as you draw the three axes of an isometric, you automatically set a viewpoint and the target. If the first line you draw is the vertical Z-axis, and if the X- and Y-axes are drawn at any equal and opposite angle from the vertical, your viewpoint is from a high or low position in one of the quadrants of the Cartesian system. The angle of the X- and Y-lines set the height of the viewpoint. A steep angle means a high point of view, and a moderate angle means a lower point of view. The target is the intersection of the three lines. This is the 0,0,0 point of anything you draw. It acts as a benchmark or workpoint in three-dimensional space.

With a little practice plotting coordinates from an isometric viewpoint, you can quickly draw isometric sketches that can be very useful in the field. The advantage of even the roughest isometric is that it is three-dimensional and therefore easier to understand than a set of two-dimensional projections, and it is scaled so that it is proportional and visually accurate.

These scaled three-dimensional sketches are useful when communicating with workers in the field because they can help you visualize two-dimensional drawing. They can also help you think through the construction of a particular detail. For example, note how the drawings in Figure 5-14 are drawn with longer or shorter versions of the same three lines.

Keep in mind that everything on a construction site relates to the same three parallel lines. You can draw just about anything on a set of drawings by following five simple steps (see Figure 5-15):

1. First, draw a vertical line: the Z-axis. The positive direction is up.
2. Then draw two angled lines from opposite directions that intersect the Z-axis at the same point. This sets the horizontal plane.

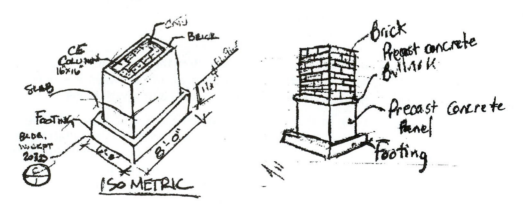

Figure 5-14. Isometric sketches use the Cartesian principles to help visualize two-dimensional plans, study construction details, or communicate the solution to a particular problem.

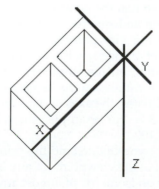

Figure 5-15. An isometric of any object in construction can be drawn quickly.

3. Label one line the X-axis and the other the Y-axis, and set the positive direction of Y. Because positive Y is north and positive X is east, you know where west and south are in three-dimensional space.
4. Divide the three axes visually into equal units from the workpoint. The workpoint is the intersection of the three lines.
5. Now plot the outline of the object roughly in three dimensions before you add detail. The edges of the objects are parallel to one of these three axes.

Axonometrics for quick 3D

An axonometric is another example of a three-dimensional drawing. An axonometric differs from an isometric because two axes of the Cartesian coordinate system are always perpendicular. The two perpendicular lines can be any two of the three axes and can be oriented in any direction, depending on the particular angle of the drawing. The third dimension is a line drawn at an angle from these perpendicular lines. Like the isometric, the parallel edges of the object align with one of these three lines. Unlike the isometric, however, two sets of lines are really drawn in two dimensions.

For example, Figure 5-16 shows two different axonometrics of a concrete block. Note how each has two perpendicular axes and one axis that is drawn at an angle to these perpendicular axes (lines). The perpendicular lines define a flat two-dimensional plane, while the third line gives the third dimension. All three lines are divided into equal units, like the isometrics, and the lines of the object are again parallel to one of these three lines.

An axonometric is really an extrusion. An extrusion can be made from any two-dimensional plan, elevation, or section of any object. For example, the framing detail shown in Figure 5-17 is extruded downward from the plan view of three studs. However, you can draw an axonometric from the bottom up, top down, or from side to side because the lines that parallel the perpendicular axes can be repositioned into any position along the third axis. It's like stacking a series of two-dimensional drawings. There are five basic steps:

1. Draw two perpendicular lines. These are the axes of a two-dimensional plane.
2. Draw a line at any angle from these two lines. This line is the third axis of the three-dimensional space.
3. Divide the three lines using equal units of measure. These units will act as guides for plotting the drawing.

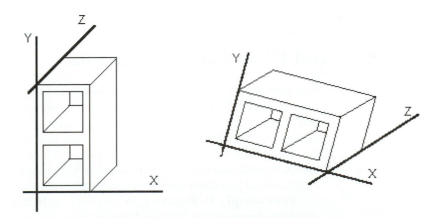

Figure 5-16.   Axonometrics have two perpendicular axes and a third that is at any angle from the perpendicular. All lines in the object are parallel to one of these three lines.

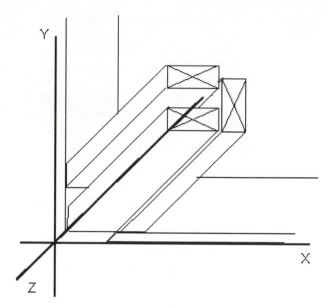

Figure 5-17. Axonometrics are extrusions and are valuable for visualizing a detail quickly in three dimensions. They can be made from any two-dimensional drawing with a few quick parallel lines.

4. Draw a rough two-dimensional plan, elevation, or section at the base point of the extrusion on the perpendicular plane.
5. Add the third dimension by drawing the third line parallel to the angled axis.

You can use the rolling parallel and a scale to draft 3D drawings accurately. When the same units of measure are used on all three axes and the lines are carefully plotted, the axonometric becomes a scaled three-dimensional drawing. It can be useful for some detailing and means almost any two-dimensional drawing can be converted easily to three dimensions with the addition of a few parallel lines.

You can also use this method on the jobsite to convert something quickly on a construction drawing to three dimensions. In fact, almost any two-dimensional drawing can be turned into three-dimensional objects by adding this same series of parallel lines. First, trace the 2D drawing or detail and then quickly add the third dimension with a few lines. It explains a detail or gets your point across in the field because the angular lines extrude the flat drawing and give it a third dimension.

Visualization and Clear Communications

The idea that three dimensions can support clearer and more effective communications is fairly obvious. The additional dimension adds both the context of the detail and depth to the visual information. Most important is that 3D drawings can be generated quickly and used easily in the field to explain any part of the construction process. When you master this skill you will find yourself at another level of management skill, one that has been traditionally relegated to the role of the architect and engineer but is increasingly becoming important to the constructor.

For example, in Figures 5-18 and 5-19, note the difference the third dimension makes in your ability to visualize the assembly of the wall section. In two dimensions, shown in Figure 5-18, your mind must convert the lines into three-dimensional objects before you can begin to understand how they are constructed.

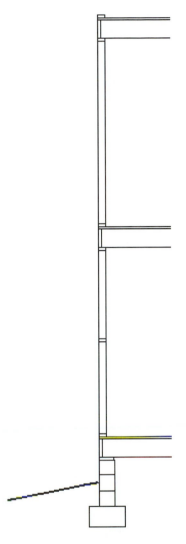

Figure 5-18. A two-dimensional wall section requires skill to interpret and visualize and is subject to error.

When they are drawn in three dimensions, as in Figure 5-19, the conversion is complete and you can visualize the construction information immediately. Similarly, note how the isometric in Figure 5-20 is easier to understand, even without words, than its two-dimensional equivalent in Figure 5-21. Again, the extra dimension helps you communicate construction information quickly and efficiently to workers in the field.

Most important is that you can convert this wall section into a scaled three-dimensional drawing very quickly, with or without drafting tools. As an axonometric, it is a simple derivative of the two-dimensional wall section. In other words, the horizontal and vertical lines were already drawn when the wall section was drafted, so the third dimension is simply a matter of adding a series of angled parallel lines.

With practice, axonometrics and isometrics can be drawn almost as quickly as a 2D drawing. Some would even argue that a 3D drawing is faster to draw because there is less need for abstract visualization. Certainly with the advent of the

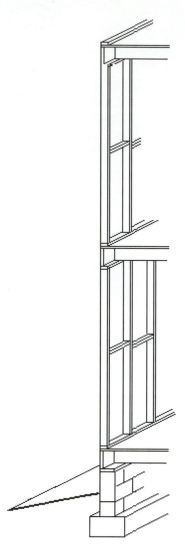

Figure 5-19. A three-dimensional wall section can be visualized immediately and understood by anyone.

computer and the power of the new parametric software just entering the market, 3D images will be the medium of choice in the near future. They can also be more effective in helping to analyze a construction detail. First, they do not require the extra step of visualizing and interpreting a flat diagram. You have the ability to see the full ramifications of a detail as you think through alternate methods of constructing it. Second, 3D drawings amplify your power to communicate even very complex ideas to outside consultants for faster communication and collaboration. If you can explain something to an engineer or architect in half the time, it stands to reason that you will save half their consulting fee plus the value of your time. Finally, 3D will communicate more effectively with the workers who will be building the assembly they represent. Many workers do not need drawings and may even refuse to look at them, preferring to be told what to do in simple and direct language. A 3D field drawing does not have to be read and interpreted, only glanced at, to be understood.

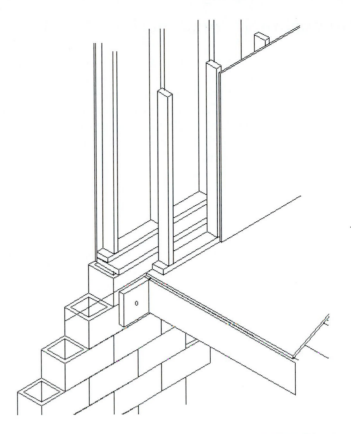

Figure 5-20. An isometric is easy to draw and, even without notes and dimensions, quickly communicates a lot of information.

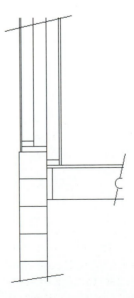

Figure 5-21. A two-dimensional detail contains the same information but requires interpretation.

Three-Dimensional Construction Details

If there are tricks to drawing in three dimensions, the first is the fact that you have to train your hand and your eye to see the parallel lines. There is no shortcut to drawing; it just takes practice. The best way to start practicing is by drawing the boundaries of the Cartesian system as a cube and noting the coordinates of the axes, planes, and quadrants on the outside of the box. Your box should look like Figure 5-22. Try different angles of parallel lines and note how each represents the box from a different viewpoint.

You can also practice by drawing simple rectangles and putting them together in different combinations to make up a construction detail. In fact, almost everything on a jobsite can be made from a box. For example, the foundation detail on the left side of Figure 5-23 is made up of all the boxes shown on the right of the same figure.

Putting together a three-dimensional construction detail is therefore a matter of assembling the boxes that represent the pieces of the total construction. Gradually layer the visual information. Start with the layout lines for the pieces, then draw in the first pieces that would be placed in the construction. Once the first pieces are in place, add pieces to the assembly in exactly the same sequence as their construction. And that is the second trick to three-dimensional drawing. You do not draw the detail as much as build it piece by piece. You are less an artist and much more a constructor who is using pencil and paper (or a computer program) to assemble the three-dimensional image. Building a detail in this way helps you visualize the construction and reinforces the accuracy of the actual drawing. You can do this in four steps (shown in Figure 5-24):

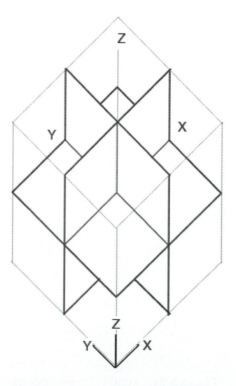

Figure 5-22. Drawing the Cartesian cube is a good way to practice isometrics. First, draw the three axes and then try to make all sides and quadrants equal.

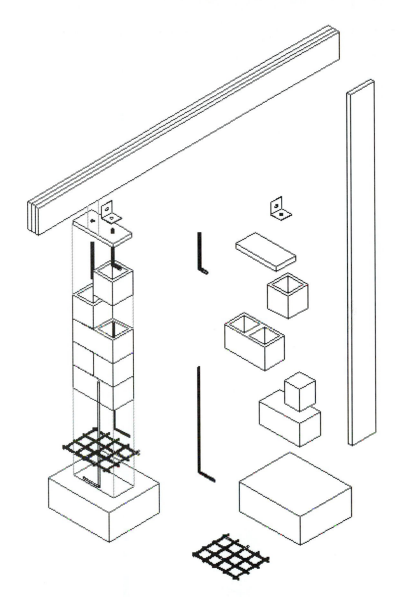

Figure 5-23. Construction details are built as an assembly from a collection of isometric boxes. Each box is a piece of the construction.

1. Use the method described above to lay out the three axes for the isometric or axonometric coordinate system, as shown in step 1 of Figure 5-24. To save time, you can draw just the quadrant in which the detail is to be assembled. This will make it easier because you will be able to ignore negative values. Your layout should include both the lines of the axis and the units that divide them into the three-dimensional grid that will contain the drawing. The scaled axes are the boundaries of the virtual world.

2. Use a pale blue pencil to lay out lightly the boundaries and alignments of the construction. To guide your work, plot the coordinates of the critical points that govern the assembly by putting a dot at each main point and then connecting the dots to outline the pieces. The lines between the dots are chalklines that act as a wireframe to which all the pieces are attached. For example, for the foundation detail in step 2 of Figure 5-24, the wireframe includes the bottom of the footing, the height of the footing, and the height of the masonry pier.

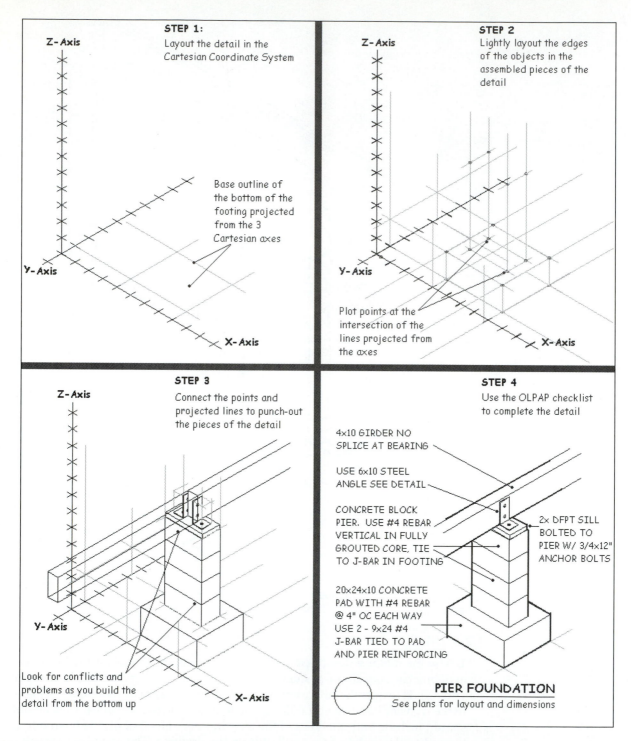

STEP 1:
Layout the detail in the Cartesian Coordinate System

Z-Axis

Base outline of the bottom of the footing projected from the 3 Cartesian axes

Y-Axis

X-Axis

STEP 2
Lightly layout the edges of the objects in the assembled pieces of the detail

Z-Axis

Plot points at the intersection of the lines projected from the axes

Y-Axis

X-Axis

STEP 3
Connect the points and projected lines to punch-out the pieces of the detail

Z-Axis

Look for conflicts and problems as you build the detail from the bottom up

Y-Axis

X-Axis

STEP 4
Use the OLPAP checklist to complete the detail

4x10 GIRDER NO SPLICE AT BEARING

USE 6x10 STEEL ANGLE SEE DETAIL

CONCRETE BLOCK PIER. USE #4 REBAR VERTICAL IN FULLY GROUTED CORE, TIE TO J-BAR IN FOOTING

2x DFPT SILL BOLTED TO PIER W/ 3/4x12" ANCHOR BOLTS

20x24x10 CONCRETE PAD WITH #4 REBAR @ 4" OC EACH WAY USE 2 - 9x24 #4 J-BAR TIED TO PAD AND PIER REINFORCING

PIER FOUNDATION
See plans for layout and dimensions

Figure 5-24. The three-dimensional detail helps you to analyze the assembly of the pieces of the detail as you build it. Step 1: Lay out the three axes. Step 2: Project lines to define the boundaries of the assembly. Step 3: Punch out the pieces and analyze the construction. Step 4: Use the OLPAP checklist to complete the detail.

3. Now use a carpenter's pencil to draw lightly a box for each of the components of the detail, including boxes around irregular shapes that are not rectangles, like the angle securing the joists to the wooden sill in step 3 of Figure 5-24. You can draw these boxes to one side and then mentally move them into place by copying them in their correct location, or you can draw them directly where they belong. Look for conflicts or problems that might occur with the assembly and supply alternatives that can be used in the field. The whole idea is that you visually analyze the detail, not just illustrate it. Of course, internal components, like the reinforcing steel, are not visible. These pieces will have to be called out in the OLPAP notes.

4. With everything lightly laid out as an assembly, punch out the boundaries of the visible edges of each of the objects by darkening the visible edges with a carpenter's pencil. (See step 4 in Figure 5-24.) You punch out the visual content of your drawing in the same way as your two-dimensional field drawings. As always, use the OLPAP checklist to make sure you include all the annotations necessary to explain the construction.

A detail like those in Figures 5-25 and 5-26 grows out of the same visual problem solving process of interaction and collaboration that shaped the rest of the drawings. In other words, it begins with some vague ideas and sketches. The sketches are reviewed and modified in preparation for scaled drawings. These are then used to investigate materials and establish costs for engineered layouts and further detailing. Finally, the details are checked in a preconstruction analysis with the main set of drawings.

What is important to detailing is that the problem solving process begins with identifying the context of the details so you can set priorities. You must recognize all the conditions in the engineered drawings that require further analysis and explanation. This is done by thinking through the construction process and the particular sequence of assembly, looking for portions of the work that require clarification. The objective is to identify the details required for the entire building so you can decide

Pencils

Using a light blue pencil for your layout lines will be a lot like using a chalkline to lay out your work in the field. These lines are necessary to align correctly the pieces to be assembled and to make sure that you know exactly where everything will go before you begin. Chalklines guide the construction on paper, on the computer screen, and in the real world. Most workers would agree that the number one reason for poor quality construction is a poorly laid out building. To get it right, you have to take the time to lay out the drawing carefully.

Drawing with a carpenter's pencil will help improve your communications skills because one of the most important kinds of construction communication involves simple hand-drawings completed with readily available tools, so you can be effective in the field. The most available surface will be a scrap of wood or drywall, and the best instrument for drawing will be some dull marker that you might have to borrow from one of the workers. A carpenter's pencil comes close to the kind of drawing tool that you may have to use in the field. If you can draw with a carpenter's pencil, you can draw with anything, anywhere—and constructors always seem to find the need to communicate about almost anything in almost every possible situation.

Drafting With Paint

The same process can be used to build a construction detail with the simple Paint program found in the operating system for almost every desktop computer. Small accessory programs allow you to draw lines in different colors, constrain the lines to horizontal or 45 degrees, and copy and paste parts of the drawing from place to place.

The tricks to using a Paint program to build a three-dimensional detail are exactly the same as those for a hand-drawing. First, you have to practice; nothing beats practice. Second, you have to remember that you are building the detail and not drawing it. Think through the assembly process with a three-axis coordinate system, lay out lines, and copy and paste the lines into position. In fact, you should not have to draw more than three lines of the same color. Once those lines are drawn, all you need to do is copy and paste them into position. It takes experience, imagination, and a mind open to a world of possibilities to draw a detail like those shown in Figures 5-25 and 5-26 with a Paint program, not so much because they are well-constructed drawings, but because both represent construction information transferred to a piece of paper.

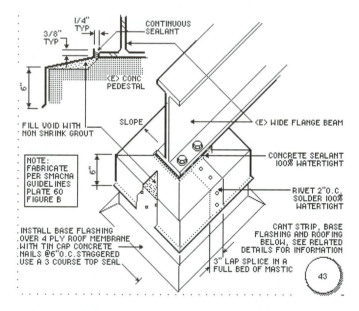

Figure 5-25. A three-dimensional detail grows out of the same problem solving process used to resolve the requirements of the entire building.

which will benefit most from a separate drawing and which will be handled best by a note or reference to the final specifications. Time is of the essence in a field drawing and there is no need to detail something that everyone already knows how to build.

Once the context of all the details is understood, the parameters of the most important problems must be defined carefully. These are the environmental and structural forces as they relate to each detail in its particular place in the total construction. These forces are the conditions that must be resolved by the detail and act as a program to define the requirements that must be met by the final design. They include the dimensions and specifications for the particular pieces of the assembly, for exam-

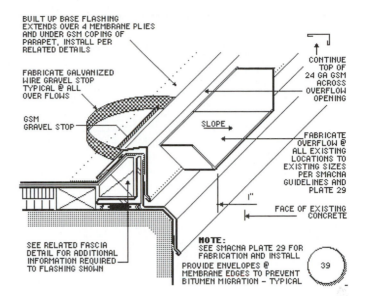

BUILT UP BASE FLASHING
EXTENDS OVER 4 MEMBRANE PLIES
AND UNDER GSM COPING OF
PARAPET, INSTALL PER
RELATED DETAILS

FABRICATE GALVANIZED
WIRE GRAVEL STOP
TYPICAL @ ALL
OVER FLOWS

GSM
GRAVEL STOP

SEE RELATED FASCIA
DETAIL FOR ADDITIONAL
INFORMATION REQUIRED
TO FLASHING SHOWN

CONTINUE
TOP OF
24 GA GSM
ACROSS
OVERFLOW
OPENING

SLOPE

FABRICATE
OVERFLOW @
ALL EXISTING
LOCATIONS TO
EXISTING SIZES
PER SMACNA
GUIDELINES AND
PLATE 29

1"

FACE OF EXISTING
CONCRETE

NOTE:
SEE SMACNA PLATE 29 FOR
FABRICATION AND INSTALL
PROVIDE ENVELOPES @
MEMBRANE EDGES TO PREVENT
BITUMEN MIGRATION - TYPICAL

39

Figure 5-26. To draw a three-dimensional detail, you have to visualize the context of all the forces associated with the problem that the detail is trying to solve.

ple, the steel inserts for the concrete coins in the foundation plan or the height of the skylight flashing on the roof.

Most important, drawing the detail is a way of thinking through the solution to the construction of these particular problems. This might begin as a mental image, but it will be resolved only when you begin to draw it, think about how the pieces come together, and resolve the forces that are shaping it.

Drawing a detail in three dimensions therefore means establishing a much broader understanding of the context and the forces shaping the building rather than simply attempting to translate visually the construction into a collection of two-dimensional projections. To draw a three-dimensional detail, you have to use the drawing to visualize the questions, study possible answers, and communicate and test the results with outside consultants. Each step in the visual problem solving process gives you a little more understanding of the total picture, and the picture it-self ultimately helps you visualize and communicate the solution.

The Construction Details for the Trainer

The objective of the details is to explain the fabrication or placement of every piece of the building. If you understand the context of all the details that will be required for the construction, you need to draw details only for those pieces that cannot be explained in any other way. In other words, since time is limited for a field drawing, your initial analysis established priorities for particular parts of the building that have to be explained. Again, there is no need to explain common or standard construction because the workers making the installation need to know only what is unique to this project.

For example, as shown in Figure 5-27, you can explain the construction of the retaining wall for the first location of the trainer directly on the foundation plan with notes and callouts and save a great deal of time. At least some of the carpenters and masons who will build this wall have built a lot of footings and walls before and really need to know only its dimensions, how much reinforcing it will take, and if there is anything different about the installation that they would not normally do. Because

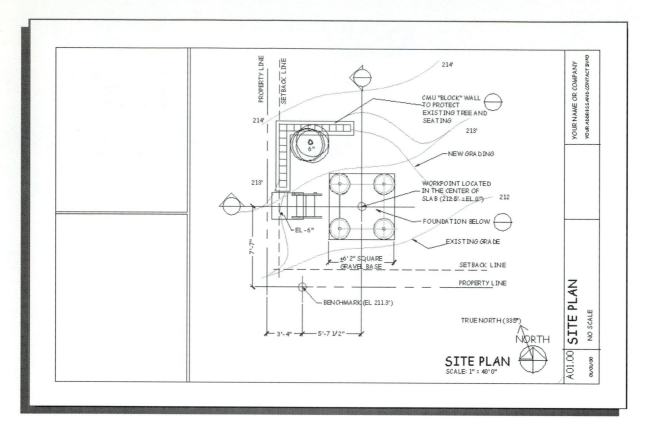

Figure 5-27. The site plan shows the detail bubbles for the building section and the details associated with the sitework.

the dimensions are already given for the wall on the plan and the vertical elevations are shown on the building sections, you have to add only a few notes to the foundation plan:

1. A note for the footing construction: 10"×16" CONTINUOUS CONCRETE FOOTING WITH 2 #4 CONTINUOUS REBAR W/ 24" LAP AND SPLICE
2. A note for the construction of the wall: 8"×8"×16" CONCRETE BLOCK WALL WITH 10 GA HORIZ LADDER REINFORCING AND FULLY GROUTED VERTICAL #4 REBAR AT 24" OC
3. A note for the J-bar tying the footing to the wall: BEND 6"×18" #4 J-BAR AT 24" OC TIE TO FULLY GROUTED VERTICAL REBAR IN WALL

Add to this list a note on the elevation about the bond, joints, and cap for the wall, and everything that a mason needs to build the wall is on the drawings. In this way, the workers' own skill and experience with this type of construction fill in the gaps. Of course, it's important to know who is building the wall and doubly important to field check its progress as it is built.

Once priorities have been established and you know what needs to be drawn on the sheets, the first step is to reference the drawings on at least one of the sheets of the drawings by a symbol with the detail and sheet number. This symbol is called a bubble. Although it will probably look different from project to project, it represents a link to the location of additional information.

These detail bubbles set the stage for the drawing and are found on the plans, elevations, and sections, as well as the wall sections, stair plans, and even other details.

The idea is to anticipate where the information will be most useful. As shown in the foundation plan in Figure 4-36, a detail bubble can be drawn as a line with a tail or an arrow pointed in the direction in which the detail faces. As shown in the wall sections in Figures 4-35 or 4-36, it can also be a circle or oval around a portion of the drawing with a leader line attached to a bubble. In some cases, a detail will be called out by a note with an arrow and a line drawn from the point at which the detail is taken.

Bubble references to the details for the building and wall sections that refer to other sheets in the set are commonly shown where they can be most descriptive. In fact, these references should be visible on every plan and elevation or section where they occur. For example, the symbols for the wall sections should be shown on every floor plan, the engineered plans, elevations, and even the building sections.

Once the location of the details is identified with a symbol, you must locate the best position for the detail in the set of drawings. Wherever possible, the detail should be directly adjacent to the point from which it is referenced. Of course, this is not always possible. First, there is only so much room on a particular sheet. Second, one detail may be referenced from several different sheets in a set of drawings. Final decision for placement again falls back to the priorities set by the overall context of all the details to be used in the project.

For example, in Figure 5-27, any details that might be shown with the site plan should be related directly to the problems associated with that particular sheet in the set of drawings. In other words, even though a foundation or retaining wall might be visible in the site plan, details on the same sheet should include the most critical and closely related site conditions. Therefore two slots are available on this sheet. In an evaluation of all the clarifications necessary to complete the construction, the highest priority should be given to the information that would be most necessary to the construction of the building at this stage of the construction. The details exclusive to a site plan include staging and marshalling, site layout, grading, drainage, walkways, landscaping, parking, and special installations should go here.

As noted above, the only way to determine which detail has the highest priority and should therefore be located on this sheet is to understand the context of all the details necessary for the total construction. What problem would need the most immediate answer during this phase of construction? The right detail will help the work to flow a little more smoothly. The wrong detail will become the first in possibly an ongoing pattern of poor communications. Workers will have to flip back and forth through the drawings, which wastes time and makes it more difficult to visualize both the process and the requirements of the construction.

Once the symbols and details are organized throughout the set, an architect with a particular design style might go to a file drawer or a collection of CAD files and literally cut and paste his or her favorite details into the appropriate positions on each of the sheets. In a standard building, this might even include some engineered details for a few special situations. Again, however, most of the information will be included on the base sheets as notes and callouts. On a large job, the architectural and engineering details will be separated because each engineer and consultant draws them individually. Most field drawings are themselves details and may be referenced from the project's construction drawing by a memorandum, clarification, or change order.

If you take a close look at the detail bubbles and the details that they reference for almost any job, it becomes obvious that even at this late stage there are several ways to build the same building. In fact, detailing a building is the Achilles heel of every set of drawings. Detailing is where the most experience and the most knowledge must be applied. When it is done correctly, you will have the best chance for a smooth and efficient project. When it is done incorrectly, you could have a disaster.

The best detail is one that requires the least labor and materials, has the most constructibility, and comes closest to the original program requirements. All of that is relative to each particular project. The details should work together as a total system. In other words, one good detail deserves another and another and another, so that they are all mutually supportive and equally efficient. One bad detail can ruin an entire project.

Depending on the conditions set by the drawings completed in step 5, the possibilities are endless for the trainer. In addition, the level of detail is critical to the efficiency of the project. There can be too many details, just as there can be too few details. Part of the art of construction detailing is understanding how much information is necessary for each particular project. Sometimes a simple note will be more than adequate; other times, several layers of details will be required to get the construction exactly right.

Figures 5-28 through 5-44 represent a collection of some of the three-dimensional details for the structure of the trainer used in this book. These drawings are examples of how you can use 3D drawings to deliver specific construction information. You can add to or change these details to adjust the level of detail in a set of construction drawings. A high level of detail will restrict the workers in the field to exact methods of installation, but a low level of detail could mean endless questions and delays. For field drafting, almost any three-dimensional drawing will be quicker to understand and more effective at getting your point across. In addition, almost all the detailing can be generated spontaneously on the jobsite, as the workers need the information in the course of construction.

Site Plan Details

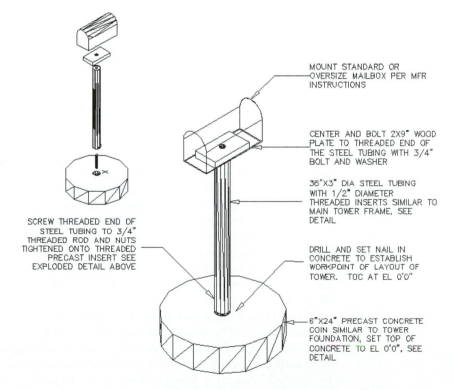

MOUNT STANDARD OR OVERSIZE MAILBOX PER MFR INSTRUCTIONS

CENTER AND BOLT 2X9" WOOD PLATE TO THREADED END OF THE STEEL TUBING WITH 3/4" BOLT AND WASHER

36"X3" DIA STEEL TUBING WITH 1/2" DIAMETER THREADED INSERTS SIMILAR TO MAIN TOWER FRAME, SEE DETAIL

DRILL AND SET NAIL IN CONCRETE TO ESTABLISH WORKPOINT OF LAYOUT OF TOWER. TOC AT EL 0'0"

6"X24" PRECAST CONCRETE COIN SIMILAR TO TOWER FOUNDATION, SET TOP OF CONCRETE TO EL 0'0", SEE DETAIL

SCREW THREADED END OF STEEL TUBING TO 3/4" THREADED ROD AND NUTS TIGHTENED ONTO THREADED PRECAST INSERT SEE EXPLODED DETAIL ABOVE

Figure 5-28. A relocatable mailbox can be fabricated out of the same material as the trainer using a threaded precast concrete base and steel tubing with threaded caps.

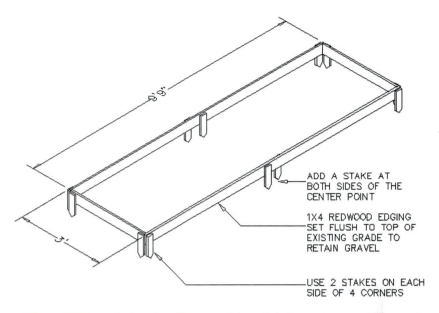

Figure 5-29. A standard gravel walkway edging detail can be used to create a path to the trainer. It might also be used as a base material in the materials yard.

Foundation Plan Details

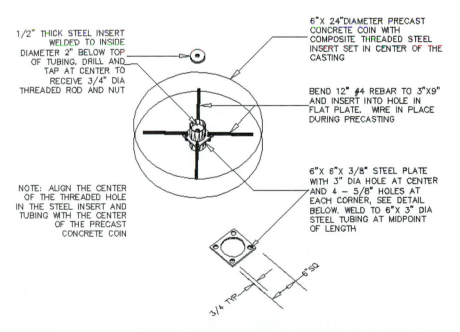

Figure 5-30. The precast concrete coins have threaded metal inserts that support the reinforcing steel for the concrete. These metal inserts can be supplemented with wire mesh, or fiber reinforcing can be mixed into the concrete itself. Note that a threaded rod extends through each of the concrete coins and is locked into position by a locking nut.

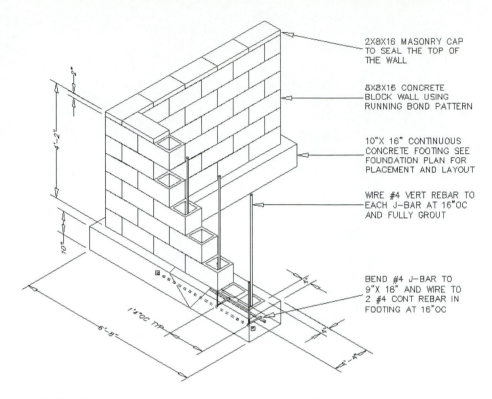

2X8X16 MASONRY CAP TO SEAL THE TOP OF THE WALL

8X8X16 CONCRETE BLOCK WALL USING RUNNING BOND PATTERN

10"X 16" CONTINUOUS CONCRETE FOOTING SEE FOUNDATION PLAN FOR PLACEMENT AND LAYOUT

WIRE #4 VERT REBAR TO EACH J-BAR AT 16"OC AND FULLY GROUT

BEND #4 J-BAR TO 9"X 18" AND WIRE TO 2 #4 CONT REBAR IN FOOTING AT 16"OC

Figure 5-31. The details for the concrete masonry wall show the layout for the reinforcing in the footing and the wall. This clarifies the information in the main body of the field drawings for the trainer, but the overall dimensions of the wall and the elevations for the main part of the construction must still be shown on the plans, elevations, and sections.

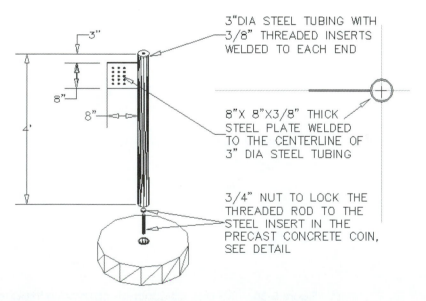

3"DIA STEEL TUBING WITH 3/8" THREADED INSERTS WELDED TO EACH END

8"X 8"X3/8" THICK STEEL PLATE WELDED TO THE CENTERLINE OF 3" DIA STEEL TUBING

3/4" NUT TO LOCK THE THREADED ROD TO THE STEEL INSERT IN THE PRECAST CONCRETE COIN, SEE DETAIL

Figure 5-32. The framing begins with the attachment of the steel tubular column of the trainer frame to the upper piece of the foundation. The height of the column can be adjusted to level the floor when ground level varies with terrain. Note that the steel plate faces inward to support the floor framing.

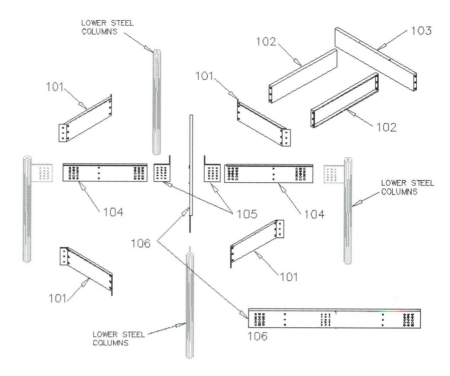

Figure 5-33. Each of the steel members for the raised floor framing would be detailed in shop drawings by the manufacturer. They are prefabricated pieces that must be assembled in the field.

Framing Plan Details

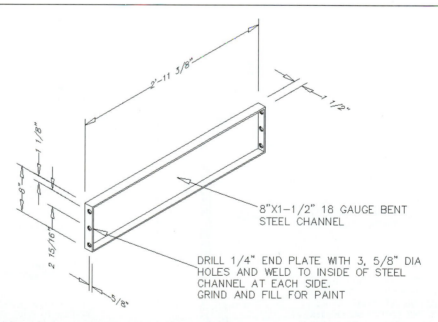

Figure 5-34. A three-dimensional detail of one of the framing members gives the sizes and locations of holes that need to be drilled or punched in the steel, as well as information about bends and welds necessary to make the pieces shown on the construction drawings. The shop drawings are piece-specific and are intended to provide shop workers only the information necessary to fabricate each framing member.

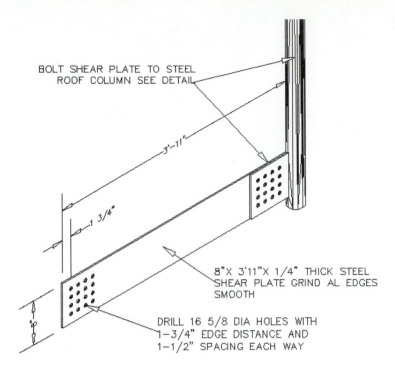

BOLT SHEAR PLATE TO STEEL
ROOF COLUMN SEE DETAIL

3'-11"

1 3/4"

8"X 3'11"X 1/4" THICK STEEL
SHEAR PLATE GRIND AL EDGES
SMOOTH

DRILL 16 5/8 DIA HOLES WITH
1-3/4" EDGE DISTANCE AND
1-1/2" SPACING EACH WAY

Figure 5-35. Some of the details for the trainer will have to show the piece in association with the actual assembly. These details freeze the assembly and isolate a particular sequence in the construction process. A good set of details has the information to support each step of the construction.

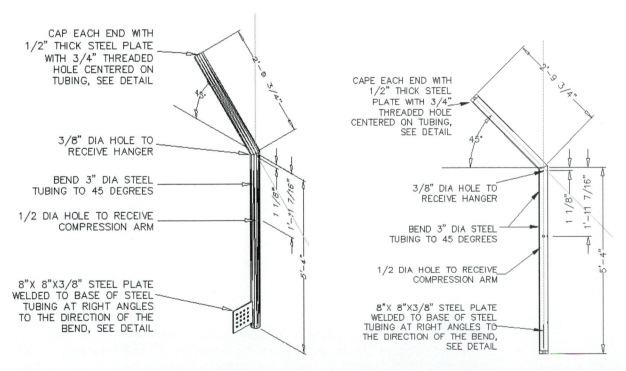

CAP EACH END WITH
1/2" THICK STEEL PLATE
WITH 3/4" THREADED
HOLE CENTERED ON
TUBING, SEE DETAIL

3/8" DIA HOLE TO
RECEIVE HANGER

BEND 3" DIA STEEL
TUBING TO 45 DEGREES

1/2 DIA HOLE TO RECEIVE
COMPRESSION ARM

8"X 8"X3/8" STEEL PLATE
WELDED TO BASE OF STEEL
TUBING AT RIGHT ANGLES
TO THE DIRECTION OF THE
BEND, SEE DETAIL

CAPE EACH END WITH
1/2" THICK STEEL
PLATE WITH 3/4"
THREADED HOLE
CENTERED ON TUBING,
SEE DETAIL

3/8" DIA HOLE TO
RECEIVE HANGER

BEND 3" DIA STEEL
TUBING TO 45 DEGREES

1/2 DIA HOLE TO RECEIVE
COMPRESSION ARM

8"X 8"X3/8" STEEL PLATE
WELDED TO BASE OF STEEL
TUBING AT RIGHT ANGLES TO
THE DIRECTION OF THE BEND,
SEE DETAIL

Figure 5-36. As shown in these two illustrations, a two-dimensional drawing can sometimes be just as easy to understand as a three-dimensional drawing, especially when there is a bend in the framing member that is along an axis that is not seen easily in an isometric drawing.

Roof-Framing Plan Details

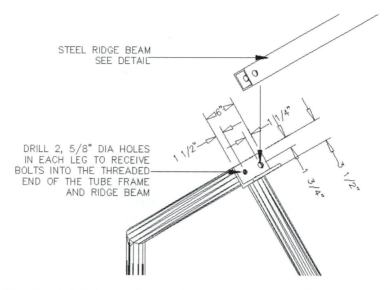

STEEL RIDGE BEAM
SEE DETAIL

DRILL 2, 5/8" DIA HOLES
IN EACH LEG TO RECEIVE
BOLTS INTO THE THREADED
END OF THE TUBE FRAME
AND RIDGE BEAM

6"

1 1/4"

1 1/2"

3 1/2"

3/4"

Figure 5-37. This detail shows where a ridge bracket fits into the assembly. This single image therefore shows more than one step in the construction. A drawing of just the bracket would give enough information to build the bracket, but the three-dimensional drawing gives a sense of where the bracket fits into the assembly.

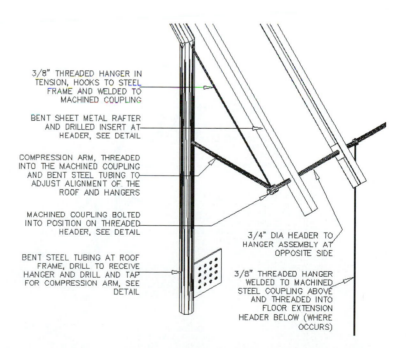

3/8" THREADED HANGER IN
TENSION, HOOKS TO STEEL
FRAME AND WELDED TO
MACHINED COUPLING

BENT SHEET METAL RAFTER
AND DRILLED INSERT AT
HEADER, SEE DETAIL

COMPRESSION ARM, THREADED
INTO THE MACHINED COUPLING
AND BENT STEEL TUBING TO
ADJUST ALIGNMENT OF THE
ROOF AND HANGERS

MACHINED COUPLING BOLTED
INTO POSITION ON THREADED
HEADER, SEE DETAIL

BENT STEEL TUBING AT ROOF
FRAME, DRILL TO RECEIVE
HANGER AND DRILL AND TAP
FOR COMPRESSION ARM, SEE
DETAIL

3/4" DIA HEADER TO
HANGER ASSEMBLY AT
OPPOSITE SIDE

3/8" THREADED HANGER
WELDED TO MACHINED
STEEL COUPLING ABOVE
AND THREADED INTO
FLOOR EXTENSION
HEADER BELOW (WHERE
OCCURS)

Figure 5-38. The detail of the roof support system for the floor extension or solar support panels shows the advantage of a three-dimensional detail. Rather than focus on the dimensions and sizes that are shown in the main set of drawings, this detail shows how several different pieces fit together.

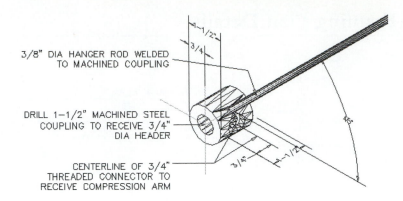

3/8" DIA HANGER ROD WELDED
TO MACHINED COUPLING

DRILL 1-1/2" MACHINED STEEL
COUPLING TO RECEIVE 3/4"
DIA HEADER

CENTERLINE OF 3/4"
THREADED CONNECTOR TO
RECEIVE COMPRESSION ARM

Figure 5-39. This is a detail of a detail, or a closer look at a particular part of the trainer that needs to be machined as a coupling for the roof system. This detail would more likely be referenced from within one of the other roofing details rather than from the main set of drawings, where it would be too small to draw and see. This two-dimensional drawing therefore takes the place of several two-dimensional drawings.

Stair Details

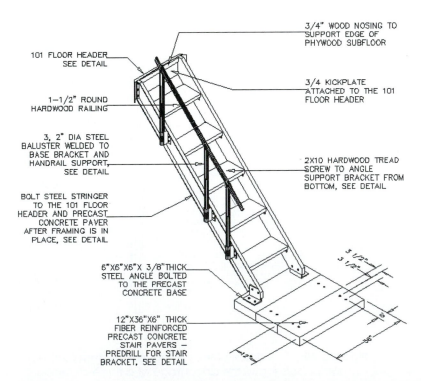

101 FLOOR HEADER
SEE DETAIL

1-1/2" ROUND
HARDWOOD RAILING

3, 2" DIA STEEL
BALUSTER WELDED TO
BASE BRACKET AND
HANDRAIL SUPPORT,
SEE DETAIL

BOLT STEEL STRINGER
TO THE 101 FLOOR
HEADER AND PRECAST
CONCRETE PAVER
AFTER FRAMING IS IN
PLACE, SEE DETAIL

3/4" WOOD NOSING TO
SUPPORT EDGE OF
PHYWOOD SUBFLOOR

3/4 KICKPLATE
ATTACHED TO THE 101
FLOOR HEADER

2X10 HARDWOOD TREAD
SCREW TO ANGLE
SUPPORT BRACKET FROM
BOTTOM, SEE DETAIL

6"X6"X6"X 3/8"THICK
STEEL ANGLE BOLTED
TO THE PRECAST
CONCRETE BASE

12"X36"X6" THICK
FIBER REINFORCED
PRECAST CONCRETE
STAIR PAVERS –
PREDRILL FOR STAIR
BRACKET, SEE DETAIL

Figure 5-40. Drawing the stair as a three-dimensional isometric puts together different kinds of information into one detail. In this case, it acts as an elevation, section, and plan because it shows how all three of these two-dimensional drawings work together in the final assembly. Dimensions are given for the pavers, but they can also be referenced by a different detail.

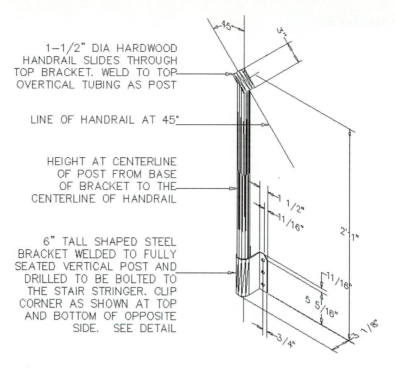

1-1/2" DIA HARDWOOD HANDRAIL SLIDES THROUGH TOP BRACKET. WELD TO TOP OVERTICAL TUBING AS POST

LINE OF HANDRAIL AT 45"

HEIGHT AT CENTERLINE OF POST FROM BASE OF BRACKET TO THE CENTERLINE OF HANDRAIL

6" TALL SHAPED STEEL BRACKET WELDED TO FULLY SEATED VERTICAL POST AND DRILLED TO BE BOLTED TO THE STAIR STRINGER. CLIP CORNER AS SHOWN AT TOP AND BOTTOM OF OPPOSITE SIDE. SEE DETAIL

Figure 5-41.   The isometric of the handrail and post for the stair is an example of a detail that might be referenced from either the building elevations in the main set of drawings, the stair plans or sections, or from another detail. Again, the one drawing shows the same information that would normally be provided on two or three two-dimensional drawings.

Wall Panels

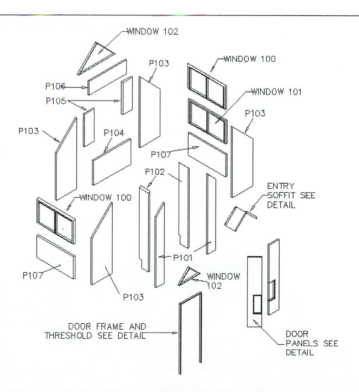

Figure 5-42.   Like the steel framing members, the manufacturer also details the wall panels for piece-based fabrication. The construction information for each panel must therefore be calculated carefully from the overall dimensions of the trainer. A typical detail for an edge condition and the basic composition of the panels are required to guide the shop drawings.

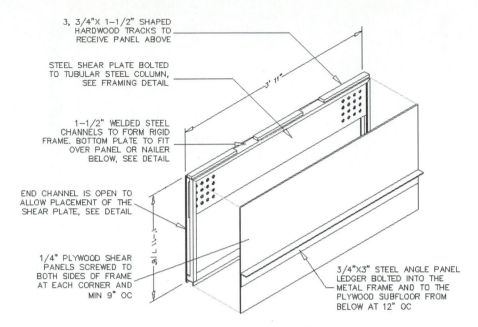

3, 3/4"X 1-1/2" SHAPED HARDWOOD TRACKS TO RECEIVE PANEL ABOVE

STEEL SHEAR PLATE BOLTED TO TUBULAR STEEL COLUMN, SEE FRAMING DETAIL

1-1/2" WELDED STEEL CHANNELS TO FORM RIGID FRAME. BOTTOM PLATE TO FIT OVER PANEL OR NAILER BELOW, SEE DETAIL

END CHANNEL IS OPEN TO ALLOW PLACEMENT OF THE SHEAR PLATE, SEE DETAIL

1/4" PLYWOOD SHEAR PANELS SCREWED TO BOTH SIDES OF FRAME AT EACH CORNER AND MIN 9" OC

3' 11"

3'-11 1/2"

3/4"X3" STEEL ANGLE PANEL LEDGER BOLTED INTO THE METAL FRAME AND TO THE PLYWOOD SUBFLOOR FROM BELOW AT 12" OC

Figure 5-43. This example is a three-dimensional detail of panel #P107. Note that it gives all the information necessary for the fabrication, including the context of the installation, because the shear plate is shown within the panel cavity. The wall panel can be preassembled, but it would have to be disassembled to be installed.

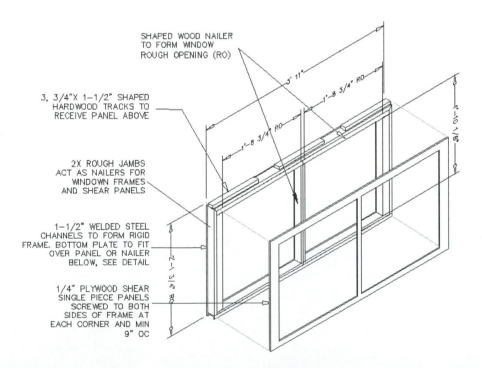

SHAPED WOOD NAILER TO FORM WINDOW ROUGH OPENING (RO)

3, 3/4"X 1-1/2" SHAPED HARDWOOD TRACKS TO RECEIVE PANEL ABOVE

2X ROUGH JAMBS ACT AS NAILERS FOR WINDOWN FRAMES AND SHEAR PANELS

1-1/2" WELDED STEEL CHANNELS TO FORM RIGID FRAME. BOTTOM PLATE TO FIT OVER PANEL OR NAILER BELOW, SEE DETAIL

1/4" PLYWOOD SHEAR SINGLE PIECE PANELS SCREWED TO BOTH SIDES OF FRAME AT EACH CORNER AND MIN 9" OC

3' 11"

1'-8 3/4" RO

1'-8 3/4" RO

4'-10 1/2"

3'-1 3/4" RO

2'-1 3/4" RO

Figure 5-44. The window panel is similar to a wall panel except that the manufacturer for the wall may not supply the window unit itself, which means that the rough opening shown in the detail must be coordinated with the sizes and specifications required by the window manufacturer.

Chapter 6

PRECONSTRUCTION MODELING

Introduction and Review

Now you know how to draft floor plans, elevations, and sections for a simple building and, most important, how to visualize and detail those drawings in three dimensions for construction. You know how to take a vague idea and translate it into a set of construction drawings and details.

Understanding how to translate an idea into a full set of construction drawings for a large building is probably beyond the skills necessary to be a good constructor—at least for the moment. Many would argue that even knowing how to put together this little set of field drawings is more than you will ever need to know. Most of the complicated or difficult field drawings will be done by the project architect or a construction engineer hired especially for the particular job.

Of course, some constructors want to control the design process, either as design-builders or single-source construction managers. For these constructors, knowing how a set of drawings goes together means they will have a deeper understanding of the challenges facing the design team. As you now know, many things can go wrong. If the project is rushed, ideas will not be exchanged or, worse yet, concepts will be developed in isolation, with the potential of contradiction and confrontation. It is also easy to not fully explore the ramifications of an engineered solution, especially when you have electrical and mechanical requirements or the aesthetic concerns that will be most important to an architect. None of these complications were present in the trainer, but you can easily imagine their effect on the work you have already completed.

Obviously the real value of being able to draw every piece of a building is that it gives you the ability to communicate its construction. Drawings give you a stronger voice in your fast-paced role as a constructor. They give you the ability to communicate with the owner and the design team by contributing your own ideas and your own experiences for the way a building is to be built. The ability to draw also places you in a proactive position with workers in the field because it helps you clarify your directives and get your point across quickly to workers at various skill levels. In fact, a field drawing does not really do a lot for anyone until it can be used to communicate something about the construction of a building. Drawings can

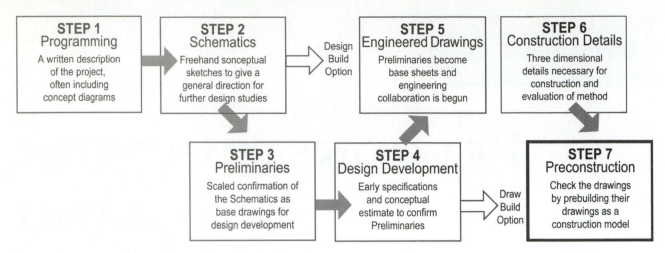

Figure 6-1. In step 7, you will check the drawings produced in steps 1–6 by preconstructing the trainer on the computer.

include jobsite sketches on scraps of wood or drywall, construction permits for falsework or scaffolding, task drawings for crews, presentations, memorandums, letters, change orders, requests for information, or the preparation of exhibits in a hearing or trial.

Most important, you can use drawings and details to define the scope of the work they represent. In other words, construction drawings are the focus of a visual problem solving method. They help everyone to see the evolution of the solution to the problem. If you encourage discussion and interaction, participants also share ownership in the information when it gets to the field.

Figure 6-1 began with the rough napkin sketches and a written memorandum that represented the project's program requirements. In step 2, these requirements were presented as conceptual sketches, otherwise known as schematic drawings. In step 3, they were drawn to scale as preliminaries so that they could be finalized in step 4 with early specifications and a conceptual estimate. Once the estimate and the revised preliminaries were approved, they became the base drawings for the actual construction set. In step 5, you added the engineered drawings to this set and used them to gather input from outside consultants to support the feasibility of the construction. In step 6, you drew three-dimensional details that showed how the pieces of the building fit together.

Step 7: Preconstruction

The goal in the last step, step 7, is to review the plans and check them to make sure all the information is available to support the workers in the field. The drawings are again the focus of the work, but this time they must be checked before they are released to the field for construction.

Checking the drawings begins with your technical ability to read plans and determine what is missing. If you can draw the field drawings for the trainer, you should also be able to read the final set of drawings and determine if you can construct it. Because you understand how to draw the building on paper, including how the line weights, dimensioning, symbols, and notes work together to document

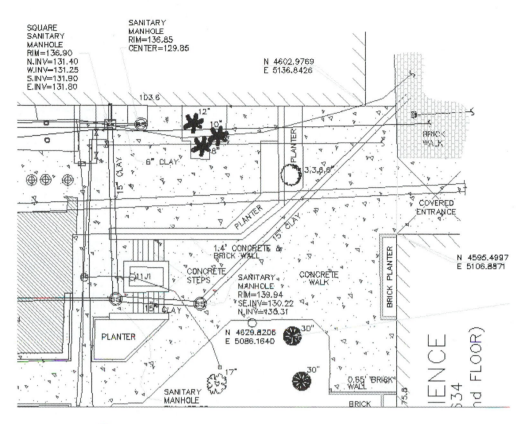

Figure 6-2.   Imagine how difficult it would be to check this two-dimensional drawing for any errors in its information.

the building for construction, you should also be able to read the plans once they are complete.

For a large building, even the most experienced architects and engineers completing the most carefully coordinated set of the construction drawings and specifications could not possibly discover all the errors and missing information the drawings might contain. The possibility that one or two people can check the drawings of a complex building and discover all the errors and omissions is too much of a challenge in today's high-speed, computer-driven construction industry.

For example, imagine checking the civil engineering drawing shown in Figure 6-2. No matter how much time you spent checking this one drawing, questions and requests for information will come up in the field. These clarifications will require immediate answers to avoid critical delays or cause a great deal of conflict in the progress of the project. Minimizing mistakes in the drawings is important to ensure a well-coordinated, smoothly running project.

Until very recently, discovering all the errors in a set of drawings could only be done in the field during the actual construction process. Now that new three-dimensional modeling software has become available, it is possible to test and prebuild any building prior to construction. For example, note how the three-dimensional model in Figure 6-3 clarifies the two-dimensional information shown in Figure 6-2. Both drawings illustrate the same thing. Four items in Figure 6-3 are important to note:

1. Like the hand-drawn images in Chapter 5, the power of the three-dimensional image is clearly superior in transferring information when compared to the

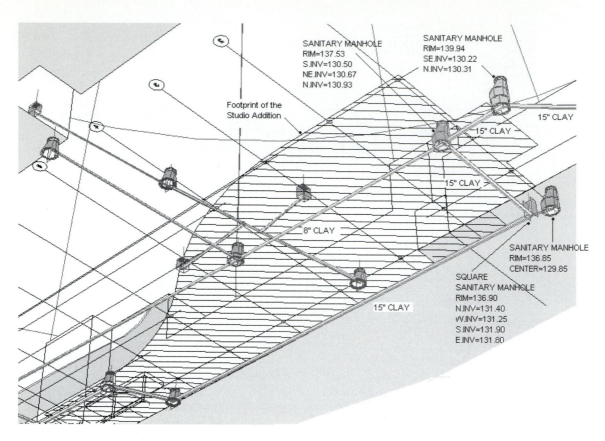

SANITARY MANHOLE
RIM=137.53
S.INV=130.50
NE.INV=130.67
N.INV=130.93

SANITARY MANHOLE
RIM=139.94
SE.INV=130.22
N.INV=130.31

Footprint of the
Studio Addition

15" CLAY

15" CLAY

15" CLAY

8" CLAY

SANITARY MANHOLE
RIM=136.85
CENTER=129.85

SQUARE
SANITARY MANHOLE
RIM=136.90
N.INV=131.40
W.INV=131.25
S.INV=131.90
E.INV=131.80

15" CLAY

Figure 6-3. A preconstruction model tests the information found in the two-dimensional plan by prebuilding the assemblies from the construction drawings.

two-dimensional version. It is faster to visualize and much easier to understand. In other words, it communicates much more clearly.

2. Since this is a computer model, the image shown is just one of an infinite number of views of the same model. For example, the model can be shown from many other views, as shown in Figure 6-4. Example views include below or above ground, in perspective or isometric, and with any pieces included or excluded from the image. The model is therefore valuable in illustrating sequences of installation or emphasizing a particular phase of construction.

3. If the model cannot be built from the information provided on the drawings, it would not be possible to build the building in the field. The preconstruction model should allow you to pretest the assembly and check the drawings and specifications for errors or missing information before you are committed to any particular phase of the work in the field.

4. Most important, if the process of building the model matches the construction process that would be used in the field, the preconstruction model embodies both the drawings and the time associated with any construction. The drawings can be tested in a way that has not been possible prior to the introduction of recent computer technology.

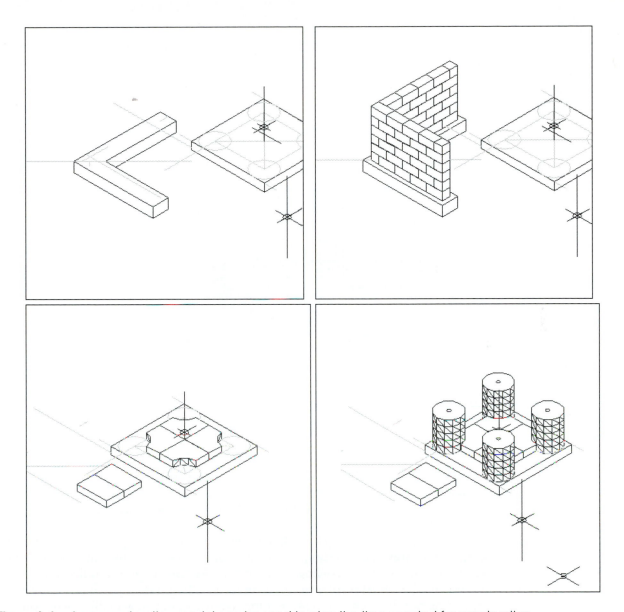

Figure 6-4. A preconstruction model can be used to plan the time needed for construction.

Preconstruction Models Are Not Architectural

Unlike architectural models, preconstruction models are fully detailed assemblies of the construction. A preconstruction model can be used to represent the building in ways that would be almost impossible with conventional drawings because the model can include every piece of framing and every brick and block, structural member, and wall panel shown on the construction drawings. You can zoom in, explode, annotate, and image digitally any particular part of the construction of a building.

In addition, preconstruction models represent the time embodied in the construction drawings. For example, the images shown in Figure 6-4 are all derived from the same model. Only one piece or another has been turned off so that it is not shown in the captured image. The ability to analyze time in the construction process and

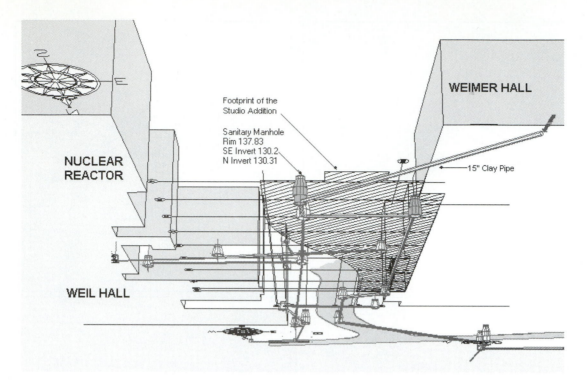

Footprint of the
Studio Addition

Sanitary Manhole
Rim 137.83
SE Invert 130.2
N Invert 130.31

WEIMER HALL

NUCLEAR
REACTOR

15" Clay Pipe

WEIL HALL

Figure 6-5. Once the preconstruction model is complete, it can be manipulated in various ways to illustrate several particular kinds of information.

examine the relationships of time to the pieces of construction is a powerful management tool, one that will become increasingly important as the capability of construction graphics moves onto the World Wide Web. (This subject is beyond the scope of this book.)

At first glance you might think that Figure 6-4 is nothing more than using the computer to draw the building again. After all, it looks just like another drawing. But in preconstruction modeling, you are actually constructing a full-size three-dimensional representation of every piece of the building. When you build these models, you do not draw lines to represent the construction; you actually orient yourself to the jobsite's boundaries, lay out chalklines, manufacture the pieces as solids, and then put the pieces of the building into place. The model is really a representation of a process. Materials are fabricated and staged before they are moved into position in much the same way that they are in actual construction.

Once the model is complete and all of its pieces are in place, you can view the completed assembly in its virtual environment in many different ways, as shown in Figure 6-5. This means it can be turned, sliced, and examined from various angles, as well as enlarged for detailed views of various parts of the assembly. This includes two-dimensional plans, elevations, and sections taken from the model. In other words, the three-dimensional views can be annotated and dimensioned just like a set of two-dimensional drawings. They can also be manipulated in layers to show details of a particular aspect of the construction.

The model is available to be studied, annotated, and printed from an infinite combination of layers, viewpoints, and scales, like the stair shown in Figure 6-6. You can view the model from specific heights and set that view to a particular part of your model. You can add notes and dimensions, zoom in for detail, zoom out

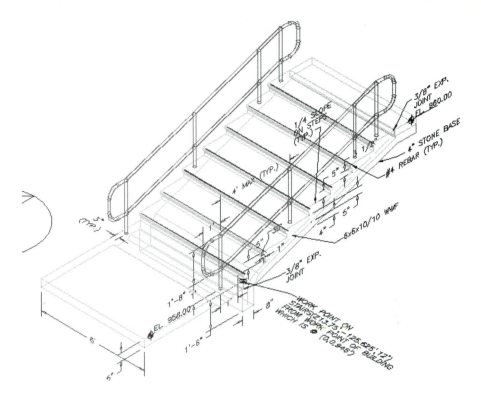

Figure 6-6. The preconstruction model can be dimensioned and noted on all planes of three-dimensional drawings.

for an overview, and turn layers on and off to show different combinations of information.

You can also do a virtual walkthrough as a series of printed images or transfer those images to an animator to create sequence animations by placing the pieces on different layers and hiding these layers for different combinations of assemblies. You can capture images of these views and save them as bitmaps for illustrations in the text of a word processor or as a slide in a computer presentation. For fast communications, you can convert model images to GIF or JPEG files and use them in HTML e-mail or project specific Web pages. With newly evolving networked technologies, the graphical communications potential is almost endless.

The Basic Requirements of Preconstruction Modeling

Preconstruction models can be built on just about any three-dimensional computer program, which should have the following important features:

1. A solid model component. Sometimes referred to as a primitive modeler, this kind of modeler creates complex objects from simple shapes like boxes, cylinders, and wedges. The pieces of the model must be controlled independently so that you can show various combinations of construction.
2. Control of the dimensions of these solid objects. The closer the tolerances for the measurements, the more accurately you can create the final construction.

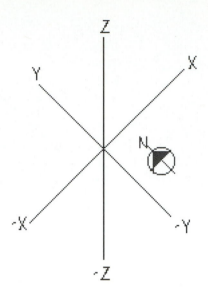

Figure 6-7. The positive Y-axis is always north for a preconstruction model, as it would be for a hand-drawing.

Some modeling programs are parametric: you can change the size of the model by changing the numerical text of the dimension, and vice versa.
3. Object level control over the final assembly. In other words, every piece of the assembly can be controlled individually. Most programs provide layer controls so that you build the model in layers and turn the layers themselves on and off to reconfigure the objects that are viewed. Object control is important because you can make objects visible or invisible, depending on what you want to show.

Almost all modeling programs use the same Cartesian coordinate system used to build the three-dimensional details in Chapter 5. The only difference is that, with the computer, the coordinates are already built into the modeling program. The addresses for the lines and solid objects in the virtual three-dimensional space can be accessed directly with the controls built into the software.

The coordinates are important not only for finding out where you are on the computer screen, but also for placing the objects in their correct locations relative to their position within that space. The coordinates mean that the modeling space is oriented automatically to the compass points of the Earth. As shown in Figure 6-7, having this coordinate system built into the program means that the positive Y-direction is north and positive Z is up. Therefore, the positive X-direction is east, negative X is west, and negative Y is south.

By definition, building a preconstruction computer model follows the same three steps you use to build the building:

1. Have a clear idea of what you will build before you build it. Visualize what you are about to build on the computer with a quick three-dimensional hand-drawing. Think of it as a field drawing for a virtual jobsite instead of a real one. For the trainer, much of this has already been done in the details, but you should have a clear mental image of what you are about to build before you attempt to build it.

> ## Computer Modeling
>
> Computer modeling is not as difficult as most people think. In fact, it is much easier to learn than two-dimensional CAD drafting and, in many ways, it is more useful. The preconstruction model requires two talents: the ability to read the drawings and visualize and lay out the work, and an understanding of how to fabricate, rotate, and assemble the pieces, like you would for any construction project. These talents are often completely intuitive for a construction professional.

2. Lay out the work before you build it. You must use stringlines, chalklines, and marks on the pieces you are cutting and assembling to place your work accurately. Any experienced superintendent will tell you that this is the key to a well-constructed building. Be sure to use the actual construction documents to do your layout. Again, like the real world, if it's not on the drawings, it's probably not in the scope of the contract, so you don't want to lay out anything based on intuition. All of this means preconstructing the building in the same sequential process that you would use in the field. Although it's easy to forget, the objective of step 7 is to check the drawings, not build the model.

3. Stage and marshal the construction as you would the actual project. Follow a work breakdown structure and a schedule so that the model is built so that it can be used to communicate the construction process after it's complete. In fact, the true value of a preconstruction model is not the final product, but what you learn as you proceed through its assembly. The model is not very useful when it's finished because it has to be deconstructed, digitized into a common graphical file format, and transferred to another program before it can communicate any real information.

Preconstruction Modeling with AutoCAD

AutoCAD will be used to build the preconstruction models for several reasons:

1. It is widely available in the industry and has become a de facto standard for most CAD drafting. Although its three-dimensional environment is not as well known, AutoCAD (ACAD) offers a simple and precise modeling environment in which to test a set of construction documents.

2. The ability to customize the program means that it can be used for modeling without having to learn a lot of unnecessary commands. This begins with the personal toolbar shown in Figure 6-8. A personal toolbar reduces the number of commands you have to learn to navigate, lay out, and build your projects. In other words, you use only the tools necessary to build the building. This rapidly increases your proficiency because you focus on just the fundamentals. At the same time, it is important to remember that there are thousands of commands, settings, menus, icons, and special features in ACAD that

Not Just AutoCAD

Many of the features in AutoCAD can be found in other programs. Although they look a little different or are called by another name, they will perform essentially the same function. For example, Softimage or think3 are much more powerful at rendering, while Bentley or Intergraph are more complex because they integrate estimating and scheduling.

Figure 6-8. A custom toolbar will reduce the number of commands you have to learn to those necessary for preconstruction modeling.

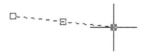

Figure 6-9. Hotgrips simplifies model construction.

you will not need to know. Many of them are actually more powerful than the ones you will use.

3. One of the most important features of recent versions of ACAD is called Hotgrips. Hotgrips allows you to stretch, move, rotate, scale, or rotate an object with a single control. Hotgrips eliminates at least five two-dimensional commands that you have had to learn to build a model. To use Hotgrips, you identify an object like a line of a solid by clicking it. (See Figure 6-9.) Select one of the blue handles of the object to set its base point, and then use the space bar to cycle through the five possible commands that will change the object's position according to that base point.

4. Another important feature of ACAD for modeling is the ability to control assembly points by snapping objects together. Combined with Hotgrips, object

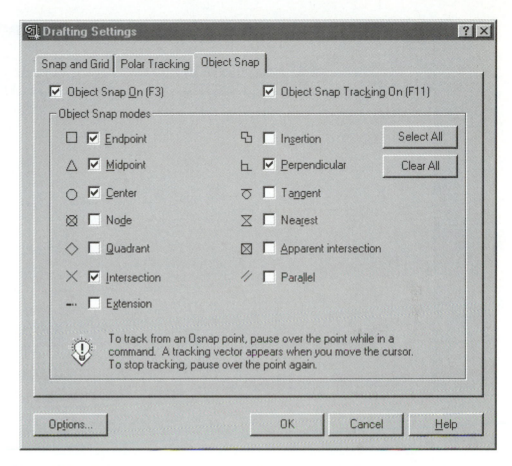

Figure 6-10. Five key object snap settings facilitate preconstruction assembly.

snaps (OSNAP) control the way lines and objects fit together with eighteen different snap settings, five of which are most useful for preconstruction modeling. As shown in Figure 6-10, these snaps are intersection, perpendicular, endpoint, center, and midpoint. Snaps are important because objects must snap into their correct position so that they can be viewed from any viewpoint in three-dimensional space. You can quickly turn OSNAP on and off by clicking on the OSNAP button located below the Command lines on the ACAD window. (See Figure 6-11.)

5. With Tiled Viewports, you can split your window into multiple views of the same or different objects, as shown in Figure 6-32 (p.203). Multiple viewports allow you to see the model you are working on from different directions. With this tool, you can make sure that the pieces of an assembly come together correctly. You can use Hotgrips to drag and drop pieces from one viewport to another. For example, you can set up one viewport on a staging area in one corner of the site, and you can drag and drop materials into the other viewport for assembly. A materials yard means that you have a common place to fabricate pieces and store them for use anywhere on the model. You can repeatedly copy pieces into the model and even export them to other models so you have to build them only once.

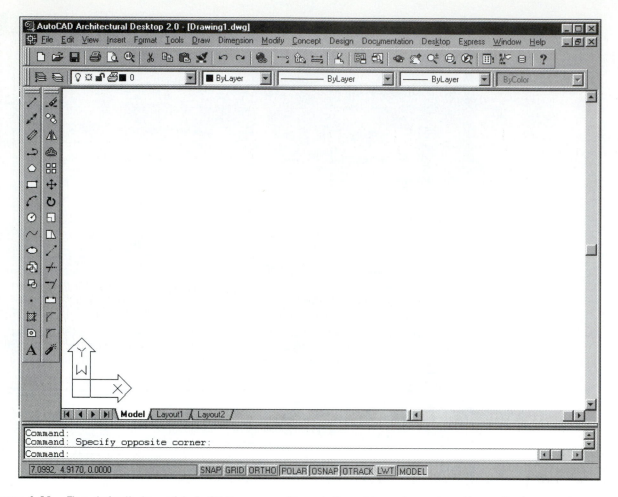

Figure 6-11. The default view of AutoCAD opens with a clutter of two-dimensional icons that are not necessary in preconstruction modeling.

The Modeling Process

The idea of a materials yard in multiple viewports suggests how the method used to build a preconstruction model simulates the construction process. The yard and its relative size help you plan visually for materials storage and delivery, including thinking through the distance the materials need to be moved for immediate access by workers and the general approach to the work as a whole. Some students will even add job trailers and entry gates to plan access and unloading.

The preconstruction model therefore begins with orienting the work to the available site. The project has to be aligned with the benchmarks and workpoints that will control the assembly of the building. Once stringlines and batterboards are set up, the storage areas and transfer routes for the materials can be identified clearly.

The OLPAP checklist is also useful for guiding preconstruction, just like it is with field drawings. For example, to begin the sitework for the trainer:

1. Orient the work with a north arrow pointing in the positive Y-direction. You can then set the benchmark, lay out the property lines, and plot the workpoint. The workpoint is the basepoint for most of the objects that make up the preconstruction model and is usually located at coordinate 0,0,0. In some cases, it

> ### The Construction Model
>
> Staging, orientation, layout, prefabrication, and assembly are usually figured out in the field. Sometimes they require you to work around obstacles or move originally surveyed references as the project progresses. The construction model therefore does more than represent the building: it also represents the methods that might be used in the actual construction.

might be important to add a construction fence to set the boundaries of the work area.

2. Lay out the construction. For the sitework, this includes stringlines attached to batterboards to lay out the footprint of the building. From this, you can then lay out paving, walkways, and special site conditions.

3. When the layout is ready, you can fabricate the pieces for the assembly. It's important to create distinct objects for each piece of the construction. As you will see by the end of this chapter, however, this will place heavy demands on your computer's ability to calculate a complex model.

4. Assemble the pieces using Hotgrips, OSNAP, and tiled viewports. Snap the pieces onto the stringlines or chalklines. Chalklines are object-specific control points similar to those used in the field by carpenters and others responsible for the frame of the building.

5. Publish the results by moving your viewport and printing or capturing an image for use in illustrating the construction.

With a little practice, you can use the OLPAP checklist, Hotgrips, OSNAP, and tiled viewports to prebuild almost any building.

AutoCAD as a Preconstruction Modeler

As you saw in Figure 6-11, when you open an unmodified version of ACAD, the default window is the two-dimensional X-Y plane. You can tell this by looking at the world coordinate system (WCS) icon in the lower lefthand corner. What you are looking at is the two-dimensional plan view of a three-dimensional space. One of the hardest things for your eyes to do when you look at this blank screen is to visualize where you are within virtual space.

In fact, you are suspended in the air above an infinitely deep world, but there are no visual references to guide your perception. The entire virtual world, or at least the Z-axis of that world, is literally in your face and all you can see is a white (or black) background. It's as if you are looking down from a helicopter, through a cloud, at the flat face of an infinite two-dimensional plane on which you can draft anything you want. Most CAD operators never see beyond this plane. Like the Flatlanders in Chapter 1, their world in confined to drafting lines on the X-Y plane in almost the same way that you might draw lines on a flat piece of paper. But as you know from your three-dimensional drawings, you need the Z-axis to bring an object into the third dimension.

Surrounding the blank background of this screen are the menus and toolbars used to draft in ACAD. These icons are on the side and top of the working window. Each icon is a button that initiates a command. Almost all are necessary for a CAD

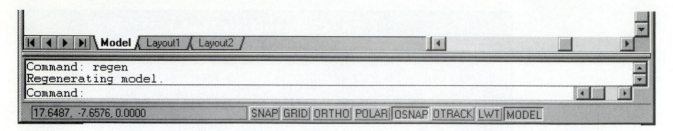

Figure 6-12. The Command line at the bottom of the AutoCAD window records your mouse clicks and prompts you for input.

operator, but only a few will be used to build a preconstruction model. Even more commands are built into the keys. The four most important key commands are:

1. The F1 or Help key is used for AutoCAD's extensive on-line help and tutorial support. Commands and tools add a great deal of power to the basic controls introduced in this chapter.
2. Use the Escape key to cancel the last command. When nothing seems to be happening or the computer seems to be locked up, the solution is almost always to hit the Escape key.
3. The Delete key will erase any object that is selected. First select that object and then hit the Delete key to erase it. You can select as many objects as you want before you hit the Delete key; they will all be erased together.
4. Enter the letter "U" on the command line at the bottom of the ACAD window and press Enter to Undo your last commands. You can undo commands all the way back to your last save.

When you make a menu selection, click on an icon, or press a key command, the command itself is displayed as a prompt on the command line at the bottom of the ACAD window. (See Figure 6-12.) The word or abbreviation that appears is a code word called a line command that can be substituted for any of the tools and menus available in ACAD. There are more line commands than visible icons and menus. The line commands give you direct access to buttons or menu selection and are used by CAD experts because they increase drafting and modeling speed. You will probably use two line commands a lot in preconstruction modeling: the HIDE and REGEN commands. They simplify working with solids because the first will remove hidden lines from a view, and the second will regenerate those lines so you can see through the solid objects.

If you work with this program, you will find that a lot does not meet the eye in ACAD. Most of ACAD's obscurely documented tricks take some experience to learn.

CAD drafting is similar to what you did with hand-drafting, except that the computer mediates your view of the drawing. To draw CAD plans and details in two dimensions, you would have to learn as many of the default menu selections and tools as possible. CAD drafting involves entering lines and other two-dimensional objects like arcs and circles to describe a building. When these objects are recorded in a file, the CAD operator adds dimensions, notes, and detail references in exactly the same step-by-step method used to put together field drawings. It is an extremely tedious process that takes total concentration, which is part of the reason it is so prone to error.

For preconstruction modeling, none of this is necessary because the number of commands is reduced to those necessary to build the model. You ignore almost all the menu selections and most of the icons and toolbars that are visible in the default ACAD window. In fact, you can close these toolbars to simplify the interface prior to building a personal toolbar that includes the basic commands you need to build a model.

Go to the View > Toolbars menu or right click on any toolbar to get the dialog box shown in Figure 6-13. Uncheck all the toolbars listed, except "View" and "Object

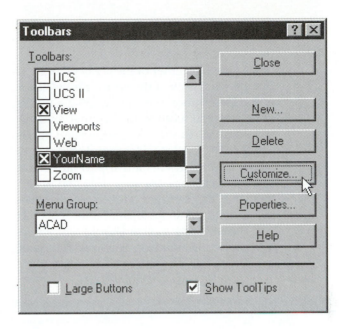

Figure 6-13. You can control the visibility and content of toolbars to simplify preconstruction modeling.

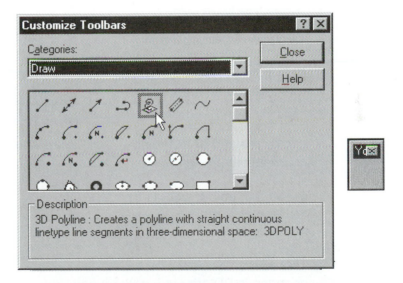

Figure 6-14. Customize a toolbar by choosing a category, then dragging and dropping an icon onto a new toolbar.

Properties." Notice that as you uncheck the toolbars, they disappear from the ACAD window. (You might want to check and uncheck some of the other toolbars on the list to see the range of other commands available.) Now click the "New" button and name a new toolbar after yourself in the naming box. When you click OK, a small blank square appears at the top center of the ACAD window. Drag the new toolbar next to the Customize Toolbars dialog box, shown in Figure 6-14, by its dark blue title bar.

To customize this toolbar, incrementally add the tools necessary to build a pre-construction model. For example, start by adding the Polyline tool by clicking on the "Customize . . ." button in the dialog box shown in Figure 6-13. Then choose "Draw" from the Categories pulldown menu at the top of the Customize Toolbars dialog box shown in Figure 6-14. Note that you can use the scrollbar to the right of the Draw icons to access more tools. There are many tools from which to choose in each one of these tool categories.

At the top center of the array of Draw tools is a button called "3D Polyline." You can tell what each of the buttons is by clicking on it and reading the text that appears in the Description box below. Drag and drop a copy of the 3D Polyline button onto your personal toolbar (the original remains in place). Many tools look exactly alike, so be sure to read the description and get the right one.

Add the Circle tool for round objects and detail symbols, and the Dtext tool for callouts and notes. These tools appear farther down in the Draw category pulldown menu. In the object snaps category, drag and drop the Object Snap Settings icon to your new toolbar. In the Standard category, scroll to the bottom of the large array of tools and drag and drop the "Pan Real Time" and "Zoom Real Time" tools onto the new toolbar.

The resulting toolbar should look something like Figure 6-15 in the preconstruction modeling window. Your personal toolbar and the View toolbar should be on

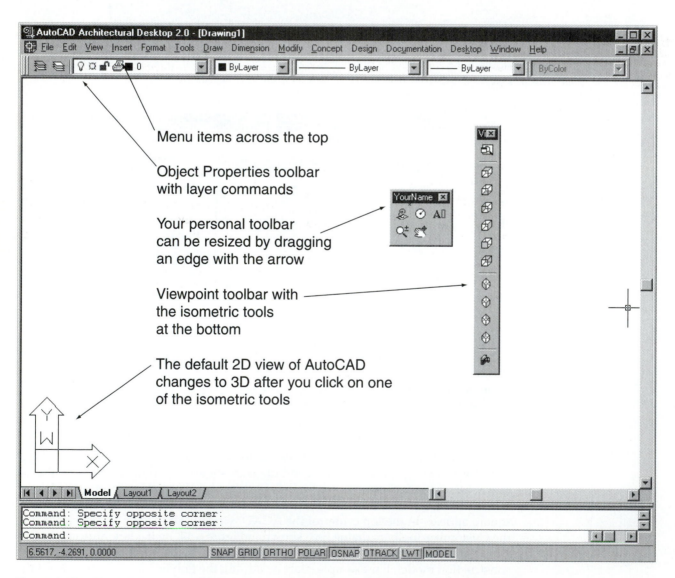

Figure 6-15. The initial window shows only the toolbars you need to begin building the preconstruction model.

Figure 6-16. This icon is for 3D in AutoCAD.

floating palettes. If they are docked, you can make the palettes float by "tearing them" away from their docked position by dragging them to the center of the window. The Object Properties toolbar is probably best docked at the top.

Note that the default two-dimensional WCS icon is visible in the lower left corner. When your tools are ready, the next step is simply a matter of entering three-dimensional space so you can see where you are and visualize where to start the construction. Click on the icon for the SW Isometric View in the isometric group of the Viewpoint toolbar. This will change the WCS icon in the lower left corner to the three-dimensional version shown in Figure 6-16. The W on the Y-axis shows that this is the isometric version of the WCS icon. The icon changes to different isometric orientations as you click the Isometric buttons on the View toolbar. It can also be changed to a user coordinate system (UCS) for making and slicing objects. (This subject will be discussed in more detail later.)

The Preconstruction Modeling Method

Once you're in the three-dimensional environment, follow the OLPAP checklist and think through the construction process. The preconstruction modeling method is almost exactly the same as the process you would use on the jobsite. If you've never built a building before, this process might be a bit intimidating, but the benefit of a preconstruction model is that it gives you the next best thing to a hands-on experience before you get to the field. Follow the process logically to see how things turn out. Chances are you will find that building construction is nothing more than being organized and logical.

As a guide, you can use something called a work breakdown structure (WBS). Almost all buildings are built according to something close to the following outline:

1. Staging and marshalling

    Setup

    Orientation

    Layout, batterboards, stringlines

2. Sitework

    Excavation

    Services and utilities

    Grading and drainage

    Backfill

3. Foundations

    Formwork

    Footings

    Stem walls

    Slabs

    Drainage

4. Framing

    Columns

    Beams

    Joists

    Subfloors

    Studs

    Rafters

    Roof beams

5. Weatherproofing

    Doors and windows

    Siding

    Roofing

6. Fixtures and equipment

    Plumbing

    Mechanical

    Electrical

    Special equipment

7. Furnishings and finish work

    Exterior finishes and landscape features

    Interior finishes

    Cabinets

    Furnishings

Staging and marshalling

In construction, this phase might include finalizing permits, startup meetings, hiring workers, planning the site, and scheduling the equipment. In preconstruction modeling, setting up the site means preparing the virtual site for construction, including general orientation to the program. In other words, make sure you are in an isometric view, set the units to architectural, format the text to correspond to model space, and organize the layers to receive the various pieces as they are constructed. These steps are necessary because ACAD opens with generic settings that have to be changed so that you can use the program to support building construction (see Figure 6-17):

1. First set the units of the Cartesian system to feet and inches. Go to the Format Units menu and click on the architectural button. The tolerances will default to what seems like a pretty extreme setting of 1/16". If you change the setting to something more reasonable, like $^1/_2$", the program will automatically round up its dimensions to match the tolerances. (This chapter does not cover dimensioning a model, but it is something to keep in mind.)

2. Set the style and size of notes to be used for the preconstruction model. Choose Format > Text Style. Then click the New button, name the style, and select a font like Arial from the pulldown menu. Set the height of the font to 12 points (for now). The letters are drawn as three-dimensional objects the same size as the model, so the appearance of these notes will vary as you zoom in and out in the viewport.

3. Open the Layers dialog box by clicking on the Layers tool button in the upper lefthand corner of the standard toolbar. The first layers button allows you to switch from layer to layer according to a selected object. Clicking on the Layers

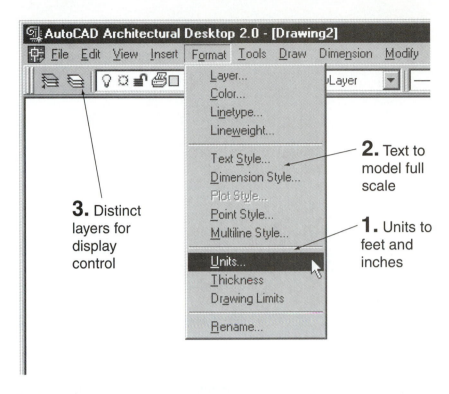

Figure 6-17. The basic setup for three-dimensional modeling includes setting the units, text, and layers for the model.

tool brings up the Layers dialog box. Use this dialog box to create a layer for each of the major components of the model. Basic layers for each item on the WBS include stringline, chalkline, workpoint, and object lines. There can never be too many layers for a model that must be deconstructed.

Once the program is set up, you should save this file as a template to use for other projects and then save a second file specifically for this project.

Sitework

Preconstruction begins when you orient the model to the WCS. For most buildings, this includes adding in boxes for adjacent structures, property and setback lines, and topography and other geographic features. For the trainer, this is simply a matter of setting the benchmark and workpoint and then laying out the stringlines necessary to begin the foundation.

Object Selection
Select objects in one of two ways. First, click on one or more objects, as you have been doing, and second, drag a selection box or marquee around or through them. In ACAD, if you drag from left to right, you must surround the object to select it. If you drag from right to left, you need only to touch the object with the selection box to select it. If you want to "de-select" any object, hold the Shift key down as you click and the handles will disappear.

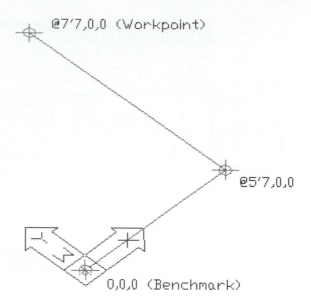
@7'7,0,0 (Workpoint)

@5'7,0,0

0,0,0 (Benchmark)

Figure 6-18. The relative coordinates from the 0,0,0 benchmark to the workpoint at 7'7,5'7,0 are preceeded by the @ symbol.

There are many ways to lay out the construction. For the Trainer, for example, you can use the 3D Polyline tool on the Chalkline layer to set the coordinates for the benchmark and workpoint. First, click on the Polyline tool on your personal toolbar and then input the absolute coordinates of 0,0,0 in response to the command prompt "Specify start point of polyline." As shown in Figure 6-18, this sets the benchmark as the start of the line.

The next prompt asks you to "Specify endpoint of line or [Undo]." Enter the relative coordinates from the benchmark to the workpoint as dimensioned on the site plan. The dimensions extend first along the X-axis 5'0" and then along the Y-axis 10'0". As shown in Figure 6-18, relative coordinates are entered in the format @X,Y,Z. The polyline therefore ends at the workpoint for the trainer.

You can add the text that calls out the benchmark and the workpoint on a different layer with the Dtext tool. First, click on the icon and then click on the spot where you want the text to go. The rotation is usually 0, so press the space bar to accept the default, then enter the text and press the Enter key or space bar twice to enter the text. Notes are useful as model references and reminders. They are placed on the X-Y plane in the 12 point default text style set up earlier.

You can also use Hotgrips to move lines into position, like any other object. For example, you can use Hotgrips to build the layout for the foundation by first fabricating the batterboard and then moving it into position. In the field, batterboards look like fences that surround the site. In ACAD, they are just polylines on the stringline layer. Move them into position by clicking on the line, then clicking on one of the blue boxes (or handles) to get a red grip and then pressing the space bar to switch from Stretch, Move, Rotate, Scale, and Mirror. Note that you can make a copy in association with these commands. You can also use relative coordinates to stretch or move the object precisely. An ORTHO button at the bottom of the ACAD window will restrict the movement of lines and objects in the X- and Y-directions. This will help you align the batterboards and draw out the perpendicular stringlines.

Remember, the Escape key cancels a command in progress or resets the command line. You can also type the U key and press the space bar to undo the last part of a command. The Edit > Undo menu or the Control key and Z also delete the last command.

Once the batterboards are located, use Polyline and OSNAP to snap stringlines and form the intersections of the corners of the foundation pieces. With the ORTHO

> ## Zoom and Pan Tools
>
> You may find it useful to zoom in close and pan around the foundation as you lay it out. Most CAD programs have zoom and pan tools to move around as you input the coordinates and build the model. For example, in ACAD, the 3D Pan tool on your custom toolbar can be used to move laterally to different parts of the window. You can also use the 3D Zoom tool on the same toolbar to zoom in and out as you pan. Note that when you click the 3D Zoom tool, you can make alternate selections, like E for extents or W for window to zoom in different ways. To select one of these alternatives, type in the first letter of the selection and press the Enter key or space bar. To select the default command in parentheses, press the Enter key or space bar without entering a letter. You can also access zoom and pan tools by right-clicking anywhere on the background of the modeling window.

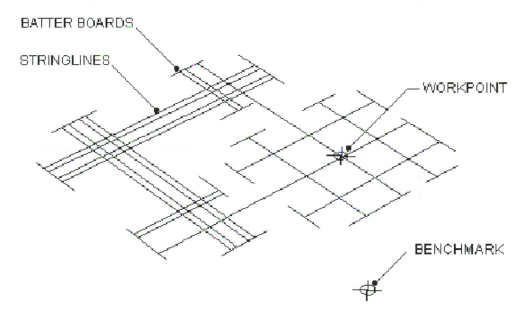

Figure 6-19. The layout for the batterboards and the stringlines for the foundation should test the information on the construction drawings.

and OSNAP buttons on, it is fairly easy to lay out the foundation so that it is accurate and square. As you can imagine, it is much more difficult to do this in the field. Of course, none of these batterboards or stringlines are necessary to build the computer model, but since you are checking the entire process, they can be an important part of making sure that all the information necessary to build the foundation is in the construction drawings.

When the layout for the trainer foundation is complete, it should look something like Figure 6-19. Once the stringlines are set, the site is ready for excavation. In the field, it is important that the batterboards are positioned so that they can be removed for excavation. The idea is to remove the strings, dig down to an approximate depth, and then reinstall the strings to check the position and depth of the bottom of the excavation.

When you break down the construction into its components, the Layer tool and dialog box allow you to control visibility, color, and line weight, as you can see

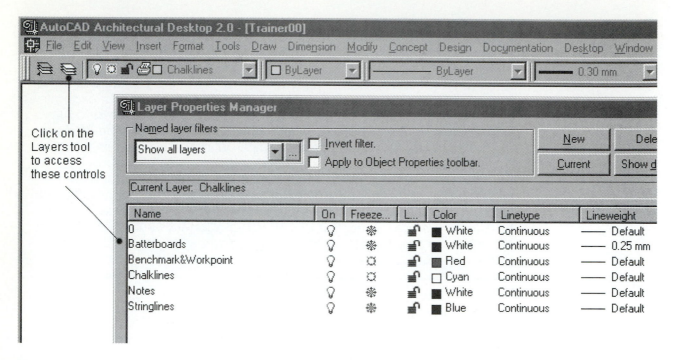

Figure 6-20. The Layers tool brings up a Layer Property Manager that allows you to control the visibility and color of the preconstruction components.

in Figure 6-20. Click on the snowflakes to freeze and unfreeze layers and make them invisible or visible. Click on the color box to change the color for distinct objects. The line weights are more valuable for plotting drawings and are not always visible in a preconstruction model.

The depth of an excavation and the slope or angle of repose surrounding the cut are functions of the existing soil conditions. If the soil is hard and stable, it should be relatively easy to move in an excavator and cut the holes according to the grades established in the foundation plan and sections. The excavation should also include at least 6 inches of clearance to work around the footings. Some jobs might require more room; others might need much less. The rule to remember with excavation is that you pay to remove the soil and then pay to put a lot of it back, so you do not want to dig out anything unless it is absolutely necessary.

Cutting the foundation for a preconstruction model can be as simple as building a wireframe below the ground to represent the area to be excavated. As shown in Figure 6-21, this is done by first deciding the point for the toe of the slope at the bottom of the hole, the angle of repose for the cut, and the top of the slope based on the soil conditions. If there is a lot of room, a gentle angle will not be important. If there are buildings nearby or it's possible for the soil to cave in, you may have to consider special shoring or temporary retaining walls.

Figure 6-22 shows a wireframe of the excavation for the trainer. The bottom of the footing sets the bottom of the excavation, and the volume of soil that must be removed is the negative volume represented by the model. Use the Polyline tool on an Excavation layer to trace the footing perimeter at the intersection of the stringlines on the XY-plane. (See Figure 6-23.) Then use Hotgrips to move the perimeter lines down the Z-axis to the bottom of the footing. New polylines can then be extended back up to the finished grade with a taper angle from the dropped perimeter of the footing.

The intersections of the stringlines should already mark these locations, so it's simply a matter of snapping new lines into place. In the field, carpenters would drop

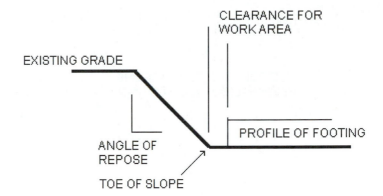

Figure 6-21. The extent of the excavation will depend on the angle of repose, soil conditions, and proximity of adjacent structures.

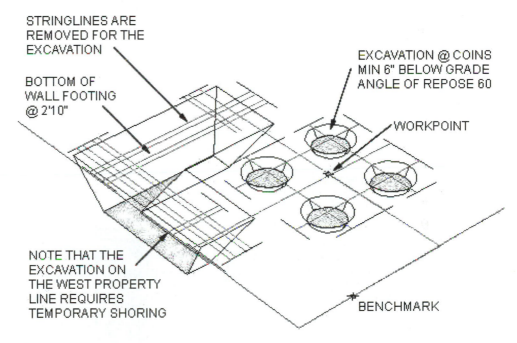

Figure 6-22. The wireframe for the excavation shows the extent of the excavation required for the construction.

plumb bobs down from the stringlines to locate the concrete forms. You can simulate this by dropping lines from the critical stringline intersections.

For the trainer, note how the model shows that the angle of repose on the west side cuts across the property line. The excavation will thus require a temporary retaining wall to prevent intruding on the neighboring property. The temporary retaining wall is not something that needs to be shown on the drawing, but it would be efficient to note the condition for the actual construction.

Foundations

To prepare for the foundation's construction, add solid modeling tools to your toolbar. First, right-click on your personal toolbar and then click on the Customize button. From the Solids category, drag and drop the Extrude, Slice, Box, and Cylinder tools. (Ignore the Wedge tool for now.) Be sure to read each description carefully because many tools look alike. Select the Modify category and add the Union and

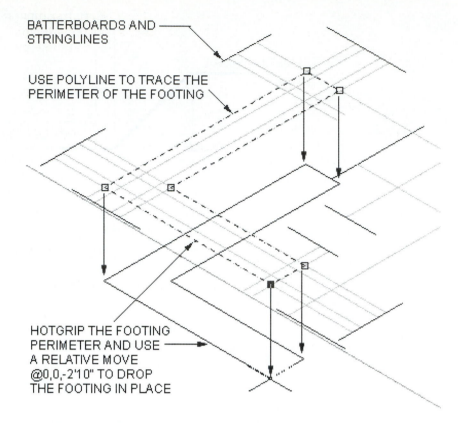

BATTERBOARDS AND
STRINGLINES

USE POLYLINE TO TRACE THE
PERIMETER OF THE FOOTING

HOTGRIP THE FOOTING
PERIMETER AND USE
A RELATIVE MOVE
@0,0,-2'10" TO DROP
THE FOOTING IN PLACE

Figure 6-23. Use the Polyline tool on a separate layer to outline the footing, then Hotgrip the footing perimeter and move it down to the bottom of the footing.

Figure 6-24. Add solid tools to your custom toolbar.

Subtract tools at the bottom of the array of icons. With these tools, you can build, cut, and shape almost any object in a building's construction.

Your personal toolbar should look like Figure 6-24 when you are finished. Note that the tools do not need to be in exactly the same order as they appear in this illustration. You can drag and drop the tools onto any part of the toolbar and order them any way that you want. You can also reshape the toolbar by moving your cursor over one of the edges and dragging the edge when an arrow appears at the cursor's position.

With these solid modeling tools, you can build almost any piece of a building. First, use the drawings to lay out the construction. Second, fabricate the pieces in a separate area so they can be copied and moved into position. For example, to build the foundation, you should have the chalklines prepared for the assembly and the pieces of the foundation fabricated as solids. When these pieces are ready, all you have to do is snap them into place.

For the trainer's foundation, you need only the Polyline tool to lay out the chalklines; the Box tool for the footings and concrete block; the Slice, Union, and Subtract tools to modify the boxes; and the Circle and Extrude tools as alternate ways to make a solid. You can also use these tools to make and then trim and shape the rectilinear objects, including long or thin objects like 2×4's, plywood, or other pieces of formwork or falsework required to build the foundation. Other solid objects include cylinders and wedges, which are sometimes combined with boxes to create complex shapes. For example, cylinders are useful to drill holes in objects with the Subtract tool.

You can use the Box tool to build segments of the footings and then join them with the Union tool (see Figure 6-25):

1. Click the Box icon on the personal toolbar and follow the command prompts.
2. Specify any corner of the box that defines the footing by clicking on an intersection of the chalkline layout or inputting the coordinates to start the construction.
3. The command line will immediately ask "Specify a corner or [Cube/Length]." Enter an "L" for length and follow the prompts for length, width, and height.

   Length = X-direction in feet and inches, either negative or positive

   Width = Y-direction in feet and inches, either negative or positive

   Height = Z-direction in feet and inches, either negative or positive

4. Build a box for the length, width, and height of the footing in two pieces. This should be fairly easy if your chalklines are placed properly.
5. To join the two boxes into a single footing, click on the Union tool on your personal toolbar. Follow the command prompts. First, select the objects to join and then press the space bar or the Enter key.

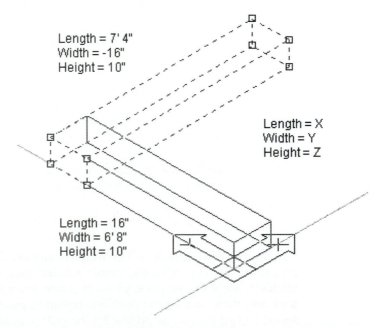

Length = 7' 4"
Width = -16"
Height = 10"

Length = X
Width = Y
Height = Z

Length = 16"
Width = 6' 8"
Height = 10"

Figure 6-25. Use the construction drawings to build the footings from two solid boxes. Then use the Union tool to join them.

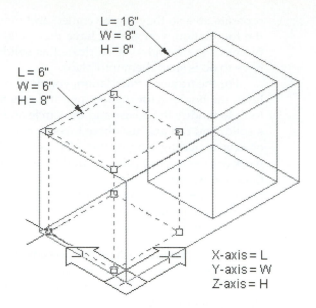

L = 16"
W = 8"
H = 8"

L = 6"
W = 6"
H = 8"

X-axis = L
Y-axis = W
Z-axis = H

Figure 6-26. The concrete block is made when two boxes are subtracted from a third.

Remember to use the HIDE and REGEN line commands as you work with solids. The 3D Zoom and 3D Pan tools will not work when an object is hidden, so you have to use the REGEN command to bring the objects back to wireframes and to use these tools.

To make a concrete block, use a new layer called Wallblock and the Box tool. Build three boxes to the lengths, widths, and heights shown in Figure 6-26. Position the smaller boxes with Hotgrips and relative coordinates, and then use the Subtract command to form the hollow concrete block. To use the Subtract tool, click on the icon, select the larger box, and press the space bar. Then select the smaller boxes to subtract them.

After fabricating the concrete block, you need to duplicate it, and then slice the copy in half to make two half-blocks. Use the Slice tool and OSNAPs to cut the block (see Figure 6-27):

1. Click on the Slice icon on your toolbar. At the command prompt, select the concrete block.
2. When you press the space bar, five options appear on the command line (Object, Z-axis, View, XY, YZ, and ZX). Each describes a different cutting plane. The plane that will cut this block vertically at the center is YZ.
3. Make sure OSNAP > Midpoint is checked in the OSNAP Tab of the Drafting Settings dialog box. Then enter a Y on the command line and press the space bar.
4. Click on the concrete block at the midpoint. Enter a B to keep both sides of the slice and press the space bar. You will see a line appear at the plane of the slice.
5. Use Hotgrips to move the pieces apart. The two half-blocks are shown in Figure 6-27.

You can also extrude solids from two-dimensional shapes. In Figure 6-28, for example, the coins used in the trainer's foundation are extruded from two concentric circles made with the circle tool. On a new layer called ConcCoins, click the Circle tool, and then click on the chalkline layout to position the center of the larger circle. Input a 12 on the command line for the radius, or input a D for Diameter and a 24 for the diameter. Press the space bar to complete the command. Now do the same for the smaller 3" diameter circle in the center. To extrude the circles, click on the Extrude

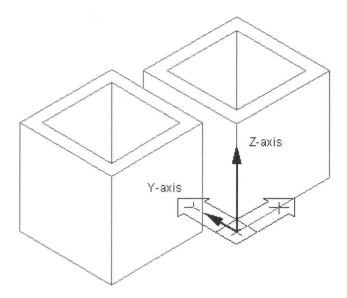

Figure 6-27. Slice the concrete block along the Y-Z plane to make two half-blocks.

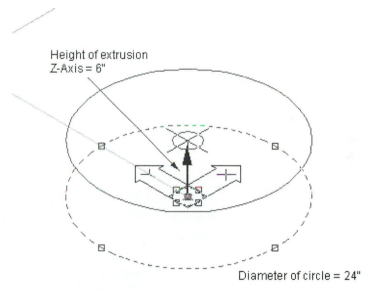

Figure 6-28. The Extrude tool will turn any two-dimensional object into a three-dimensional object by adding the third dimension.

tool, select both circles, and enter a 6 for the height of the extrusion and a 0 for the angle of the taper.

In Figure 6-29, extrude the steel inserts that are cast into the coins in the same way. This time, however, extrude two concentric circles on a Steelinsert layer to make two concentric cylinders. Then use the Subtract tool to eliminate the center cylinder and form the steel tubing. The threaded steel plug was inserted with Hotgrips after being extruded from its own set of circles in the same way. The diameter of the plug's outside circle is 2.75", and the diameter of the hole is 1". (The threads themselves require a double helix that is beyond the needs of a preconstruction model.) The rectangular rebar flange was fabricated using the Box tool. The Subtract tool was used to remove the five cylindrical shapes for the 3" diameter insert and the four $^{5}/_{8}$" holes. Figure 6-29 shows the finished steel tube and flange with its plug as it was detailed in the hand-

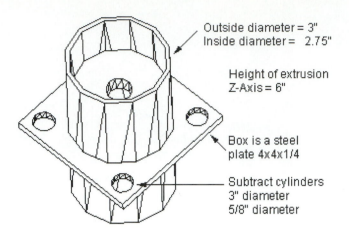

Outside diameter = 3"
Inside diameter = 2.75"

Height of extrusion
Z-Axis = 6"

Box is a steel
plate 4x4x1/4

Subtract cylinders
3" diameter
5/8" diameter

Figure 6-29. The steel insert is an extrusion of two concentric circles grouped with a welded plug and with a 1" diameter hole.

Figure 6-30. You can keep several objects together with the Group command.

drawing in step 6. You can use Hotgrips to insert it into the coin and group it with the concrete coin.

When the steel insert is in place in the concrete coin, use the GROUP command to group the precast coin and the insert as a single assembly. Enter GROUP on the Command line in either upper- or lowercase and then press the space bar. In the dialog box shown in Figure 6-30, enter a Group Name, check the Selectable checkbox, and click New. The box disappears, and the Command line prompts you to select the

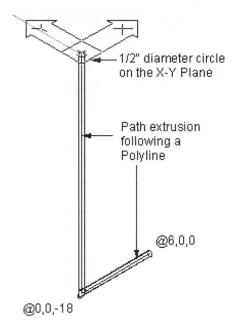

1/2" diameter circle
on the X-Y Plane

Path extrusion
following a
Polyline

@6,0,0

@0,0,-18

Figure 6-31. A path extrusion extrudes an object along a polyline.

objects for the group. Again, press the space bar to enter the objects. When the dialog box reappears, simply click OK. (With the PICKSTYLE variable set to 1, selecting either the coin or the insert will select the entire group.)

Figure 6-31 shows a path extrusion for the J-bar that connects the footing and the concrete block stem wall. To make this extrusion, use the same Extrude tool. This time, however, use a Path to control the length and direction of the extrusion.

1. Use the Circle tool to build a $^1/_2$" diameter circle on the X-Y plane. Select the Circle tool, and then click on a chalkline to position the center of the extrusion.
2. Use the Polyline tool to create a three-dimensional two-leg polyline in the shape of the rebar on the X-Z plane. The polyline should start in the center of the circle.
3. With the Center option in OSNAP, click on the center of the circle. Then use relative coordinates to draw the line.
4. When both the circle and the line path are ready, click on the Extrude tool, select an object, and press the space bar. Then enter a P for path and select the Polyline.

Use the Box and Subtract tools on your personal toolbar to build all the pieces for the frame of the trainer according to the drawings and details. These pieces include the gravel base, the stair slab with threaded inserts, and the shaped concrete slabs between the coins.

Assembling the foundation: Fabricating these pieces in a materials yard on the virtual jobsite will help you visualize the extent of the assembly and the amount of storage that may be necessary at different stages of the project. For the foundation, the best way to proceed is to follow the probable sequence of the installation.

Once the pieces are fabricated, it's simply a matter of assembling them according to the drawings. Keep in mind that you must simulate the construction process and therefore think through the methodology that will be used in the field. It is easy to get carried away with building the model and forget that you are really

Multiple Views

Assembly is easier with multiple viewports. Split the screen into two viewports by selecting View > Viewports > 2 Viewports, and then enter V for vertical. Click on a viewport to make it active, and use Zoom and Pan to position the fabricated pieces in one viewport and the stringline and chalkline layout in the other. You can now use Hotgrips to snap the pieces into place by gripping them in one viewport and dragging them to the other. Change your viewpoints regularly so you can see the pieces come together from different angles.

preconstructing a building to test the construction drawings. Therefore, the assembly process is as follows:

1. Select an object or group of objects either directly or with a selection box.
2. Get a Hotgrip by clicking on one of the handles. Then use the space bar to cycle to the command you want (either Move or Rotate).
3. Enter a C to make a copy. Leave the original and drag the copy to the assembly area.
4. With the OSNAP button turned on below the Command line, you can snap the object to the intersection of a stringline or a chalkline.
5. Use Hotgrips and a relative move again to make adjustments or place the pieces into their final position.

The HIDE and REGEN commands are even more important when assembling solids because, in many cases, you get so many lines you no longer know which lines belong to which object. Remember, 3D Zoom and 3D Pan will not work when objects are hidden. You must use REGEN before you can use these tools. You can also control visibility by freezing and thawing layers in the Layers Property Manager dialog box. Unlike turning layers off or on, freezing layers makes objects invisible to both the HIDE and REGEN commands.

Figure 6-32 shows the final assembly of the trainer foundation with the concrete block wall under construction. Note that the actual assembly occurs in the left viewport; the materials yard containing the pieces is in the right. In the example, the concrete blocks are dragged from a southwest view on the right to a northwest view of the foundation on the left. These views vary with the current tasks. Many pieces can be preassembled in the materials yard and installed as a prefabricated group. Breaking down the work into these kinds of components and figuring out the most efficient way to put things together takes a great deal of experience and skill. In many ways it is the very essence of what it takes to be a good constructor. For some, it comes naturally; for others, it takes a lot of practice. This book and the trainer are designed to give you practice, so try to think through the management of the assembly and not just putting together the pieces. With good drawings, many skilled workers will be able to fabricate these pieces.

You will need to check the dimensions and elevations of your assembly regularly. Just like a real building, a slight error in the layout is something that will haunt you all the way through the finish work, so you want to make sure everything is installed according to the dimensions on the drawings. To check dimensions and the position of objects, you need the two new tools shown at the bottom of the personal toolbar in

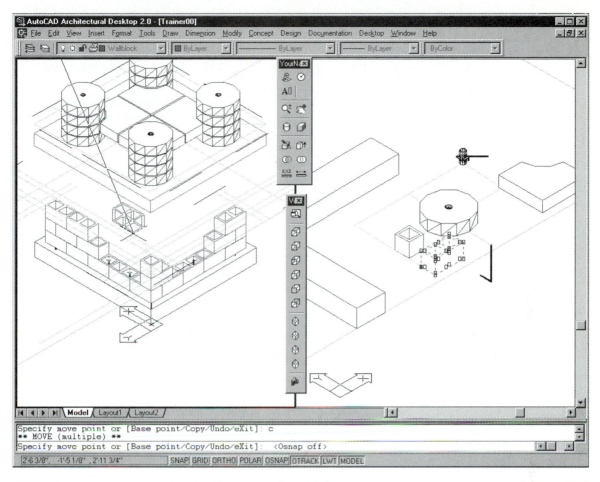

Figure 6-32. You can use Hotgrips with Move and/or Rotate to drag materials from the materials yard to the assembly area and thus visualize the construction method.

Figure 6-32. Right-click a toolbar and choose Customize. Then click the Customize button, and drag and drop the Distance and Locate Point tools from the Object Properties category. With OSNAP on, these tools can be used like a measuring tape to check distances or the coordinates and alignment of a particular point. Note also the Area and Mass Properties icons, which can be useful in calculating square footages or volumes. Your personal toolbar should now be ready for final assembly. Figure 6-33 shows the foundation complete and ready for the framing.

You may have noticed that your computer seems to be getting bogged down as you zoom in and out and move around the modeling environment. Each new viewport means that the modeling software and the computer's hardware need to recalculate all the lines associated with all the objects visible in that new position or view. In addition, when you execute a HIDE command, it takes longer to hide the lines in the object because both software and hardware must recompute the position of all the hidden lines in that view.

One way to avoid this slowdown is to freeze the layers that are not being used so they are not calculated while you are working on other parts of the model. In ACAD, you can freeze the layers for the stem wall footing, concrete block, concrete slab, gravel base and the excavation because they will not be necessary to complete the framing. In other words, you remove everything from view except the pieces that are

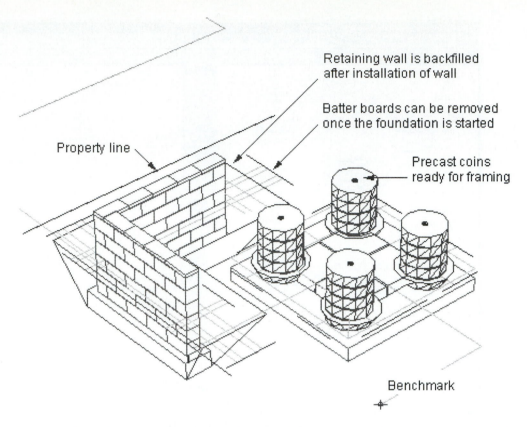

Retaining wall is backfilled
after installation of wall

Batter boards can be removed
once the foundation is started

Property line

Precast coins
ready for framing

Benchmark

Figure 6-33. The completed foundation ready for framing. Note that the benchmark and the layout lines are still available for future assemblies.

necessary to the work at hand. Freezing a layer removes the objects on that layer from the calculations. Turning a layer on and off with the light bulb removes the objects on the layer from plotting, but they are still part of the calculations and their ghosted images will sometimes block the view of another solid. Figure 6-34 shows the layers that you can freeze and still complete the framing in the next section.

Framing

Fabricating the pieces for the framing of a building means reading the construction drawings, planning your approach to the assembly, and then fabricating the parts necessary to build the main structure. Of course, the framing materials attach to the foundations to support the main structure, so most of this planning is done by pure logic. The framing materials are brought onto the jobsite as soon as the foundation is complete. For example, a traditional single-story, woodframe building starts with the sill plates on a slab or foundation wall; goes through the floor joist, subfloor, and wall studs; and then goes up to the roof framing.

For preconstruction, follow the plans, sections, and details and imagine putting them together in the same logical sequence. The objective is to test the notes and dimensions on the construction drawings. If the model can be built from the plans, chances are more likely that the building can be built with the same drawings in the field. At the very least, you will find the conflicts and missing information early in the

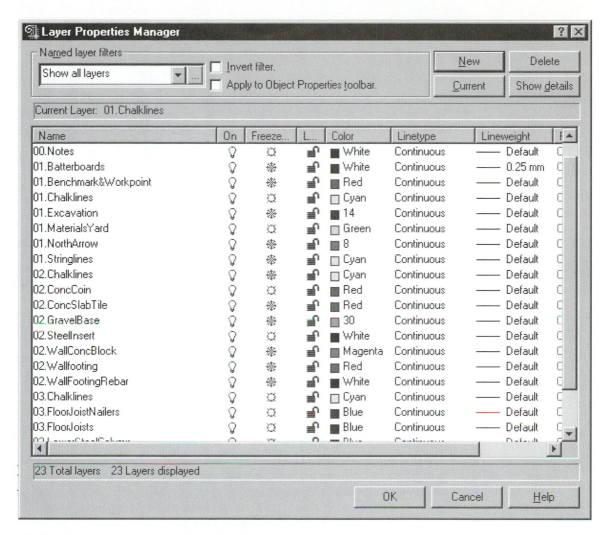

Figure 6-34. Freezing layers suppresses recalculation of the objects on that layer and speeds computations of the visible lines during modeling.

planning phase and thus alleviate some of the potential communications problems that will occur in the field.

For the trainer framing, this testing begins in Figure 6-35 with the four lower columns that bolt to the threaded rods secured in the steel inserts of the precast concrete coins. The columns are made according to the drawings and using the Extrude tool in exactly the same way used to make the cylindrical pieces of the foundation. The pieces that make up the floor framing system attach to these columns, along with the stair header and main stringers.

Use the Box tool to make the pieces of the floor framing. The Subtract tool can be used to drill holes in the steel plates by subtracting solid cylinders once they are in position. Like the foundation pieces, the pieces for the framing can be fabricated in a common area and moved and rotated into position to complete the assembly. Be certain to put the pieces on different layers. As shown in Figure 6-34, these layers should be numbered and titled according to the WBS. You will thus be able to turn various layers on and off in the future to access specific areas of the model and display

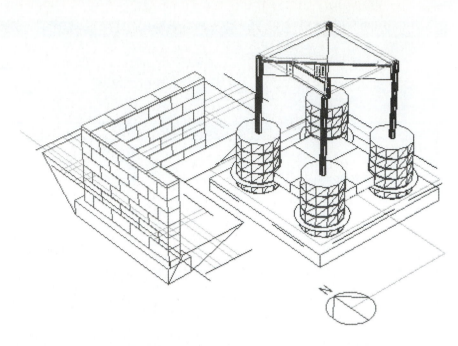

Figure 6-35. Once the foundation pieces are in place and squared, you can use the construction drawings to install the raised floor framing, in preparation for the stair and roof framing.

particular combinations of pieces. None of this can be done without chalklines, however, either in the real world or in preconstruction. In Figures 6-35 and 6-36, note the layout lines used to assemble and snap pieces together within the framing. When the floor is in place, it acts as a platform for installing the bent-steel columns that frame the roof shown in Figure 6-36.

You will find it much easier to fabricate and assemble these pieces if you move the WCS to the surface or plane of the work area. This technique simplifies the relative coordinates for the piece that you are building and allows you to shift your reference to the specific planes of their construction. For example, Figure 6-37 shows how a stair baluster can be trimmed and mitered by shifting the Cartesian coordinates to set up the Slice tool with a chalkline, which is exactly the way you might cut these pieces in the field.

1. Find the face (X-Y plane) of the piece of wood (or box) where the cut would occur.
2. Orient your square to draw a line or chalkline for the cut (or slice). The cut is perpendicular to the surface marked with the layout line.
3. Cut the post along the plane of the saw following the layout lines. The saw defines a new cutting plane.

In AutoCAD, repositioning the X-Y plane to make these modifications shifts the coordinates to a new set of three-dimensional references called a user coordinate system (UCS). As shown in Figure 6-16, the WCS is the default XYZ position for ACAD and is shown by a W on the UCS icon. The UCS is user-defined and has no W in the icon.

To move the UCS, enter UCS on the Command line, then enter M for Move, and press the space bar. In response to the command prompt, select new origin. With OSNAP on, click on the point where you want to locate the new UCS origin. To rotate the UCS, press the space bar or right-click to repeat the UCS command, but this

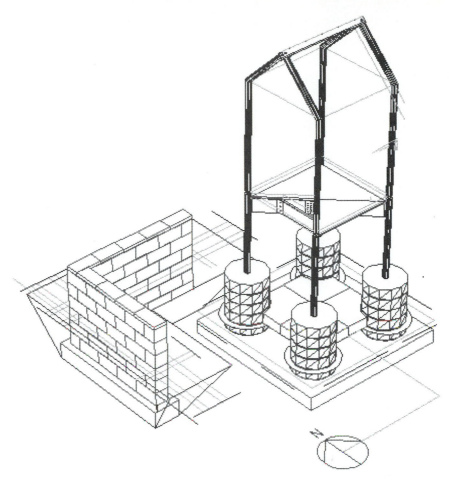

Figure 6-36. Once the floor framing is in place, the upper columns, ridge brackets, and roof beams can be set in place, in preparation for the rafters and skylight headers.

time enter N for New to get a new set of eight different command prompts. These are all axes of rotation. Input one of the axes and then the number of degrees you want to rotate it. Positive numbers rotate counterclockwise; negative angles rotate clockwise.

Figure 6-38 shows the steps necessary to fabricate and place the welded tab on one of the lower columns. Copy and rotate this column around the Z-axis of the WCS for each of the four corners to start the framing. The fabrication of these pieces follows the same OLPAP checklist steps for the main construction:

1. Move the UCS to a new origin at the center of the column. Then reenter the UCS command, with N for New, Z for the Z-axis of rotation, and negative 45 degrees for a clockwise rotation. This will align the plane with the center of the welded plate.
2. Lay out a chalkline where the steel tab attaches to the column by running a chalkline down from the end along the outside surface of the column. Draw a polyline down the center of the column and then Hotgrip > Move > Copy the line in the X- or the Y-direction the distance of the radius.
3. The tab itself can be fabricated once the chalkline is in place. Use the Box tool to make the steel tab. With OSNAP on and the layer the same as the column,

Figure 6-37. The WCS can be moved to a new position, called a user coordinate system (UCS), to facilitate fabrication and assembly.

click on the endpoint of the chalkline. Enter the length, width, and height according to a UCS oriented in the direction of either side of the tab thickness.
4. Weld the tab and the column together with the Union tool, and either delete the chalklines or turn off the Chalkline layer.

Study the drawings to determine which materials need to be fabricated to complete the framing. You can fabricate these pieces using the same tools and techniques already introduced. A single manufacturer would probably produce all the steel according to shop drawings drawn either by its own employees or by an engineer or professional detailer. Shop drawings would also be useful for the construction of the stair, especially if it were to be built by an outside manufacturer or fabricator. These shop drawings would have to be reviewed by the constructor prior to fabrication. In other words, these drawings are redrawn by the manufacturer to verify the actual pieces to be fabricated. Shop drawings would be necessary only for a very complex set of field drawings. Most field drawings act as shop drawings for the main construction.

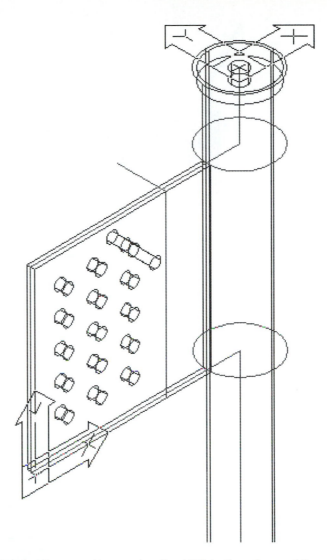

Figure 6-38. Fabrication requires moving the UCS to the plane of the work and creating layout lines to build the pieces.

The pieces produced for the assembly could be set up in a materials yard either on or off site, depending on the staging requirements. Figure 6-39 shows the materials yard for the trainer at this stage. Note that the materials for the foundation are also included. Only one of each piece of the frame is necessary because Hotgrips allows you to move and copy before dragging and dropping the piece from one viewport to the other.

Assembling the frame: Once the pieces are fabricated, you can complete the assembly for the trainer's frame. Again, it should be done in the most logical sequence of construction and should include staging the materials and thinking through the most efficient method possible. Finding out what works and does not work is part of the preconstruction model, so it is important to remember that you are testing the drawings. You want to make sure the information necessary to build the building is readily available to the workers in the field. If information is not available on the drawings or it is in the wrong place, be certain to write a note so that it can be corrected later.

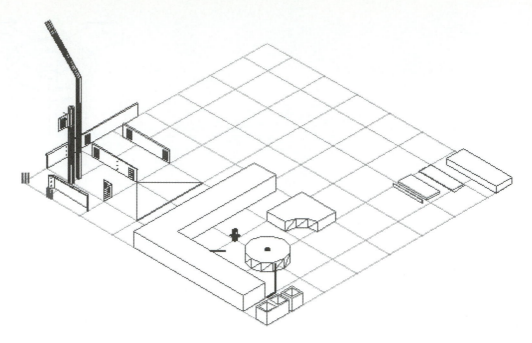

Figure 6-39. Setting up a materials yard is useful because it means piece fabrication can be done away from the main model. This can make it easier to see the piece because it would be isolated from the work area.

Figure 6-40. The 3D Rotation tool is necessary to orient the pieces for assembly.

To assemble the frame of the trainer, you need the new tool shown in the second row of Figure 6-40. This tool allows you to rotate the objects in three dimensions so that they can be snapped into position with the OSNAP tool. To add this tool to your personal toolbar, right-click any toolbar, choose customize, and click on the Customize button. Select the Modify category, and drag and drop the Rotate 3D tool onto your toolbar. Now use the framing plans to assemble the trainer. First, set the lower columns onto the inserts in the precast concrete coins. Then drag and drop the steel framing for the floor from the materials yard.

1. Select the piece and click a handle to get a Hotgrip. Use the space bar to cycle to the Move command, and enter a C for copy.

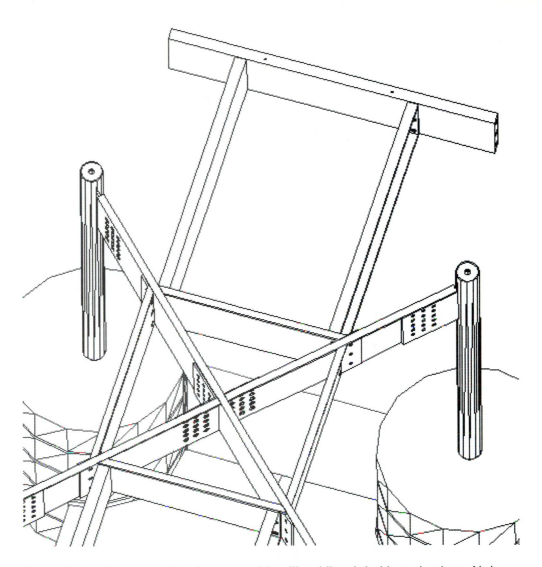

Figure 6-41. Close-up of the floor assembly without the stair stringer in place. Note that the columns are rotated copies of one piece in the materials yard.

2. Drag the copy to the work area in the adjacent viewport and click to place the piece close to the point of assembly.
3. To rotate the piece, click on the new Rotate 3D tool and select the object.
4. Follow the command prompts, and choose an axis for rotation and a point on the access. The rotation angle is the degree of rotation that you want to turn the object.

Once the object is oriented in the work area, use Hotgrips and OSNAP to snap the piece into position. This cannot occur unless there is a chalkline already in place to position the object. Think of this as a marker that ensures the alignment of the pieces for correct placement.

Figure 6-41 shows a close-up of the floor framing and lower columns in position, and Figure 6-42 shows the stair stringers and treads without the floor panels. Figure 6-43 shows the completed assemblies for the floor, with the roof columns and ridge

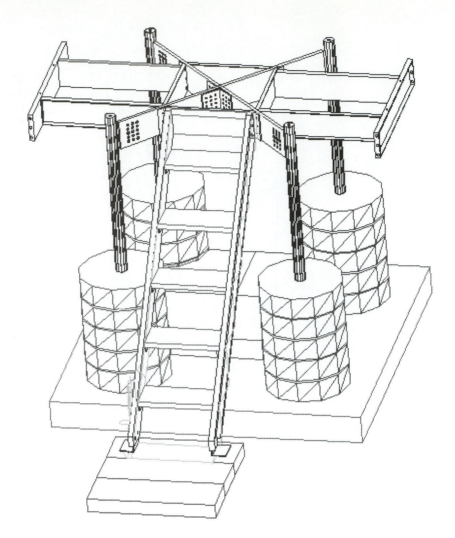

Figure 6-42. The stair stringers and stairs are in place with the completed floor framing. The subfloor is omitted.

beam in place. The trainer is now ready for the floor panels, the rafters, and suspension pieces for the roof framing.

Roof framing: With the details drawn in step 6, the pieces for the roof framing are fairly straightforward. All these pieces can be fabricated with the tools in your personal toolbar. For example, to make the steel rafter shown in Figure 6-44:

1. Use the Box command to make a solid box that is $1\frac{1}{2}"\times3"\times72"$ long. This box represents the outside edges of the metal rafter.
2. Use the Box command again to make a box slightly smaller than this box. This box will be subtracted from the inside of the first box to form the extruded C-shaped rafter. The size of the subtracted solid varies with the thickness of the steel.
3. Use the 3D Polyline tool to position the Slice tool and cut away the flanges at the ridgeline. Use the Box and Union tools to make and join the tabs necessary for the attachment. (See Figure 6-45.)
4. Make a box for the bushing and put it in place at the opposite end of the bent tabs before drilling it with a $\frac{3}{4}"$ cylinder. (See Figure 6-46.) To drill the pieces, lay out the center of the hole on the face of the bushing with a chalkline and

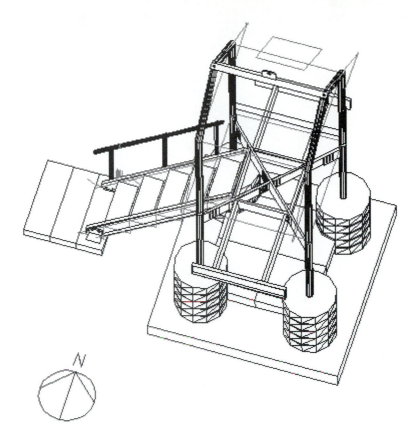

Figure 6-43. The completed framing for the floor and stair, with the roof columns and ridge beam in place.

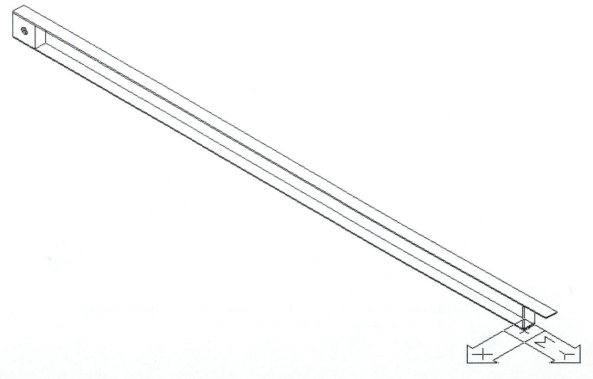

Figure 6-44. The rafters can be fabricated with the Box and Subtract commands. Make one box for the outer shell and another to subtract and form the C-shape of the rafter.

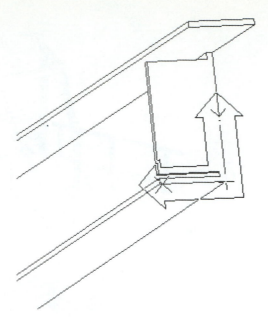

Figure 6-45. The tabs are formed using the Slice command and then making flat tabs to Union tabs into place.

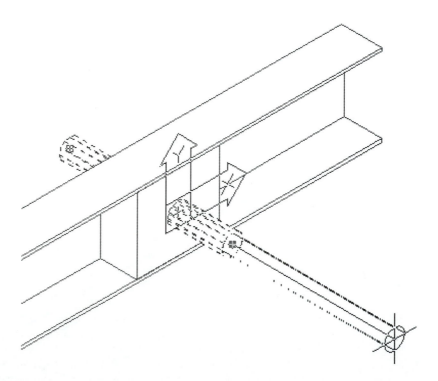

Figure 6-46. The bushing and the steel rafter are drilled at the same time with a cylinder that is subtracted from both.

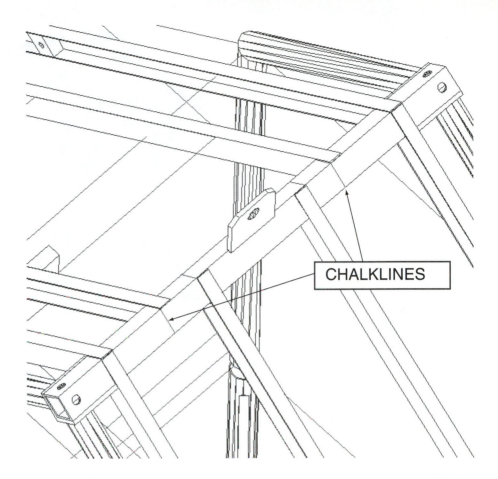

CHALKLINES

Figure 6-47. Chalklines are used to set the rafters on the ridge beam in almost the same way they would be located in the field.

> move the origin of the UCS command to position the base of the cylinder. Once it is in place, use the Cylinder command to make the cylinder through the two objects and the Subtract command to create the hole.

Once the rafters are ready, you can use the same details to fabricate the ridge beam brackets, compression arm, and the suspension rod so that they too are ready to be moved and copied into position. These pieces have to be fabricated exactly according to the drawings to get them to fit in place and thus have the roof assembled correctly. If the drawings are wrong, the roof will not fit together correctly. The accuracy of the dimensions on the details is therefore essential to prevent incorrect fabrication or placement in the field. Either error can delay the construction schedule.

Assembling the roof framing: No new tools are necessary to assemble the roof. The process is more complicated, however, because the rafters have to be rotated in three dimensions through several intermediate steps to get them to fit onto the ridge beam. If the ridge beam and rafters were manufactured correctly, this assembly should start with the selection of each piece from the materials yard. Get a Hotgrip and then use Move and Copy to place that piece near the work area. Once the piece is adjacent to the assembly, it's easier to orient it before snapping it to the chalklines that mark its final position.

Figure 6-47 shows the ridge beam with chalklines marking the location of the rafters. The rafters snap onto these chalklines in the same way that you would mark

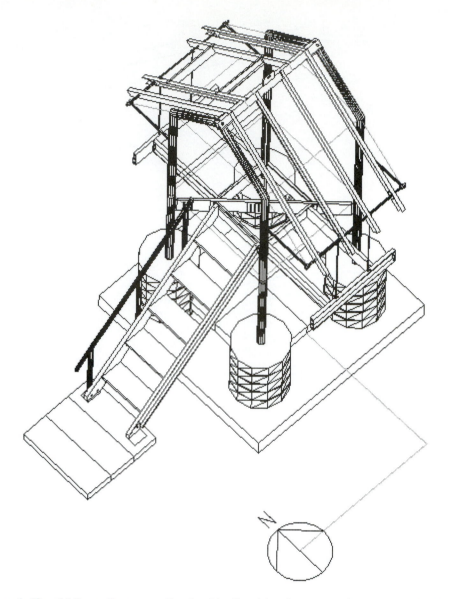

Figure 6-48. All the rafters are attached to the ridge beam and are supported by the compression arms.

Check for Different Views

Check your work from different angles continually as you complete these assemblies to make certain they fit together correctly. When you put items together in three-dimensional space, what looks right in one view will often be aligned incorrectly when it is viewed from a different perspective. The tiled viewports help to check your work, but it is still a good idea to use the View toolbar and Zoom and Pan to check the final assembly quickly.

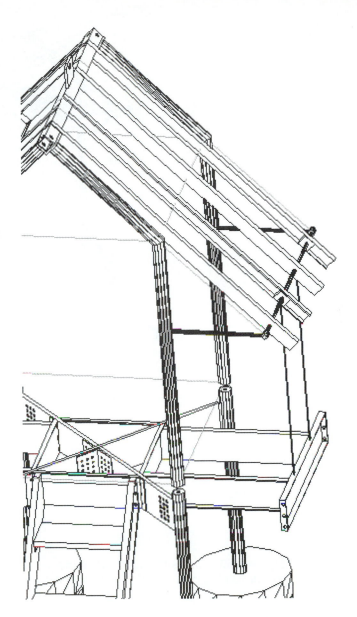

Figure 6-49. The upper ends of the rafters are attached to the ridge beam. They work with the compression arms and horizontal header to support the floor extension.

the ridge beam prior to attaching the steel rafters. Figure 6-48 shows all the rafters in place with the compression arms, horizontal threaded header, and tension rods. Figure 6-49 shows a closer view of the horizontal header, suspension rods, and compression arm as they work to counteract the weight of the floor extension. With all the pieces for the roof assembled, use a Hide command to view the roof as the completed structure shown in Figure 6-50.

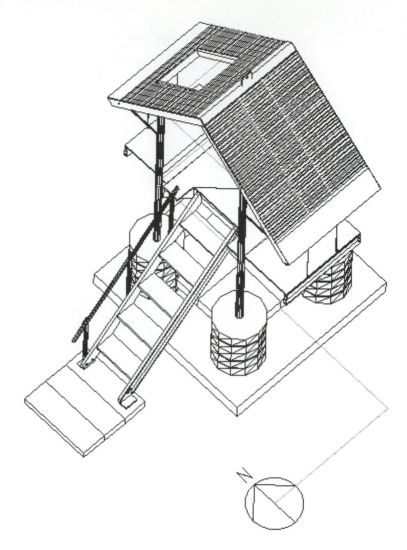

Figure 6-50. Once the framing is in place, the corrugated metal roofing and sheet metal flashing can be installed to seal the roof in preparation for the walls.

Wall and Ceiling Panels

Figure 6-51 shows fourteen wall panels, six ceiling panels, two windows, two clerestories, and a prehung door assembly for the trainer used in this book. Each of the wall panels has a wood frame with an insulated core sandwiched between an interior and exterior skin. The strength of the panel comes from the integration of the frame and the skin as a single unit. Its energy value is determined by the specifications for the core insulation and its thickness.

The drawings for the trainer show a 2×2 wood frame, with a $1\frac{1}{2}$″ injected foam core sandwiched between an interior skin of perforated high-density fiberboard and an exterior skin of $\frac{1}{4}$″ marine grade plywood. A wood frame is used because it has a better insulating value than lightweight steel and will be easier to adjust and secure to the trainer's steel frame. The panels do not have internal mechanical or electrical ducting or wiring and can be prefabricated easily to match the dimensions shown on the drawings.

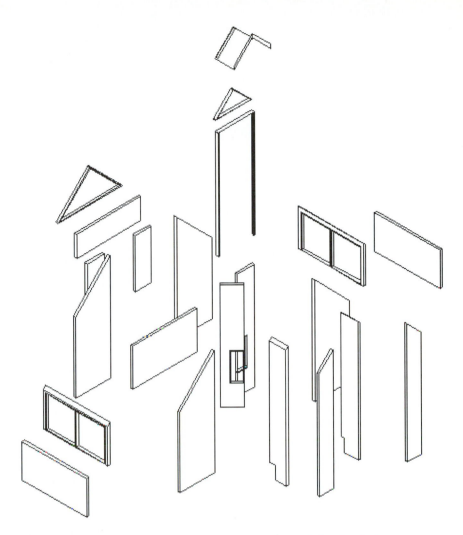

Figure 6-51. The dimensions of the prefabricated panels for the trainer must be calculated from the field drawings. To make sure they are correct, shop drawings would probably be required before the panels are actually manufactured.

Because the panels are prefabricated, they would be built to the overall shapes of the panels as they fit in the wall and should fit together in the field for rapid construction and deconstruction. The panel sizes might be shown in a schedule in the drawings or determined in shop drawings by the manufacturer. In either case, it is the overall shape that is most important to check in the preconstruction model, so constructing each panel is simply a matter of interpreting the drawings and slicing a box to match the required dimensions. This process is fairly straightforward for the rectilinear panels. Simply use the Box tool to create the specified shape, and then rotate and move that panel into position. For the sloping panels that have to match the roofline, however, the Slice tool will have to be used in conjunction with different positions for the UCS.

The most important thing to remember for making these shaped panels is to position the UCS prior to making the slice. Figure 6-52 shows how to build one of the smaller panels that fit on each side of the recess for the door.

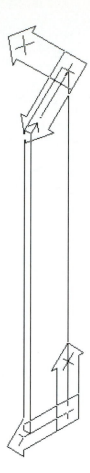

Figure 6-52. To shape a panel, move the UCS into position prior to using the Slice tool.

1. You can build the panel either flat on the X-Y plane of the WCS and then rotate the panel, or you can turn the coordinate system vertically to orient the UCS to the position of the panel's assembly onto the frame.

2. To change the position of the UCS, enter UCS on the Command line, enter M for Move, press the space bar, and follow the command prompt to select the new origin. If you want to rotate the UCS, repeat the UCS command, enter N for New to select an axis of rotation, and input positive or negative degrees of rotation.

3. Once the UCS is in position, use the Box tool to make a box with the overall dimensions of the wall panel. First, click on the Box icon. Use the origin of the UCS (0,0,0) as the starting point for the box. Then enter "L" for length at the command prompt. The orientation of the UCS is not important, as long as you enter the X value as the length of the box, the Y value as the width, and the Z value as the height. Use negative numbers to shape the box in the negative direction of any axis.

4. When the overall size is complete, shape the panel by moving the UCS to the point of the Slice. Use the relative move coordinates, preceded by the @ symbol, to reposition the UCS from its current location to the point of the cut. The dimensions for these moves should be shown on the drawings. If not, you should note the omission so they can be added later.

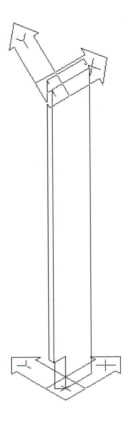

Figure 6-53. The UCS tool can be rotated into an infinite number of positions so that the Slice tool can shape the panel. Moving the tool in three dimensions helps build visualization skills.

5. Once the UCS is in position, click on the Slice tool, select the panel, and press the space bar. You can slice the panel along the X-Y, Y-Z, or Z-X plane of the current UCS by selecting 0,0,0 as the point defining any one of the three planes you might choose, and entering a "B" to keep both sides of the panel after the slice. Keeping both sides means you can confirm that the slice occurred the way you wanted it to. If it did not, Undo the command and try again.

Figure 6-53 shows another example of shaping a panel using the UCS and Slice tools. Again, there is no need to detail the internal structure of each panel because all will be prefabricated and delivered from the manufacturer as completed units. Because the objective is to test the drawings, it is important only that the overall dimensions are shown clearly and that the final collection of panels fit together as required.

As shown in Figure 6-54, the window units and clerestories are simple frame construction. The woodframes cap the ends of the panels and set up the rough openings for the manufactured windows and the skylight. Even though the details for these windows are shown in the drawing, it would not always be necessary to test the finish details and fit of the final installation once general constructibility has been determined. There was a time when windows and doors called for the best skills of a construction crew and involved a good deal of the finish work in the field, but now the placement and trim for prefabricated doors and windows are not very demanding. Except in unusual situations, these details are usually design issues that do not

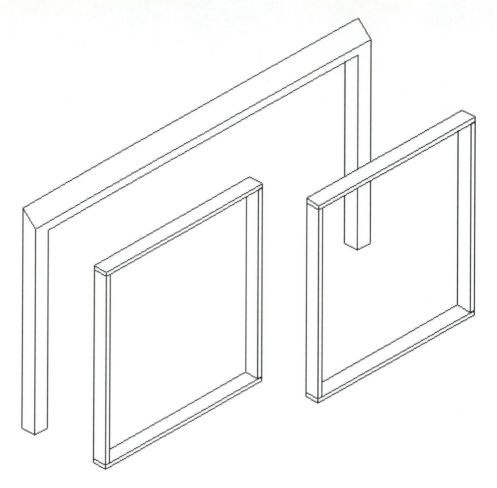

Figure 6-54. The frames around the windows and clerestories cap the panel ends and set up the rough opening for the fixed glass units.

have a great impact on general estimates and the schedule because all the work is cut to fit the rough installation.

Probably the most difficult pieces to visualize are the ceiling panels for the trainer shown in this book. Figure 6-55 shows the $\frac{1}{2}$" insulated ceiling panels for the trainer. You have to be thinking of these panels upside down as you calculate their dimensions. In most construction drawings, this is done with a reflected ceiling plan. A reflected ceiling plan is like a mirrored floor plan. You look down at a reflection of the ceiling above. These plans show the location of ceiling finishes, trim, light fixtures, or anything else that might be important to locate but difficult to show on a floor plan or any other detail for the building.

When the reflected ceiling plan is of a slope ceiling, the actual size of the ceiling will not be accurately represented because the plan shows the horizontal projection of the ceiling and not the actual dimension of its sloping surface. To calculate these dimensions, you have to extrapolate them from the room's interior horizontal dimensions and the geometry of the sloping ceiling. As shown in Figure 6-56, for example, a room with a finished interior dimension of 10'0" square and a 45-degree sloping ceiling would have a ceiling panel 10'-0" wide and 14' 1$\frac{3}{4}$" long because the long dimension of the ceiling is the hypotenuse of a triangle.

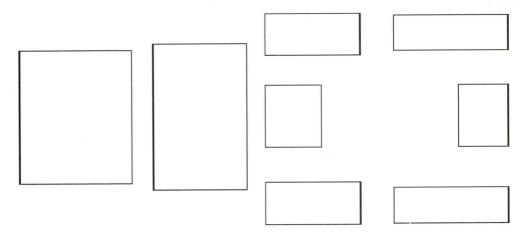

Figure 6-55. The ceiling panels for the trainer are shown as flat projections that can be precut and snapped into place once the insulation is placed in the rafters.

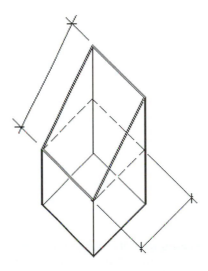

Figure 6-56. The dimensions of the ceiling panels must be calculated according to the slope of the roof and the horizontal dimension of the room.

Panel Assembly

Assembling the wall and ceiling panels for the trainer comes after the installation of the roof framing and roofing. This assembly sequence ensures that they would be protected in case of inclement weather. In almost any building, assembly would begin with the exterior panels first to get a weather seal for the building and to allow the rough-in for the electrical and plumbing systems to begin.

Figure 6-57 shows the first wall panels for the trainer, with the roofing and roof framing omitted so that you can see the actual placement. The logical progression would probably begin with the prehung door and the panels immediately adjacent to the doorframe. Then the wall panels would be completed for the window wall and frame on the opposite wall. These panels are screwed to the steel roof columns with continuous sheet metal plates. Both have been omitted from the illustration, but they are visible in the three-dimensional details. Installing the shear plates to the columns

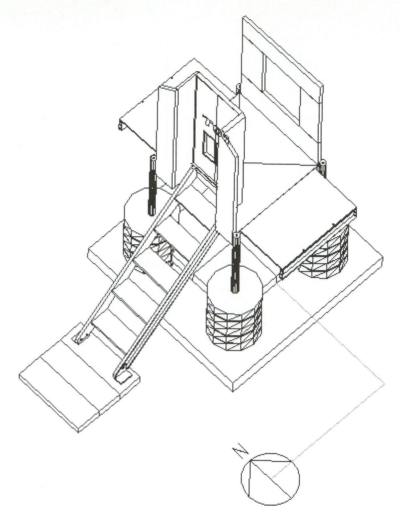

Figure 6-57. The roofing and roof framing have been omitted to show the placement of the main door and window panels.

and the panels is not really necessary in the preconstruction model if the main components fit together.

Once the main units are aligned and attached to the trainer's frame, the wall panels and windows can be put in place for the floor extension. These wall panels and the clerestories are shown in Figure 6-58 with the roof columns and ridge beam. The panels and window units would be installed in sections from the inside of the room, but final adjustments would have to be made to the alignment on the outside prior to applying the foiled building paper and siding shown in the details.

The ceiling panels with the rafters in place are shown without the roofing in Figure 6-59. These panels would be snapped into position from below after the space between the rafters had been insulated.

Preconstruction Models Embody Time

This chapter introduced a modeling concept that is just now possible on an ordinary personal computer. The idea can be adapted for use with almost any basic solid modeling program and linked to schedule and project estimates for a completely visual

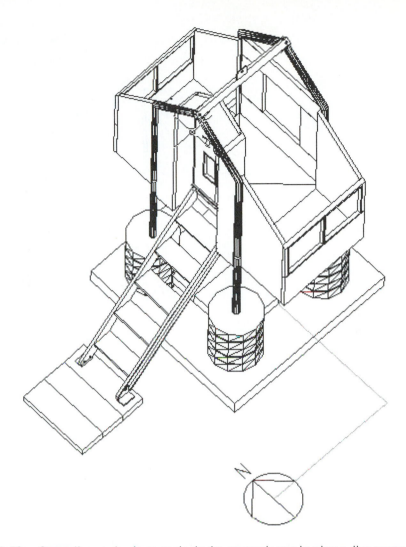

Figure 6-58. Once the main door and window panels are in place, the panels for the floor extension and clerestories can be mounted.

approach to preconstruction analysis and construction management. This powerful new tool promises to add a new dimension, the fourth dimension of time, to the visual problem solving process covered in this book.

A preconstruction model embodies time in a way that can be used to illustrate and visually analyze almost any aspect of a construction problem. In the preconstruction of the trainer shown in Figure 6-60, you have not only tested the construction drawings for errors and omissions, but you now have a graphical database that will allow you to manage your projects visually in the field. The completed model embodies both the time and materials inherent in the total construction process.

Unlike architectural models that help you visualize space, preconstruction models are built following a standard work breakdown structure to simulate both the process and the physical pieces that enclose that space. Layer and object controls allow these pieces to be turned off and on individually in any sequence for analysis. Most important, the resultant sequence helps you communicate time in ways that were not possible just a few years ago. You can coordinate a complex crane lift or an animation of a monthly progress report. The model can also be useful to demonstrate your particular approach to any part of a project's construction

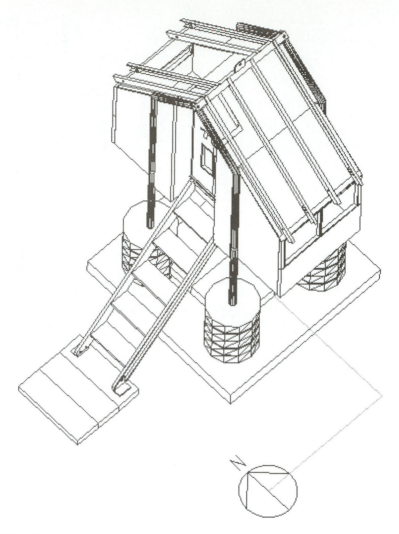

Figure 6-59. To complete the interior space, the ceiling panels are snapped into position once the rafter insulation is installed.

to a client, regulating agency, or subcontractor. The model could give you a distinct competitive advantage in a project proposal, allowing you both to illustrate your company's capabilities and to fine-tune your methodology and pricing strategies.

Preconstruction modeling can be useful for project planning, field documentation, and facilities operations. Built from the actual contract documents, it can help you visually analyze estimates, simulate schedules, or animate value engineering alternatives. It can become an all-inclusive visual tool for almost every aspect of construction. Most important, preconstruction models resolve the seven-step visual approach to problem solving discussed in this book. They do so with a three-dimensional solution that can now be taken into the field and viewed on the trainer's own computers.

In other words, you have come full circle. The result of your work is a graphical database that includes all the dimensions and specifications of the completed building. This database could be made available on jobsite computers, just like the networked trainers in this simulated project. This process suggests a multidimensional construction document that closes the loop on the early program requirements in

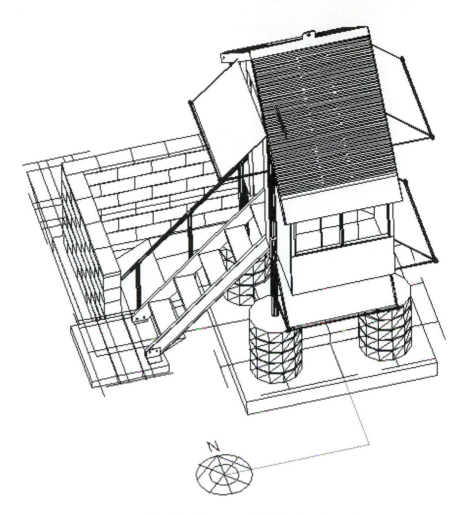

Figure 6-60. The final model does more than represent architectural form. It embodies the time and materials inherent in the total construction process.

step 1. The preconstruction model in step 6 gives three-dimensional form to the schematics and preliminaries that were used to resolve and scale the vague ideas in steps 2 and 3. And just as the design development drawings of step 4 represented those ideas in the engineered drawings completed in step 5, the solid objects now floating in virtual space as a construction model embody the skills and experience of the consultants and other professionals who contributed to the field drawings. The 3D details added to those drawings in step 6 thereby guided the construction of the preconstruction model in step 7, first to test the documents for missing information, but ultimately to introduce itself as a new tool for managing the eventual construction.

The potential of the idea is enormous. And it all rests on a simple set of hand-drawings and a seven-step visual approach to problem solving.

Index